Stone Conservation

Principles and Practice

Stone Conservation

Principles and Practice

Edited by

ALISON HENRY

Managing Editor

JILL PEARCE

Routledge
Taylor & Francis Group

LONDON AND NEW YORK

First published 2006 by Donhead Publishing Ltd

Published 2015 by Routledge
2 Park Square, Milton Park, Abingdon, Oxon, OX14 4RN
711 Third Avenue, New York, NY 10017, USA

Routledge is an imprint of the Taylor & Francis Group, an informa business

ISBN-13: 978-1-873394-78-6 (hbk)

Typeset by Aarontype

British Library Cataloguing in Publication Data

Stone conservation: principles and practice
1. Stone buildings – Conservation and restoration
2. Building stones – Biodeterioration
I. Henry, Alison
691.2
ISBN-10: 1873394780

Library of Congress Cataloguing in Publication Data
A catalog record for this book has been requested

Contents

Acknowledgments

The Publisher and the Editor would like to offer their gratitude to Peter Burman for the original ideas which inspired this book. It emerged from Peter's insight that the annual Stone Conservation course at the University of York offered a snapshot of the art and science of conserving stone structures. Peter's enthusiasm for the project had as its inspiration the remarkable late twentieth-century flowering of the conservation of traditional materials in cathedrals and country houses. Peter was also at that time the founder chairman of both the Building Limes Forum in the UK, and the York Art Workers' Association, and a past master at bringing together architects, art historians, craftsmen, conservators, artists and other professionals in a relationship which enabled the whole to be greater than the sum of the parts; hence, this interdisciplinary book on stone conservation.

Foreword

From time to time a new book on a technical subject needs to make an appearance. Although a very substantial body of literature exists on the conservation of stone buildings, sculpture and other artefacts, this is a good moment for specifiers and practitioners to have an authoritative review made available to them.

A habit of reliance on existing available resources and a natural reluctance to publish new material that is not fully developed sometimes mean that important information or ideas are not disclosed soon enough to those who need them. But there is no point in time when everything is known about a subject. Publication is of its time and published ideas and technical information become 'dated', but this should not discourage. There is real value to those whose work involves the ongoing care of historic stone to know what was current practice in the eighteenth century, or during the great technological advances of the nineteenth century, or during the development of conservation techniques and philosophies in the twentieth century. There are truths, part truths and errors to be sifted, studied and re-evaluated from the rich archives of this subject to which must then be added our own experience and knowledge. An authoritative group of authors have made this contribution in *Stone Conservation*.

A large part of the value of a work of this kind can only be measured by the effect it has on thinking and practice in the future. Many practitioners in this field work in a rather isolated way, not by choice but by the nature of the work. This book will reduce that isolation, provide background and context, and aid decision making and good practice. The beneficiaries will be buildings, monuments and sculptures of stone.

Professor John Ashurst DArch RIBA
Ingram Consultancy

Chapter One

Introduction

Alison Henry

Most of the world's greatest buildings as well as many of its humbler architectural gems are built of stone, so it is no wonder that the subject of stone conservation continues to arouse great interest amongst conservation professionals, practitioners and the general public.

The science of stone conservation spans three centuries: the nineteenth-century saw attempts to consolidate stone using waxes and Baryta water; during the twentieth century lime-based techniques were refined, and synthetic consolidants and sophisticated cleaning methods were developed; today we have at our disposal such techniques as the use of calcite-forming bacteria, hydroxylating conversion treatment and advanced laser and poultice cleaning.

But architectural stone conservation is not just a science; it is an art and a craft skill, and for many people therein lies its attraction. Underpinning all aspects of this multi-disciplinary activity is a decision-making process that is crucial to successful conservation. In a world of rapidly developing scientific techniques and new materials, it is all too easy to get carried away with enthusiasm for actually doing the practical work. Sometimes too little thought is given to its aims and objectives and the effect that the work might have on the significance of the building as a whole. This book aims to redress the balance by presenting stone conservation as a process that starts long before the first specification is written or the first spatula is wielded on site.

The emphasis is on stonework, both plain and decorative, in an architectural context. Whilst an appreciation of the geology of building stone types and an understanding of the mechanisms of stone decay are fundamental to successful stone conservation, these are not covered in depth in this volume for want of space.

The philosophical principles on which stone conservation is founded can be traced back to antiquity. Peter Burman and Michael Drury provide a fascinating account of the development, through the centuries, of conservation thinking and craft skills, paying particular attention to re-evaluating the role of the great nineteenth-century British architects. They argue that the work of the 'restoring' architects was not as black-and-white as is often portrayed. Many of these villains of the conservation movement in fact carried out sympathetic repairs to many buildings, particularly churches, but were constrained by the contexts in which they were working, which often demanded radical interventions in buildings that were close to ruin.

Michael Drury develops the themes of restoration, conservation and preservation, which is a challenging task given the generally ambiguous use of these words today. How often, for example, do we hear someone talk of restoration when what they really mean (according to the British Standard definitions) is in fact conservation? The picture is clouded even further if one considers the choices to be made when deciding to treat individual stones: at what point does restoration or preservation (of individual stones) stop and conservation (of the building) begin? You might be tempted to think that terminology is not important so long as we, the professionals and practitioners, know what we mean. But terminology is important if we are to counter the generally negative connotations of conservation amongst the general public, who often confuse conservation with preservation and see it as something that is stultifying and restrictive. The concept of conservation as a proactive means of managing the inevitable change in the historic environment is something that escapes the majority of people.

Michael Drury goes on to use the example of the conservation of the West Front of Salisbury Cathedral to illustrate how these philosophical ideas influence decision making, and how they can be used to develop a conservation policy for a project. However, it is not only outstanding buildings that deserve such an approach; the humblest of projects will benefit from the same thought processes, even if they are not formalized into a written document.

Jerry Sampson, who, I believe, must surely be descended from Sherlock Homes, explains how, with a detective's eye, an enormous amount of information about the history and development of a building can be gleaned from its fabric. This information, combined with the results of documentary research, can help provide an understanding of the building, which then allows informed judgements about its significance to be made. This is an essential pre-requisite of any conservation project: only by appreciating the value of something can we truly determine whether the interventions we make are beneficial or harmful. We might clean, repair, and consolidate stone in the name of conservation, and in the process wipe out evidence of part of a building's history because we did not appreciate, for example, that there were fragments of polychromy surviving beneath the lichen growth or carbon deposits that we removed. The significance of a building lies not only in the physical condition of its constituent parts but also in its history and development, and many buildings still have much to tell us if only we would use our eyes (or those of an experienced buildings' archaeologist) before starting work.

The same principles apply in understanding the nature of the substrate and the causes of its deterioration; it is often unwise to attempt to treat a symptom until the cause of a problem is fully understood. Nicholas Durnan and Colin Muir explain the range of survey, monitoring, testing and analysis that might be needed as part of the decision-making process long before work starts on site.

The subject of stone consolidation has probably aroused more interest and controversy than any other aspect of stone conservation. Being able to spray a consolidant onto crumbling stone and thereby halt further decay sounds so simple, and yet is fraught with problems. When I speak to members of the general public, I often find that they are incredulous that there is no simple, universal means of consolidating stone in this way. It is a measure of how rapidly things change in conservation that twenty years ago silanes seemingly held such promise for stone consolidation, yet today their use is limited to a few special cases. Clifford Price's chapter provides an overview of the development of stone consolidants that takes us into the 'post-silane' era of the early twenty-first century. He suggests that in the future we should move away from trying to develop long-lasting panaceas, and that we should instead aim to develop methods that would meet very specific needs, even if perhaps only for a relatively short period of time. As things change fast in the world of science and conservation it is conceivable that new techniques will be developed that will enable further (and possibly better) treatment of the stone in the future. An interesting example of this, although not specifically related to consolidation, is the large number of rusting iron reinforcements that have been removed from stone buildings in the past and replaced with stainless steel, often involving major cutting out and stone replacement; in many similar situations today, such a problem might well be dealt with by cathodic protection with practically no stone replacement required, a solution unheard of twenty years ago.

Another area in which public aspiration and practical reality often fail to meet is in the cleaning of stonework. Kyle Normandin and Deborah Slaton's chapter starts by explaining that masonry cleaning of historic buildings must distinguish between soiling, which is detrimental to the building (either because it conceals structural problems or because it actively contributes to stone decay), and benign patinas, which contribute to the character and sense of age of a building. They emphasize the need to understand the nature of the substrate and the causes of any soiling before moving to trials of possible cleaning methods. The full range of current masonry cleaning systems is summarized. Although written from a North American perspective, the systems currently used in the UK are fully covered. The authors provide a useful methodology for selecting a cleaning technique as well as a matrix summarizing stone types and possible cleaning methods. Whilst many new methods have appeared in recent years, the concluding section contains a decades-old caution that still applies: use the gentlest possible method to achieve the desired level of cleaning.

When existing stones are severely decayed, the decision may be made to replace them in whole or in part. Ewan Hyslop considers the decision-making process involved in such cases, highlighting possible alternatives to replacement. Even if it is decided, after due deliberation, that stone is to be replaced, finding a suitable match can be difficult, especially if the quarry that supplied the original stone is no longer open, or if the specific beds of stone from which it was obtained are worked out. He explains how petrographic analysis can be used to characterize the original stone, and to find replacement stones that will not only initially look similar to the original stone, but will perform and weather similarly too. Sometimes, procuring a suitable stone means re-opening abandoned quarries. This is usually met with howls of opposition from local residents fearful of noise, dust and heavy lorries. However, in many cases extraction of small quantities of building stone from not much more than a hole in the ground in the corner of a field can go on practically unnoticed, with the occasional load of stone moved to a shed in a farmyard by a tractor and trailer. Such quarries can provide distinctive local stone for distinctive local buildings. We need to decide whether we would prefer a small number of 'super-quarries' restricted to the backyards of an unfortunate few, but causing significant environmental impact and exporting tons of stone well beyond their region of production.

Moving on to consideration of individual stone types, the chapters by Nick Durnan, Colin Muir and Jonathan Kemp provide a conservator's perspective on the conservation of limestone, sandstone and marble. With a wealth of practical experience between them, they illustrate the specific approaches and techniques suitable for these different stone types. They show how the more traditional methods of cleaning, repair and consolidation are being augmented by newer methods, always bearing in mind the underlying need to fully establish the precise nature of the stone in question and the causes of its deterioration.

Christopher Weeks, in his chapter on the conservation of polychrome stone, stresses the importance of initial survey work to establish the presence and extent of paint on external architectural stonework. It is perhaps significant that as the call for thorough investigation prior to starting any conservation work is being increasingly heeded, remnants of paint schemes are coming to light on buildings where no one ever previously considered looking for them. In an earlier chapter, Jerry Sampson mentions the example of Beaminster Church in Dorset, where paint fragments were unexpectedly discovered on the quatrefoil band of the tower. As more such discoveries are made, both in the UK and abroad, the need to understand fully the special requirements for cleaning and consolidating polychromy and the implications that the presence of polychromy has for the conservation of the underlying stone, must increase. This chapter is an excellent start in this direction.

David Carrington presents a surprisingly dynamic picture of the current state of church monument conservation. Again, we come back to the need to understand the processes acting on a monument in its wider context before considering remedial action. All too often decisions have been made that have considered a monument in isolation, rather than considering whether or not decay might be reduced or arrested by improving the environment in which the monument is located. Indeed, the result of many past interventions was to provide barriers and coatings to physically isolate a monument from its environment. He cites examples of monuments which had been completely dismantled and rebuilt on a lead damp-proof membrane, but which continued to deteriorate because of a leaking roof. He also suggests that conservators in this field are increasingly considering alternatives to damp-proof membranes and surface coatings, such as improved ventilation and drainage.

Graveyard memorials have been attracting much attention in recent years, partly as a result of increasing interest in family history research, and partly due to some serious accidents, including fatalities, caused by the collapse of unstable memorials. For many graveyard managers, health and safety in the graveyard has become a pressing concern. There is often a tendency to react swiftly in the face of perceived threats, and as a result many graveyard memorials have been made safe by laying them flat on the ground. Advice on alternative methods of improving safety has been published by Historic Scotland, and this is summarized in Chris Daniels' chapter. Raising the profile of graveyard memorials has also had the benefit of increasing funding for their repair, with some local authorities and dioceses running grant schemes for the repair of memorials of architectural or historic interest. Although the amount of money available is minute in proportion to the need, successful projects can serve as exemplars and may help to bring in funds from private sources. The specific issues pertaining to these structures are explained. These are effectively situated in the unusual environment of an unprotected 'museum' with twenty four-hour unrestricted access and often hopelessly inadequate funding for maintenance. The range of techniques and materials currently in use for conservation of such graveyard memorials are also described.

Various recurring themes emerge from these chapters, particularly the need for thorough investigation and assessment of significance before work starts, and for a thorough understanding of the nature of the material being treated, its environmental context and the causes of its decay. However, the process of stone conservation is not complete until the details of the treatment carried out have been documented and lodged with the appropriate authorities. In this way we can learn in future from both successful and unsuccessful projects.

It hardly needs stating that well-trained and highly skilled conservators are essential for successful stone conservation. Through their workmanship, the efforts of architects, archaeologists, geologists and other consultants come to fruition. Sadly, whilst there are numerous stone-masonry courses in the UK, opportunities for stonework conservation training are limited, and many conservators learn on the job. While such training may be sufficient to help them develop practical craft skills, it is unlikely to produce conservators with the knowledge required to make informed judgements about how to treat a particular piece of stone or an entire building. The situation is not helped by the lack of recognized qualifications in stone conservation. The accreditation scheme for conservators in the UK promoted by the Institute of Conservation is a step in the right direction, but it needs to be underpinned by more training opportunities. But no matter what stage we are at in our conservation careers, whether practical or professional, we all have more to learn. Ongoing education is the key to successful stone conservation, and it is hoped that this book will make a positive contribution to that process.

The author

Alison Henry BSc Hons, Dip Arch Cons, PGDip Arch Stone Cons, IHBC

Alison combines her role as Historic Buildings Advisor at South Somerset District Council with running a stone conservation practice. She worked on the conservation of the West Front of Salisbury Cathedral and now specializes in church conservation in Dorset and Somerset. Alison is also a part-time lecturer in conservation at Weymouth College and a member and former chair of the Institute of Historic Building Conservation's Technical Sub-Committee.

Chapter Two

The Historical Context

Peter Burman and Michael Drury

INTRODUCTION

The purpose of this chapter is to outline the philosophical principles that can be traced throughout history and continue to lie behind successful or appropriate decision-making on the conservation and repair of stone structures and stone sculpture today.

The principal ideas behind the chapter are:

- The continuing influence of Classical antiquity on the conservation of stone structures.
- The break (real or apparent) in traditions during the nineteenth century, as a result of the general process of industrialization, and its effect on principles and practices.
- The successive re-evaluations of traditions, which, in Britain, began with John Ruskin and William Morris, both of who came to have an enormous influence on intellectual thinking and craft practice.
- The influence of the Modern Movement on craft traditions and principles.
- The continuity in craft practice during the medieval, Renaissance, Baroque and Neo-Classical eras, especially in France, Germany, Italy and the United Kingdom.
- The late nineteenth- and twentieth-century evolution of international charters dealing with conservation of stone structures and sculptures, and the development of ideas about authenticity and about universal and local values.
- The influence of such newly prominent disciplines as art history, archaeology and conservation science on craft traditions, principles and practice.

- Where we are now, in the early twenty-first century, with respect to philosophical principles and what effect these are having (or might subsequently have) on practice.
- Whether we can begin to discern, out of the welter of contemporary activity, more detailed guidelines or touchstones; or whether, on the whole, we shall simply have to accept a plurality of practice where strong personalities or institutions in effect dictate (varying) policies.

Every one of these topics could be the subject of a substantial study in its own right. The present chapter, therefore, can be seen as a report on progress within a highly complex field where theory – most excitingly – still has a chance to influence what is actually done to historic buildings and sculpture.

THE INFLUENCE OF ANTIQUITY

It would, of course, be highly convenient for us if Marcus Vitruvius Pollio, in his first-century BC work *De architectura,* had set out clear principles for dealing with the repair of earlier structures; nevertheless, what we have from him is of immense value as being the only architectural treatise surviving from Classical antiquity; the successive translations from Latin into Italian, English, French, and German are themselves classics of European literature.

What is of great significance about *The Ten Books of Architecture* (as the title is generally translated into English), is the respect in which it has been held since its rediscovery in the fifteenth century. From this, a continuity of approach has developed, and continues to be relevant to the present day. It is striking how the really thoughtful architectural geniuses of modern times, from Christopher Wren to Richard Rogers, have seen themselves as working to some extent in a Classical tradition.

What, then, did Vitruvius have to say that might be valuable to us today in this context? For example, he wrote in detail on the role of the architect and perhaps in that sense made it possible for the profession of 'architect' to develop in the way that it did; he made it clear that both practical and theoretical skills were important:[1]

> ... architects who have aimed at acquiring manual skill without scholarship have never been able to reach a position of authority to correspond to their pains, while those who relied only upon theories and scholarship were obviously hunting the shadow, not the substance. But those who have a

thorough knowledge of both, like men armed at all points, have the sooner attained their object and carried authority with them.

Also, we derive the most enduring definition of the qualities of architecture from this work; Vitruvius says that the different departments of architecture must be built '... with due reverence to durability, convenience, and beauty', and that '... durability will be assured when foundations are carried down to the solid ground and materials wisely and liberally selected.'[2] The second book deals largely with the fundamental building materials – brick, sand, lime, pozzolana, stone and timber – and this has continued to be a source of inspiration and reference.

On the subject of stone, Vitruvius deals principally with quarries and with the qualities of stone from particular quarries; this may not be thought to be of particular relevance to us today, but what is of interest is the soundness of his observations, and the nature of the phenomena observed. Speaking of certain soft and easily worked stones he says:[3]

> Under cover they play their part well; but in open and exposed situations the frost and rime make them crumble, and they go to pieces. On the seacoast, too, the salt eats away and dissolves them, nor can they stand great heat either. But travertine and all stone of that class can stand injury whether from a heavy load upon it or from the weather ...

Also of value is the advice about working with the dimensions of time and with the seasons, indicative of an understanding that was part of the traditional wisdom of the stonemason in the whole of Europe until nineteenth- and twentieth-century contracting pressures gradually squeezed it out. Vitruvius writes:[4]

> Let the stone be taken from the quarry two years before building is to begin, and not in winter but in summer. Then let it lie exposed in an open place. Such stone as has been damaged by the two years of exposure should be used in the foundations. The rest, which remains unhurt, has passed the test of nature and will endure in those parts of the building which are above ground. This precaution should be observed, not only with dimensioned stone, but also with the rubble which is to be used in walls.

The soundness of the Roman architect's observations and the Roman craftsman's practices is illustrated by the number of masonry bridges, gateways, walls, temples and other structures still standing today, some two thousand years later.

Vitruvius's qualities of 'durability, convenience and beauty' echo down the centuries from the first century BC to the present day. The first to reuse and reinterpret these terms was the architect, humanist and antiquarian Leon Battista Alberti (1404–72), whose own principal work is called *De re aedificatoria* – its emphasis being on building rather than architecture, though the difference is a subtle one. Alberti's book was written in Latin between 1443 and 1452 and the classic English translation is that by Giacomo Leoni in 1755, also given the title *The Ten Books of Architecture*. Intriguingly, the tenth book is called 'Of the Defects in Buildings, whence they proceed, and their different Sorts; which of them can be corrected by the Architect, and which cannot'. Those defects that can be corrected by the architect are, generally speaking, what today we would call structural; those that cannot be corrected by the architect, in Alberti's view, are defects caused principally by time, the elements, natural calamities, and neglect, which in effect we now seek to deal with skilfully and appropriately in our very changed circumstances. It is fascinating to observe the wrath with which Alberti speaks of neglect:[5]

> I call Heaven to Witness, that I am often filled with the highest Indignation when I see Buildings demolished and going to Ruin by the Carelessness, not to say abominable Avarice of the Owners, Buildings whose Majestie has saved them from the Fury of the most barbarous and outraged Enemies, and which Time himself, that perverse and Obstinate Destroyer, seems to have destined to Eternity.

This formulation is particularly powerful for us, because it is just these defects which our apparatus of conservation policy, principles and practice is designed to combat through various means including:

- Techniques of cleaning, consolidation and stabilization to ward off the effects of time;
- Protection by various means against the actions of the elements;
- Disaster preparedness and well orchestrated plans to deal with the effects of fire, floods and earthquakes; and
- Quinquennial inspections, condition surveys, maintenance cycles, and procedures to deal efficiently and effectively with the effects of neglect.

Nevertheless, all four categories continue to pose their practical difficulties, even where we have theoretical ways of dealing with them all to one degree or another.

THE BREAK IN TRADITION

The consequences of the Industrial Revolution were certainly manifold so far as building culture is concerned. From the late eighteenth century onwards there was an immense expansion in building activity embracing all kinds of industrial buildings – mills, factories, harbours, warehouses, transport infrastructure, housing for the industrialized labour force, and so on – and their methods of construction gradually became more mechanized, more repetitive, and less dependent upon the skills of the individual craftsman. There were other developments, too, which took building culture away from its local links. The development of canals and then railways allowed materials to be transported with relative ease and economy to distant building sites. So, for example, Welsh slates became, at the beginning of the nineteenth century, the least expensive and commonest roofing material even though there were local materials which had traditionally been used and were still available. Also, teams of workmen became more mobile, enabling architects to use their most trusted contractors, clerks of works, and craftsmen anywhere in the country, transporting them to the project sites. Pugin liked to use a firm from Lambeth, in South London; later in the century Philip Webb often used Estcourt, of Gloucester. Moreover, specialist suppliers sprang up in every field, and due to the ubiquity of the British Empire and the effectiveness of the merchant navy, their manufactures could be shipped throughout the world. For instance, the cast-iron columns, balconies, fountains, railings, and decorative architectural elements of a firm like MacFarlanes of Glasgow can be found in Sydney, Cape Town, Bangalore, Singapore and Hong Kong.

However, the break in tradition can be exaggerated, and part of the thesis of this chapter is that many craft traditions survived the industrial revolution and the internationalization of the building trade. Nevertheless, their survival in England – as elsewhere, whether in developing or developed countries – was a precarious thing, and this is where the influence of John Ruskin (1819–1900) was important.

RE-EVALUATING TRADITION

The contributions made by leading nineteenth-century figures in the architectural and emerging conservation worlds, in terms of their treatment of our ancient buildings and their contribution to the survival of craft traditions, are worthy of re-evaluation. It is important to remember that by the early nineteenth century many of our churches, in particular, were in a sorry state and that only through the intervention of architects now perceived as 'restorers' did many of them survive. It is likely that even the worst of these restorers would have carried out essential repairs, now largely forgotten. In the last decades of the nineteenth century, conservation thinking grew in parallel with the Arts and Crafts movement. There was a symbiotic relationship between the two, the Arts and Crafts movement giving priority to the craft traditions that enabled the conservation lobby to bring real solutions to problems of repairs, while the conservationists provided a training ground for young arts and crafts practitioners to learn the ways of traditional construction at first hand. The following figures are particularly important in the historical emergence of the contemporary conservation movement.

John Ruskin (1819–1900)

Following his acclaimed *Modern Painters* of 1843, Ruskin had become the most important Victorian writer on art. Later publications dwelt increasingly on architectural matters and he consequently became an influential figure in the development of the Gothic Revival. Later, following his disillusionment with the multitude of church restorations associated with the movement, he became equally (if not better) known for denouncing it. He opposed such 'restoration' for the destruction of medieval craftsmanship with which it was associated and for the repression of individual creativity that he saw as an inevitable consequence of the Gothic Revival that supplanted these earlier traditions. The Arts and Crafts Movement developed in the latter part of the nineteenth century as a response to his teaching, inspired by *The Seven Lamps of Architecture* (1849)[6] and *The Stones of Venice* (1851–1853)[7]. These publications also inspired the early conservation movement, which shared many of the same principles.

Sir George Gilbert Scott (1811–1878)

Scott's was the largest of the Victorian architectural practices and his new buildings, both secular and ecclesiastical, appeared alongside the multitude of medieval churches and cathedrals that he restored. His was 'the most successful architectural career of modern time' according to his obituary in *The Builder*, but to Ruskin and to William Morris he epitomized his generation's obsession with restoration. When visiting the churches and cathedrals Scott restored, one can almost hear the echoes of righteous indignation that emanated from the early committee meetings of the Society for the Protection of Ancient Buildings (SPAB) in the late 1870s. At Tewkesbury Abbey, where his plans for restoration were the catalyst for the founding of the Society, or at the great parish church in Cirencester, or at Boxgrove Priory in Sussex or at any one of countless other parish churches across the country, it is easy to see, in the repetitive, machine-made tile pavements, uniform pews and stereotypical Tractarian re-orderings, only the impersonal output of a huge office. It is harder to appreciate how many of these churches Scott saved, and how much of his work is now unseen and hence forgotten: the towers and arcades he underpinned, the flying buttresses he rebuilt, the rainwater drainage systems he installed, the roofs he re-covered. And although the standard of his restorations varied – as the output of any huge enterprise must vary depending on the ability of the individuals involved – the results of his best work are still as good or better than our most talented conservators and masons can achieve today. To the team at Salisbury Cathedral in 1995,

Figure 2.1 Medieval Purbeck 'marble' capitals to the central west doorway at Salisbury Cathedral, repaired during Sir George Gilbert Scott's restoration by piecing-in new carved foliate lobes into the original medieval stems.

the early stages of the West Front repair and conservation project revealed an impressive aspect of Scott's restoration of more than 125 years before. The Purbeck 'marble capitals' of the central doorway had been carefully repaired by his masons, although replacement would have been far simpler. Scott's desire to save original material resulted instead in a programme of piecing-in, the geometry of which exhibits an almost unbelievable complexity; into the medieval stems of the capitals were introduced new carved foliate lobes, jointed so tightly that they had been overlooked for more than a hundred years.

It is high time Scott's credentials as a careful and well informed historic buildings architect were re-examined. Indeed a study of his own writing on the ethics of restoration soon reveals his underlying sensitivities, as his words to the Dean of Lincoln in 1859 exemplify:[8]

> Restorers, even when disposed to be conservative, often mistake the true meaning and object of restoration, which is not to make a building look as if it were new, but (so far as concerns the fabric) to put it in seemly repair; to replace features which have been actually destroyed by modern imitations, *where they can be indisputably traced*; to clear the ancient surface from modern over-laying, and to check the progress of decay and dilapidation. The more of the ancient material *and the ancient surface* remain, and the less new introduced, the more successful the restoration. If more cannot be saved, even one or two old be-mossed stones, in a window or a cornice, give value and truthfulness to the work; but when it is possible, *all* or the *great majority* of the old stones should retain their *untouched and unsmartened surface* ...

William Butterfield (1814–1900)

William Butterfield was often the choice where the patron of a restoration project had High Church leanings. This was certainly the case in southeast Wiltshire, where the patronage of the Herbert family at Wilton House in the 1840s-1860s had thus far favoured T.H. Wyatt. But in the 1870s they turned to Butterfield and it is interesting to consider the relevance of his commission for the restoration of, for example, St. Mary's in Dinton, Wiltshire[9] in 1875, and to compare his work there to any one of the other fifty or more churches restored in the nineteenth century in southeast Wiltshire alone.

In 1848, Butterfield had built what was arguably the nineteenth century's most influential church at All Saints, Margaret Street in London[10] and, with it, High Victorian Gothic sprang into being. His work is characterized by structural polychromy, with colour being integral to the construction rather than applied afterwards. Externally, bands and zigzags of coloured brick break up the walls. Internally, materials and patterns vary prodigiously, all precise and hard yet vibrant with colour: geometric roundels of tiles, polished granite piers, and stripes of brick and tile proliferate. Perhaps Butterfield's best known building is Keble College Chapel in Oxford, a *tour de force* that established Butterfield as the leading architect in the Tractarian movement nationally.

Butterfield's work at Dinton in many ways constituted an exemplary repair. Although his style is instantly recognizable, and although his stamp is indelibly left on the interior with its furnishings in his simple stripped-down geometric gothic style, he was mindful of the sequential development of our parish churches and respected it. He also thought the average new church of the time to be 'noisy and pretentious'.[11] At Dinton, he dug the church out from rising ground to the north, carefully rebuilt the north porch (re-setting the arch), repaired the transept gables, re-roofed, re-plastered, re-hung the bells and re-floored the church throughout. The condition of St Mary's had been poor prior to Butterfield's efforts, and the universal condemnation of the great nineteenth-century restoring architects is undeserved by him, at least on the evidence of his excellent work here.

John Loughborough Pearson (1817–1897)

The work of John Loughborough Pearson as a restorer also seems deserving of study, and of respect. His restoration of the important late Saxon and Norman church of St Mary, Stow, in Lincolnshire was carried out in phases, beginning in 1851 – a very early date for scholarly restorations of this kind. The entry in the *Buildings of England* volume for Lincolnshire reads as follows:[12]

> The chancel is a prodigious piece of late Norman display, extensively but accurately restored by Pearson in 1851. It is of three bays, divided outside by flat buttresses, inside by composite shafts. The entablature outside is Pearson's design. Along the inner walls runs blank arcading with colonettes carrying scallop capitals. The string course above has small scallops just as on the outside of the nave south wall. The east wall above the arcading is largely Pearson's reconstruction, as is the great vault. The ribs and transverse arches are lavishly decorated; forty of the stones in them (some of each pattern) had been discovered in the walls, re-used after the collapse of the original vault.

Similarly, the authors of the *Yorkshire: York and the East Riding* volume write of Pearson's work at St Edith, Bishop Wilton, that:[13]

It was restored for Sir Tatton Sykes in 1858–9 by J. L. Pearson, and it was as conscientious a job of preservation as few men of that time would have done ... The Norman south doorway is as lavish as the chancel arch. It is a reconstruction from old materials. Animals, faces, human figures, beakhead, abstract beakhead and more. Notice the monkey playing on a tambourine, a man warming his hands at a fire, David and Goliath's head, and a centaur. The way in which Pearson kept the old and new clearly separated is exemplary.

George Edmund Street (1824–1881)

Street took Butterfield's High Victorian expressiveness, and added his own experience of continental precedents to achieve a robust style that has become known (perhaps for its rigour as much for its strength) as 'muscularity'. Forceful as his compositions were, his inventiveness ensured originality in each succeeding commission, best seen perhaps in his sequence of seven new churches on the Yorkshire Wolds for Sir Tatton Sykes, Pearson's client at Bishop Wilton.

But like Butterfield and Scott, Street restored many more churches than he built, and his work is widespread. At about the time Butterfield was at Dinton in Wiltshire, Street was at Britford, a church of Romanesque origin only a few miles away, which he carefully repaired for the Earl of Radnor. If Butterfield was the preferred architect of the Tractarian movement, Street was the one most highly regarded by the Ecclesiological Society. His protégés included William Morris, Philip Webb, Norman Shaw and John Sedding, from whose offices in turn emerged many of the architects of the Arts and Crafts movement. Through Street's influence, among others, craft traditions began to re-emerge, with fine ironwork and decorative designs being produced. Street wrote an early article (1857) in the *Ecclesiologist* denouncing destructive restoration[14] and although his own restorations were sometimes destructive in terms of ancient material, his influence on the key figures of the early British conservation movement suggests that his reputation deserves constructive re-assessment.

William Morris (1834–1896)

Deeply influenced by Ruskin, Morris led the crusade against the restorations of the Gothic Revival, launching the SPAB in 1877 in response to George Gilbert Scott's plans for restoring Tewkesbury Abbey. Not only did this mark the beginning of the conservation movement in Britain, it also undermined the Gothic Revival itself, for Morris, like Ruskin before him, deplored the replication of medieval style in the repair of old buildings. He insisted that new work should speak for itself as an honest contribution of its time, causing architects to think again about the validity of mimicking the past. His followers began to strip down the stylistic references in their buildings. Soon, through Morris's friend and colleague Philip Webb and the young architects of the Arts and Crafts movement they trained and inspired, there emerged the beginning of what has become known as 'rational building', a design process founded from first principles on sound building construction.

Morris himself studied architecture in the office of George Edmund Street at the time Webb was working there as Street's chief assistant. Morris gave it up because 'He found he could not get into close contact with it; it had to be done at second hand'.[15] During his lifetime Morris was perhaps best known as an author and poet, but today he is mainly remembered outside conservation circles as the leading designer of the Arts and Crafts Movement.

Philip Webb (1831–1913)

If William Morris was the figurehead of the SPAB and the early Conservation Movement, Philip Webb was its architect, in the broadest sense of the word. Enormously creative, he was a practical man and developed many of the early techniques of repair upon which the Society eventually founded its reputation. Initially seen by its many detractors as a 'do-nothing society', it was Webb who led the response that changed people's minds. Although Webb, unlike most architects of similar stature, took few pupils in his office, most early conservation architects learned their skills through Webb at the SPAB. Webb's students included William Weir, Detmar Blow and Alfred Powell, the trio favoured by the Society to represent their interests. They worked on site under Webb's guidance on early SPAB repair projects from 1892. In the earliest cases, such as the rescue of East Knoyle church tower in Wiltshire, Blow and Webb developed their repair technique through correspondence, which is still preserved in the SPAB archive. The tower was in danger of collapse; so, working internally from the bottom up, the masonry was removed in small sections and gradually replaced with what became known as a 'Webb sandwich'. Both Blow and Weir used this technique several times elsewhere, and Blow's drawing of the interior of the tower at Clare church in Suffolk shows the work in progress in 1898.[16] It indicates the contents of the 'sandwich' as a concrete of old materials between single courses of tiles, with occasional bonding courses and concrete sections divided using hard brick.

Figure 2.2   East Knoyle church tower, Wiltshire, today. It was repaired in 1892
by Detmar Blow and Philip Webb, architects, by internal rebuilding.

George Gilbert Scott Junior (1839–1897)

The younger George Gilbert Scott was among those architects who
supported Morris and the SPAB, treading a careful balance to avoid
flagrant disloyalty to his father all the while. As the Gothic Revival began to
be supplanted – in domestic architecture at least – by the red brick and
white painted joinery of Queen Anne, Scott Junior was one of the group of

Figure 2.3   Clare church tower, Suffolk, 1898: internal repairs were carried out by Detmar Blow as architect and contractor; the image is from his sketch inscribed 'View of interior of Belfry, Clare Church Tower, Suffolk. Built in the 13th Century, added and enlarged in the 15th Century which later work gave way under the strain of bells was made good with a new inside 10 foot off the bottom'.

progressive young architects that included Richard Norman Shaw (1831–1897), who showed the way. Churches had been the buildings that reflected the stylistic development of his father's generation, but for Shaw and to the younger Scott it was to be domestic architecture. Although the Gothic Revival continued, predominantly through church architecture, progressive thinking was now looking elsewhere.

Scott was a careful conservation architect, as his specification for work at Knapton church in Norfolk indicates:[17]

> The utmost care to be taken to prevent injury to the structure or to the decorative portion of the roof and especially to the coloured decorations. Such portions of the old carved work as are mutilated are not to be replaced ... .'

Through architects like George Gilbert Scott Junior, the great divide between the SPAB and the leading architects of the Gothic Revival began to narrow. Sensitive to the vulnerability of our ancient buildings, he was able to show his clients how change might be brought about without necessarily incurring the wrath of the conservation lobby.

John Thomas Micklethwaite (1843–1906)

Another supporter of the SPAB, Micklethwaite published *Modern Parish Churches* in 1874 and denounced the muscularity of the High Victorian Gothic style. George Frederick Bodley (1827–1907) had set the terms for the last phase of the Gothic Revival in Britain, one in which refinement was substituted for strength and originality. Micklethwaite was of that school. Hand in hand with this development came the 'Anti-Restoration Movement', its opposition being primarily to the conjectural replacement of genuine Late Gothic work with earlier, 'purer' styles. In 1872 Micklethwaite complained 'there are still some who would pull down good, genuine "perpendicular" to make way for sham "early English".'[18] Highly regarded by the SPAB for his espousal of such principles, Micklethwaite was chosen by the Society when it was asked to nominate a conservative architect for work to the chancel of Cherry Hinton church in Cambridgeshire. He campaigned on their behalf in many other cases during his long involvement with the Society, and his work at Inglesham church, Wiltshire, from the mid-1880s was exemplary.

Hugh Thackeray Turner (1850–1937)

Turner trained in the office of Sir George Gilbert Scott and became chief assistant to the younger Scott before taking up the post of Secretary to the

SPAB at the time that the committee published its first authoritative guidance, entitled *Notes on the Repair of Ancient Buildings.*[19] He seems likely to have been largely responsible for the text, though presumably he wrote it in close consultation with the key members of the Society of that time. Undoubtedly, this significantly included input from the SPAB's elder statesman and the originator of most of the conservation techniques evolved over the previous quarter of a century, Philip Webb. Turner's own contribution lay perhaps more in his ability, as the Society's first long-standing Secretary, to focus the efforts of the SPAB. As a result of his voluminous letter writing and quiet diplomacy, the vitriolic outbursts of Morris that characterized the SPAB's early years (and gained it the publicity that the fledgling Society so desperately needed) were tempered by quiet efficiency and organization.

But Turner was also a capable Arts and Crafts architect in his own right, as were other young architects on the SPAB committee in the 1890s such as William Lethaby, Ernest Gimson, Detmar Blow, Alfred Powell, Charles Winmill, and later William Weir. If mechanization and the great nineteenth-century building programme had threatened the continuity of craft practice, these early conservation-minded architects of the Arts and Crafts movement were in the vanguard of those who re-established the value of craftsmanship. Although the thread of traditional craft techniques may have worn thin earlier in the century, it remained unbroken, thanks to the scholarship and immense capability of leading Gothic Revival architects – despite their own often over-zealous restorations. A re-evaluation of their methodology, taking into account the context of the contracting world in which they operated, is long overdue.

THE INFLUENCE OF THE MODERN MOVEMENT

The key figures at this time included the architect Albert Reginald Powys (1885–1936), who was Secretary of the SPAB from 1908 until his early death in office in 1939. He is an interesting figure because his own modest work as an architect and his surviving letters and lecture notes show him to have been highly sympathetic both to the Arts and Crafts Movement and to the Modern Movement through his association with other young architects who, like himself, had come through the testing fire of the First World War and survived. In 1928, he published a book called *Repair of Ancient Buildings,*[19] which has become a classic reference work, twice re-printed in the late twentieth century. This book is largely an expansion of the SPAB's 1903 publication, though leaning more heavily on the work of William Weir, one of Philip Webb's keenest disciples. Powys was one of the two British representatives at the Athens Conference of 1931 (see below), and probably had a hand in drafting the declaration it issued. The so-called *Athens Charter* of 1933, drafted by Le Corbusier, was much more directly concerned with spreading the message of the Modern Movement. It also had an influence on the use of materials and on the contemporary response to historic towns and cities, two crucial issues.

It is not sufficiently realized that the repair and conservation of historic buildings was strongly influenced by the attitudes of the Modern Movement; however, this can be readily seen when we recollect that the work of repairing and altering and adding on to buildings was largely in the hands of architects, many of whom could not help admiring and being influenced by the work of their contemporaries. Some architects managed to be ambidextrous, carrying out work to old buildings in a 'clean', contemporary fashion, while at the same time designing quite advanced buildings in a Modern idiom, which may have seemed to deny the influences and traditions of good craftsmanship. It was a time of juxtapositions.

THE CONTINUITY OF CRAFT PRACTICE TODAY

Looking back at the last half of the twentieth century, we can generalize and say that there was, to begin with, a powerful feeling that building culture was inexorably breaking free from the bonds of the past. In all those countries that had suffered destruction of towns and cities and terrible loss of life during the second World War there developed, during the late 1940s–60s, a 'cult of the new' that seemed almost unstoppable. There was a feeling that, to prevent such calamities happening again, humanity had to make a fresh start. In England, the number of building firms that could confidently tackle the repair of traditional buildings, using traditional materials and skills started to dwindle. Training in the crafts seemed to hold little appeal for young people coming out of secondary education, more money could be earned by working in a car factory, and the idea of apprenticeship, of commitment to a craft, gradually became less appealing. It became increasingly difficult to obtain traditional building materials, as well as to find craftsmen able and willing to use them.

At the same time, though, there were countervailing forces. Internationally, there began to be a great revival of interest in the past; increased leisure encouraged tourism, including tourism of a discriminating kind, which gradually came to be called cultural tourism. This encouraged people to visit gardens, historic houses, cathedrals, churches, historic towns, museums, and even craft workshops. In the 1960s: Poland was reconstructing Old Town Square in Warsaw; Germany was restoring former royal and aristocratic residences such as the Castle at Bruchsal to a high standard of accuracy and fine craftsmanship; the Soviet Russians, unexpectedly perhaps, had begun on the heroic reconstruction of the former royal palaces in and around St Petersburg. In addition, France, concerned by the phenomenon of 'acid rain', had begun paying attention to the fate of its State-owned cathedrals. The owners of country houses in Britain had started, tentatively, to open or re-open them to the public as a way of offsetting the effects of a punitive tax regime, this was also because such houses, with their gardens and their estates, were already seen as part of the common cultural heritage which deserved to be shared with the wider public and with visitors from abroad. The turning point was in the early 1970s. Against a backdrop of improved legislation in many countries aimed at protecting historic buildings, the imaginative idea of inscribing 'World Heritage Sites' on an internationally recognized list of places identified as having that elusive quality of 'universal cultural value' was instigated in 1972, and in Europe, 1975 was designated 'European Architectural Heritage Year', culminating in the Congress and the Declaration of Amsterdam.

The very word 'heritage' now seems redolent of the 1970s, when those who supported it fought back against the negative attitudes and actions of the immediate post-War period. It became clear that something else was needed besides improvements in legislation, better policy documents, and a higher degree of funding. That missing component was craftsmanship. Allied to this revival of craftsmanship, there was also a growing realization that conservators were needed in the field – working on and in buildings – as well as in the conservation departments of museums. Sadly, a certain degree of friction and a lack of common purpose also developed between those practitioners who were essentially 'craft-based' (and who perhaps had undertaken a traditional apprenticeship), and conservators (who saw themselves as members of the newly established conservation profession, and perhaps had trained in museums on museum objects and had little experience of working on or in country houses, churches or cathedrals). In the 1970s, there were few trained conservators of sculpture working in and on buildings, and consequently much of the activity was carried out by dedicated and often talented people who were essentially amateurs or by those who had originally trained in some other field and then begun to apply what they had learned there to an architectural context. Much the same was true of other areas besides sculpture, such as stained glass, textiles, wall-paintings, historic musical instruments, and so on. The ethos of this time in craftsmanship and conservation deserves to be more fully recorded and understood, especially while there are still men and women around who have first-hand memories and experiences to contribute.

But what has all of this to do with continuity in craft practices? Everything, one might say. Among the most striking evidence of continuity in craft traditions is the fact that craftsmen everywhere, working with the same materials as their predecessors, on the whole use the same tools. There is something deeply moving about entering the workshop of a master carver and to have him expatiate on his tools, how he came by them, how he still makes some of them and how he maintains them. If only tools could speak! The same is true of the stonemason, the glazier, the blacksmith, the chair-bodger, the potter, the organ-builder, the bell-caster, the hedge-layer, the plasterer, and so forth.

Although there is now a considerable literature on the techniques of conservation – though much less, it is to be regretted, on the techniques of traditional crafts – it is also striking how valuable still are the treatises of the past such as the monk and goldsmith Theophilus's *On Divers Arts*, or the painter Cennino Cennini's *The Book of the Art*.[20] It is remarkable that modern craftsmen and conservators still read and refer to them, as well as the great works of nineteenth and early twentieth-century craft literatures.

Important roles have been played in maintaining the continuity of craft practice by those craftsmen who were able to live long enough to pass on their skills and knowledge, by the survival of particular training institutions and organizations, especially in France and Germany, and by the survival of particular organizations which did not depend wholly on the need to make a profit for shareholders. Prominent among the latter have been cathedral workshops, which exist in a number of countries, with the most famous probably being the *L'Oeuvre de Notre Dame* at Strasbourg Cathedral in France, a pivotal building both in its geographical location and its art and architectural history. The fame of this workshop is due partly to the extraordinary treasures it possesses in the form of original medieval drawings and other artefacts, and partly derives from the 'living treasures' it possesses in the form of craftsmen who can literally trace their craft ancestry back to the early Middle Ages.

In England, the continuity of cathedral workshops was disturbed by the Commonwealth in the middle of the seventeenth century, though even then it appears that not all repair work to cathedrals came to a complete halt. After the Restoration of the monarchy in 1660, there was a tremendous surge in craft activity in and about cathedrals. Shortly thereafter, in London a unique opportunity arose for building a new cathedral, St Paul's, and a large number of City churches. At the beginning of the twenty-first century we can record the existence of a substantial number of cathedral works organizations, which range from a Clerk of Works and a couple of handymen at some cathedrals to teams of twenty, thirty, or forty at the top end of the scale such as those in recent years at Canterbury, York, Wells, Salisbury, Lincoln, St Paul's, Chichester, Gloucester and Exeter. They go by various different names; for instance at York it is called the Minster Stoneyard. Some cathedrals and major churches, rather than establish their own teams of craftsmen, have instead developed longstanding relationships with particular building firms, such as Ely with Rattee and Kett, Lichfield with Linford-Bridgeman, Hereford with Capps & Capps, among others.

To put a long subject in a short compass, whilst traditional craft practice has continued into the twenty-first century, the scale of activity has declined, and it appears that we need to take urgent action to revitalize the traditional building crafts, including stonemasonry and carving. In England, we could do worse than examine the seemingly much more successful training regimes in France and Germany: countries which just as much as England experienced the 'cult of the new' in the post-War period in the middle of the last century. We need to encourage the emerging co-operation between cathedral works departments and exchanges of craftsmen pioneered by the cathedrals of Gloucester, Lincoln and York. We need to welcome, encourage and support the initiatives which have been taken by the SPAB in establishing the William Morris Craft Fellowships, and for the establishment of a trust to manage Woodchester Park Mansion in Gloucestershire. The latter is an unfinished country house that provides a perfect theatre of opportunity for real repair and replacement of stonework to be carried out as part of a training programme for students from stonemasonry courses at Bath and Weymouth Colleges. We also need to raise awareness of craftsmanship in the general public consciousness, embracing the work of the Heritage Lottery Fund and the national agencies at one end of the scale, to local preservation trusts and individual owners at the local level.

INTERNATIONAL CONSERVATION CHARTERS AND STANDARDS

The *SPAB Manifesto*[22] of 1877 promoted protection in place of restoration, its final paragraphs beginning to suggest a methodology that was developed later in the nineteenth century through Philip Webb and the young architects of the SPAB who worked on site, initially under his guidance. The Manifesto still forms the basis for current conservation policy, augmented by a series of conferences, charters and standards. Of these, the Athens Conference of 1931 mentioned above was the first to consider a code of practice for conservation. The *Venice Charter,*[21] published in 1966 and adopted by the newly founded International Council on Monuments and Sites (ICOMOS), superseded the Athens Charter. It stressed the importance of setting, respect for original fabric, meticulous recording of conservation interventions and the importance of all periods of a building's history. In the last forty years, a plethora of further recommendations has followed, the most important being approved by ICOMOS, including the *Burra Charter*[22] of 1981 and the *Nara Document on Authenticity*[25] of 1994. The *Burra Charter* introduced the concept of cultural significance as the basis for conservation policy-making and management, which is now generally accepted in place of the heritage-based principles previously expounded in Venice, and which forms the basis for conservation plans. The *Nara Document on Authenticity* overlays a deepening respect for original fabric upon significance-based conservation. In the UK, the *British Standard 7913:1998 Guide to the principles of conservation of historic buildings*[26] attempts to define the objectives of conservation and sets out criteria for repair, alterations and additions to historic buildings. It also provides definitions of the terms 'conservation', 'restoration' and 'preservation' that have become widely accepted amongst conservation professionals in the UK.

COMPLEMENTARY DISCIPLINES

Until the 1970s it was rare to involve art historians and archaeologists in major building conservation projects. The Wells Cathedral West Front Conservation Programme from 1974 to 1986 marked a change of approach. The Wells West Front Committee, which guided the work for twelve years, was unique at that time in that it consisted not only of the Dean and the Master of the Fabric of the cathedral, and the Cathedral

Architect and his assistant, but also the cathedral's own Clerk of the Works and Consultant Archaeologist, plus members appointed for their knowledge of art history and sculpture conservation by the Cathedrals Advisory Commission for England (the national regulatory body at that time). The significance of this was that diverse individuals were working together as a coherent team. The team included a man with the traditional craft skills as a stonemason (the Clerk of Works, Bert Wheeler), the Cathedral Architect (whose office went back in time and continuity deep into the traditions of the Arts and Crafts Movement, Alban Caroe and his son Martin Caroe) and the Consultant Conservator (Professor Robert Baker), as well as representatives of the 'new' disciplines of archaeology and the history of art and architecture, (represented by Warwick Rodwell, Professor Peter Lasko, Pamela Tudor-Craig and Peter Burman).

The conservation team included young men and women drawn by the magnetism of Robert Baker, and by the extraordinary potency and significance of the task. Many of its members have since become leaders of the conservation profession, or fine sculptors with international reputations. All had important contributions to make, and all were allowed to make them. Regrettably, some were not necessarily acknowledged as readily as should have been the case: the conservators (being 'workmen' presumably) were not invited to the feast when the Prince of Wales came to visit and to launch the final phase of the appeal. The inter-relationship of complementary disciplines that evolved at Wells has since become established, as at Salisbury Cathedral, described further in the next chapter. Jerry Sampson, himself an integral part of both the Wells and Salisbury teams, expands upon the process in a later chapter on the role of archaeology in conservation.

GUIDELINES FOR PRESENT AND FUTURE POLICY

Have the lessons learned at Wells concerning the use of complementary disciplines helped us to formulate a methodology to guide future policy? Perhaps, as they were applied by the consultant conservator, archaeologist and architect when undertaking the conservation and repair of the West Front at Salisbury Cathedral (1995–2000). Before work started on the scaffold, a policy was developed, integrating the disciplines that had worked together successfully at Wells,[27] but also further including geology, building pathology (pathology being the study of disease), conservation science and structural analysis. Together, these disciplines informed an interdisciplinary understanding of the building's fabric and history. Such an understanding should be the touchstone for future building conservation, and only when that understanding has been attained should consideration be given to the next stage in the procedure, that of policy development.

This process has parallels with conservation planning, as espoused for example in the *Burra Charter*. Conservation plans in the United Kingdom have developed over the last fifteen years, and are now well established as the standard framework for managing change. In Ireland they are an essential pre-requisite for all state-aided conservation projects, and in the UK they have become an essential part of large-scale Heritage Lottery Fund conservation applications. In every instance, conservation planning demands that we answer four questions, namely:

1. What exactly is the building, monument, artefact or site in question?
2. What is its significance?
3. In what ways might this significance be vulnerable?
4. What can be done so safeguard its significance?

Answering the first three of these questions equates to the development of a common understanding, concerning firstly the physical nature of the subject in question, secondly its cultural relevance and thirdly its susceptibility to change. A conservation plan for a great historic structure (such as that produced for Salisbury Cathedral by Alan Baxter Associates in 2005, for example) is entirely different from a policy document dealing with the conservation and repair of that structure. A conservation plan deals with the totality of the place and sets out fundamental policies for managing change. Such policies tend to be generalized, establishing, for example, that stone replacement is to be minimized and that conjectural or hypothetical restoration is unacceptable.

The detailed proposals for conservation and repair will move on from the generalized policies within a conservation plan to the specific requirements of a project. Be it the stabilization of the Leaning Tower of Pisa or the conservation of wall-paintings in an ancient parish church, each project will generate its own policies and methodologies. Those policies must come about as a result of an informed understanding of the history, significance and vulnerabilities of the structure in question. Even within the framework of current standards and conventions, policies will vary depending on the approach taken by the individual charged with conservation decision-making for any given project. However, the single most important aspect of this policy-making process, and perhaps the overriding essential guideline for the future, is not specifically what the policies might be, but that such policies should exist before technical specifications and contract documentation are prepared.

The authors

Peter Burman MBE, Dphil, SSA

Peter Burman is an architectural historian who studied at the Department of Architecture and Fine Art, University of Cambridge, and at the International Centre for Conservation and Restoration, Rome. He has had two previous vocations, one as Secretary of the Church of England's Council for the Care of Churches and the Cathedrals Fabric Commission for England, and the second as Director of the Centre for Conservation Studies, Department of Archaeology, The University of York. His present vocation is as Director of Conservation and Property Services for The National Trust for Scotland, Scotland's leading conservation and environmental charity. He is also Chairman of the Fabric Advisory Committee of St Paul's Cathedral, London, and a member of the Historic Environment Advisory Council for Scotland (HEACS).

Michael Drury RIBA, DipArch, GradDiplConsAA, AABC

Michael Drury is an architect, involved in the care of historic buildings belonging to the National Trust as well as Salisbury, Portsmouth and Westminster Cathedrals. His writings on building conservation and on the architecture of the Arts and Crafts Movement have been widely published.

References

1   Vitruvius, *The Ten Books of Architecture,* translated by Morris Hicky Morgan, Dover Publications, New York (1960), Book I, Chapter I: 2.
2   Ibid., Book I, Chapter III: 2.
3   Ibid., Book II, Chapter VII.
4   Ibid., Book II, Chapter VII.
5   Alberti, L. B., *The Ten Books of Architecture*, the 1755 edition translated by Giacomo Leoni, Dover Publications, New York, 1986.
6   Ruskin, J., *The Seven Lamps of Architecture*, Smith, Elder and Co., London, 1849, reprinted Noonday Press, New York, 1986.
7   Ruskin, J., *The Stones of Venice*, 1851–1853. Edited by Links, J. G., Da Capo, New York, 1960.
8   Ayers, T. (ed.), *Salisbury Cathedral – The West Front, A History and Study in Conservation*, Phillimore, Chichester, 2000, p. 94.
9   Drury, M., 'William Butterfield and The Restoration of the Church of St. Mary, Dinton in 1875', *Sarum Chronicle*, Issue 4, 2004, pp. 37–49.
10 Chris Brooks, *The Gothic Revival*, Phaidon, London, 1999, p. 309.

11   Quoted in Thompson, P., *William Butterfield*, Routledge and Kegan Paul, London, 1971, p. 48.

12   Pevsner, N. and Harris, J., *The Buildings of England, Lincolnshire*, Penguin Books, London, 1989, 2nd edn. revised by Nicholas Antrim, p. 724.

13   Pevsner, N. and Neave, D., *The Builidings of England, Yorkshire: York and the East Riding*, Penguin Books, London, 1995.

14   Street, G. E., 'Destructive Restoration on the Continent', *The Ecclesiologist*, 1857, p. 345.

15   Lethaby, W. R., *Philip Webb and his Work*, Oxford University Press, Oxford, 1935, p. 122.

16   Drury, M., *Wandering Architects*, Shaun Tyas, Stamford, 2000, pp. 94–99.

17   Gavin Stamp, *An Architect of Promise – George Gilbert Scott Junior (1839–1897) and the Late Gothic Revival*, Shaun Tyas, Donington, 2002, p. 234.

18   Ibid, p. 221.

19   *Notes on the Repair of Ancient Buildings*, issued by the Society for the Protection of Ancient Buildings, published by the Committee and sold on their behalf by B. T. Batsford, London (1903).

20   Powys, A. R., *Repair of Ancient Buildings*, SPAB, London, 1929, reprinted 1981.

21   Cennino Cennini was a fouteenth-century Tuscan painter who lived and worked in Padua; in *The Book of the Art* he expounds with great clarity the techniques of the painter. He was himself an important link in the continuity of tradition, having been a pupil of Agnolo Gaddi, who was a godson and pupil of Giotto.

22   *Society for the Protection of Ancient Buildings: Manifesto*, SPAB, London, 1877.

23   *International Charter for the Conservation and Restoration of Monuments and Sites (Venice Chater)*, ICOMOS, 1964, published in English by ICOMOS in 1966.

24   *Australian ICOMOS Burra Charter for the Conservation of Places of Cultural Significance*, first published by Australia ICOMOS in 1979, updated in 1981, 1988 and 1999.

25   *Nara Document on Authenticity*, drafted by the 45 participants at the *Nara Conference on Authenticity in Relation to the World Heritage Convention*, held at Nara, Japan, from 1–6 November 1994.

26   *BS 7913: 1998 Guide to the Principles of Conservation of Historic Buildings*. British Standards Institute, London, 1998.

27   Drury, M., 'The West Front of Salisbury Cathedral: The Development of a Policy for its Repair and Conservation', *ASCHB Transactions*, Vol. 20, 1995, pp. 49–58.

Chapter Three

Restoration Versus Conservation

Approaches and Policies

Michael Drury

RESTORATION

'Do not let us talk then of restoration,' said John Ruskin, 'The thing is a lie from beginning to end.'[1] The word 'restoration' resonates with the righteous indignation of Ruskin and Morris; yet it is still in common parlance, being the term most frequently used to describe what might often more accurately be described as the conservation and repair of old buildings.

The places of Ruskin and Morris in the history of the conservation movement are ensured, but those put forward for honourable mention in the previous chapter are not limited to only Ruskin, Morris, Webb, Micklethwaite, Turner and Powys, who inspired, founded and continued the Society for the Protection of Ancient Buildings (SPAB), the earliest meaningful manifestation of the conservation movement; there are also names from the other side of the great divide, restorers like Scott, Pearson, Street and Butterfield, with whom the SPAB violently disagreed. It is perhaps indicative of the historic perspective we now enjoy that representatives from both sides can be considered worthy of respect for their respective contributions to the rescue and repair of our ancient buildings. Our feet may be more firmly planted on one side than the other, but surely the great 'restoration versus conservation' debate is behind us? Surely we are all 'conservationists' now, for want of a better word?

Figure 3.1   St Albans Abbey from the south-west, before restoration. (English Heritage, NMR)

Figure 3.2   St Albans Abbey from the south-west, after restoration by Lord Grimthorpe between 1880 and 1885. (English Heritage, NMR)

Terminology has evolved over time, and this has helped to heal the wounds. In the early days of the restoration movement, Salisbury Cathedral and its 'Early English Pointed' style was upheld as the prime exemplar of Gothic architecture. Regardless of its true origins, anything built after the thirteenth century was considered debased in terms of its Gothic purity and had to be 'restored' to such Early English style. Thus, to Morris and those around him, restoration, at worst, meant to falsify the history of a building. Even when the structure in question had originated in the favoured period, the evidence for its original form had often been lost and the restoration, being conjectural, was equally likely to mislead.

Later, as the Gothic Revival grew more sophisticated, the merits of later medieval styles were appreciated but the tendency still remained to restore to a single period, for the purposes of architectural purity. Doing this meant the removal of any later additions and the reversal of any subsequent alterations. Our great churches and cathedrals, houses and castles were no longer to stand as markers of changing times. They were to 'faithfully' reflect only the 'intentions' of those who first conceived them. In the worst instances the later changes were lost, as well as the original conception as a result of conjectural restoration. The building emerged only as the restorer's vision of what the original designers might have intended had they been blessed with the questionable taste and discernment of the restorer himself.

Because church restorations in the early stages of the Gothic Revival were so often ill-informed, to those involved in the conservation movement in its early days, the reputations of the great church architects of the late nineteenth century were also irredeemably sullied, perhaps by association as much as by their own actions. Of course the SPAB's own understanding of conservation issues became more sophisticated as their experience grew, so by the 1890s their expectations had risen. Proposals that would have appeared conservative thirty years earlier were by then unacceptable. However, with hindsight the architects of the latter part of the nineteenth century were arguably the most talented, certainly the most experienced and probably the best informed architecturally of any who have ever had the responsibility to care for our historic buildings. To suggest that we know better now is a dangerous argument.

The modern definition of restoration does not perhaps differ greatly from the one Morris himself might have given:[2]

Alteration of a building or artefact which has decayed, been lost or damaged, or is thought to have been inappropriately repaired or altered in the past, the objective of which is to make it conform again to its design or appearance at a previous date.

Nowadays, however, the term 'restoration' need not have such a negative connotation as it did in Morris's day. English Heritage's published principles of repair[3] make a distinction between restoration of features of architectural or structural importance and conjectural restoration. The former involves situations where sufficient evidence exists for accurate replacement (provided it does not result in loss of historic fabric), which English Heritage believes may sometimes be justified. By contrast, it considers conjectural restoration as always unjustified. However, there is much confusion over terminology, even amongst professionals, with 'restoration' often being used indiscriminately and incorrectly to describe processes that have no intention of returning a building to its appearance at a former time.

PRESERVATION

What do we have to put in the place of 'restoration' as it was practised by the best of the nineteenth-century restoring architects? In the late nineteenth and early twentieth centuries, preservation was the guiding light. If restoration implied change, preservation was intended to arrest change. Preservation was the touchstone of the National Trust from its inception in 1895. The SPAB advised the Trust on its first building project, Alfriston Clergy House in Sussex, suggesting that they should 'restore it so far as that odious word means preserve from decay.'[4]

As Merlin Waterson points out in his history of the National Trust:[5]

It has always been one of the strengths of the Trust that the task it has set itself is so specific, as defined in its Acts of Parliament and in the clearly articulated objectives of its founders. The Trust was set up to hold property for permanent preservation.

But preservation is a limited goal. An arrested state of change is an artificial state that has been imposed upon a building under the assumption that it is incapable of evolution in a changing world. Preservation was an appropriate philosophy to save our great country houses, castles and ruined abbeys, for which no viable future purpose was deemed to exist save appreciation of their past glory. It ensured the survival of some of the best (and least adaptable) examples, and for this we must be thankful.

Figure 3.3 The Old Clergy House, Alfriston, Sussex, in a photograph taken before repairs were carried out for the National Trust by Alfred Powell in 1896. (National Trust Photo Library)

Figure 3.4 The Old Clergy House, Alfriston, Sussex in a photograph taken before 1900, but after the repairs of 1896 (from *Old Cottages and Farmhouses in Kent and Sussex*, Batsford, London, 1900).

However, such a strategy cannot ensure the well being of the vast majority of historic buildings that deserve a future.

CONSERVATION

For a viable future, conservation offers a way forward. Instead of reversing change or arresting change, conservation seeks to offer ways of managing change. As preservation offers neither a practical nor financially viable future for more than a handful of our historic buildings, conservation is the only real option for most. The British Standard Guide to the Principles of Conservation of Historic Buildings defines conservation as:[6]

> Action to secure the survival or preservation of buildings, cultural artefacts, natural resources, energy or anything of acknowledged value to the future.

The key word is action. Conservation has subsumed preservation, and restoration too; it embraces them. Sometimes conservationists restore buildings and sometimes they preserve them, but first they ask themselves how best to ensure a building's future. Often, change is required. How can that change be accommodated without compromising the significance of the building in question? Since the Burra Charter of 1981 (see previous chapter), the importance of significance-based conservation has been recognized, for if the significance of the building is not central to its planned future, change is likely to result in no more than modernization.

Within conservation a debate remains, nonetheless, and it is perhaps the descendent of the old one. For conservation has two meanings today: as well as meaning a holistic approach to managing change, conservation has a more specific meaning when applied to the repairs carried out by conservators; in this context it refers to consolidating and protecting stonework in order to save as much as possible of the original fabric.

To stone conservators this can mean many things, all of which are discussed in detail in later chapters. But sometimes the stone in question is too far decayed and no longer susceptible to the conservator's skills; it must be replaced. To the conservation architect, this process of replacement is a necessary part of the conservation process. But to the conservator it is outside his or her remit: it is not conservation, it is renewal; and to some, renewal is just another word for restoration. Certainly replacing old stones with new ones, in quantity, could be seen as an attempt to return a building to some earlier state. To a stone conservator, it is perhaps an admission of defeat. In terms of authenticity, new stones are certainly no substitute for the originals. 'Take proper care of your monuments,' wrote Ruskin in *The Seven Lamps of Architecture* 'and you will not need to restore them. Watch an old building with an anxious care; count its stones as you would the jewels of a crown ... do this tenderly, reverently, continually and many generations will be born to pass away beneath its shadow.'[7]

These fine words inspired William Morris's SPAB manifesto, but it has to be accepted that, in time, the stones that make up great architecture may fail individually to such an extent that the stone conservator can no longer save them. At this stage, only the stonemason can save the building by replacement, and if so, how does he renew without restoration? He could, hypothetically, replace a weathered stone with a sound but equally distressed-looking one, but this presents other problems concerning the credibility of the whole. Instead, those concerned must use their best endeavours to judge how that particular stone might originally have been when new. Set in place alongside its worn neighbours, it will not pretend to be original but will maintain the architectural and structural integrity of the whole. When its neighbours also eventually deteriorate to the point of no return, they too may be replaced to a similar pattern and be reset to a similar line, replicating the originals and maintaining the building as a totality.

Ruskin did not agree, and here perhaps most conservationists may part company with their august mentor. Ruskin did, indeed, consider restoration a lie from beginning to end, and such arguments would not win him over:[8]

> But, it is said, there may come a necessity for restoration! Granted. Look the necessity full in the face, and understand it on its own terms. It is a necessity for destruction. Accept it as such, pull the building down, throw its stones into neglected corners, make ballast of them, or mortar, if you will; but do it honestly, and do not set up a lie in their place.

Ruskin's argument for authenticity became a central tenet of the SPAB's cause, carried on with vigour via Morris[9] and his followers into the twentieth century and resulting, eventually, in attitudes and laws that inform the protection of our listed buildings today. Nonetheless, the contemporary listing process is in fact at odds with Ruskin's plea for demolition rather than replication, and it leaves those responsible for upholding this legislation with a dilemma. For while the most conservative of conservation architects may wish to do all they can to retain a decaying stone for its authenticity, ultimately the architect's duty is to the building as a whole. The informed building archaeologist values the ancient stone in question for what it can tell us, but much of this information lies on the surface, where man has made his mark upon it. If this stone is so worn that it can no longer tell its story, the dispassionate archaeologist may share Ruskin's view that it might as well be used as hardcore, despite its unquestionable authenticity. Both the architect and the archaeologist will have their own views on the significance of the building in question, but it is usually conservation officers (or their equivalents in ecclesiastical jurisdictions), who are responsible for upholding the legislation. Yet, the legislation, whilst intended to protect the original character of listed buildings, can actually threaten their authenticity, since it seeks to ensure that we maintain historic buildings indefinitely. When stones wear out, the indefinite maintenance imperative requires that they must be replaced, and authenticity is thereby progressively eroded.

The point at which such intervention becomes necessary, and the degree of intervention required, will vary from building to building. At Stonehenge, for example the Ruskinian argument holds good; stones

Figure 3.5 Stonehenge 1901: 'Starting for straightening with ropes strained', from 'Gowland, W., 'Recent Excavations at Stonehenge', *Wiltshire Archaeological Magazine,* Vol. 33, June 1903, pp. 1–62. Detmar Blow (in white panama) and Dr William Gowland, the archaeologist, raise the remaining leaning stone in the central and largest of the five trilithons that form the inner ring or horseshoe. (Wiltshire Archaeological and Natural History Society)

Figure 3.6 York Minster, the east end today. (Louise Hampson)

have been re-erected when they have fallen, cracked lintels have been pinned, but no stones have ever been replaced. Most would agree with Ruskin that to do so would be 'to set up a lie in their place'. But at York, for example, there is today a well reasoned case for the replacement of a large proportion of the stones making up the east elevation of the Minster to maintain structural integrity and ensure the stability of the magnificent medieval glass of the east window.

What might be an appropriate approach at York Minster is unlikely to be appropriate at Stonehenge. The latter epitomizes that group of historic structures that have outlived their original purpose – at Stonehenge to such a degree that no one now even knows with certainty what that purpose was. Although some of the fallen stones have been re-erected and others underpinned, the stones themselves are authentic. There is no perceived need either to restore the structure to its original state or find a future use for it. The goal is to simply preserve what remains, ensuring as many as possible can experience it. York Minster, on the other hand, still performs the function for which it was originally constructed. Buildings have come and gone, changing and adapting to suit this continuity of purpose. Indeed, much of the stone in need of renewal at the east end today dates from an earlier intervention in the nineteenth century. As a result, the conservation issues concerning stone replacement at York are entirely different to those at Stonehenge.

Our conclusion must be that each case should be thought through from first principles. This is not as demanding as it might sound: conservationists are doing it all the time mentally, often without realizing what complex value judgements they are making. A simple, written policy statement is worthwhile in all instances nonetheless, establishing the issues that must be addressed. In more complicated projects, this policy statement may be a substantial document, and it is worth considering its likely content and producing a list of points it should generally address. The project-specific needs of a particular case, be it large or small, simple or complex, might then be assessed and measured against this list.

The first point to establish is that this policy statement is not a specification; nor is it a stone-by-stone schedule of necessary works. These things come later. The policy statement is, instead, intended to present the information that would enable the conservationist to understand the building, assess its significance, and consider the threats facing it in order to make informed decisions about its conservation. Attention has previously been drawn to the parallels between this process and that adopted in the preparation of a conservation plan; the differences will be examined later in this chapter.

The list below derives from experience at Salisbury Cathedral, where a policy statement was prepared for the repair and conservation of the West Front.[10] The policy statement was formulated by the Cathedral's consultant stone conservator, Nicholas Durnan, in conjunction with the author (as Cathedral Architect). The headings are summarized in the following list and each item is discussed in more detail thereafter:

- Recording
- Archaeological/historical development
- Geology
- Condition
- Decay mechanisms
- Associated elements (other than masonry)
- Structural analysis
- Trials
- Conclusions and policy making

The chapters that follow later in this book deal with many of these aspects more fully. They are summarized here as an aid for decision-making and policy formulation. There must be sufficient understanding of each aspect to enable informed conclusions to be reached.

Recording

Recording must be undertaken before work commences, as it is an essential tool for the architect as well as the archaeologist. An archaeological record should be established in all significant conservation projects, and good conservationists will always leave a clear record of the interventions that have been made. Information must be conveyed, be it to obtain approvals, or to convey instructions between architect and conservator or between other members of the team. The record might be photogrammetric, rectified photographic, measured survey or purely photographic. It may well be a combination of these methods. Photogrammetry, for example, may need to be enhanced by manual survey techniques to show elements hidden from the camera, such as parapet backs, reveals, hidden faces of turrets, or pinnacles and flying buttresses. The correct methodology will, in each instance, depend upon the information that needs to be conveyed and should be established at the outset between all concerned.

Archaeological/historical development

The record should be marked up to show archaeology relevant to the project, thereby contributing to informed decision-making (see the following chapter). Those responsible for policy-making and specifying stone-by-stone schedules need to know the developmental sequence of the fabric in question and the history of previous interventions. Quite apart from this, an archaeological interpretation of the mark-up may further our understanding of the building or structure in question. Care should be taken in appointing the right archaeologist for the job. Below-ground archaeology and above-ground building archaeology are related disciplines, but if an archaeologist's experience is predominantly below ground, he may not be ideally suited for unravelling the complex issues inherent in a building project.

Geology

For the same reasons, the record drawings must be marked up and interpreted to inform a clear understanding of the masonry's geology. All stones used in the construction sequence should be identified, and, if needed, suitable replacements sourced.. The British Geological Survey can be invaluable for this task, as they provide specialist services such as thin section petroscopy for detailed analysis (as well as more general assistance). Identifying the right advisor is essential in each instance: building stone geology is a specialist geological field and local knowledge is often essential.

Condition

The condition of the masonry will dictate its treatment, and a condition survey is an essential part of the decision-making process. Such surveys may indicate patterns of deterioration. These may or may not relate to previous archaeological or geological mark-ups that indicate perhaps a poor stone selection in earlier repair campaigns, badly chosen stone at the outset, or ill-conceived developments in the structure's historical evolution. It may also identify particular elements of the structure that are at risk; for example stones in thin-walled parapets, mullions or traceries, weathering stones, carved detail, and perhaps other elements. Those responsible for scheduling conservation or renewal may be influenced, when considering the future of a specific stone, by the knowledge that the stone in question is, for example, the last original survivor of this particular stone detail on the building.

Decay mechanisms

Why has the masonry deteriorated? What decay mechanisms are operating? How does the stone's porosity, hardness or geological composition contribute to this? Is there evidence of salt content or crystallization? How does microclimate or relative humidity affect the process? What is the temperature gradient across the stone or masonry element, from outside to inside? How does the heating of the building affect the situation? All these questions should be answered when necessary, and there may be others. Analytical techniques should be considered, and time allowed for complex processes. Samples of stone from the building might be subjected to petrographic examination, salt analysis, and so on. Only when the reasons for deterioration are fully understood should decisions concerning conservation processes be made.

Associated architectural elements

Is stone masonry the only element relevant to the conservation project in hand? A masonry elevation may include a glazed opening or a wooden door. A roof element or gutter may be in need of attention to protect the masonry, or the stone surface may have been rendered or even decorated in the past. Associated elements must be given the same rigorous attention as the stone itself. They must be recorded, their material properties understood, and their decay mechanisms analysed. Every effort should be made to ascertain the presence of surviving polychrome decoration on the stone surface at the earliest opportunity, externally as well as internally. If there is the remotest evidence of the existence of such decorative schemes, a specialist conservator should be engaged to inspect the stone surface. Simple decorations using earth pigments (or even unpigmented limewash) may have proved relatively transient and only the faintest traces may remain, but such fugitive remnants may add enormously to our understanding of the building's past and may influence conservation policy in a fundamental way.

Structural analysis

The structural behaviour of the masonry element in question must be properly understood and, if necessary, analysed by a capable structural engineer specializing in historic building work. Over time, walls subside or lean, buttresses are added, buildings are altered, core material degrades or settles, window traceries become disrupted, pinnacles twist or lean, and gables are subjected to roof racking and eaves to roof thrust. Monitoring may be required to determine whether movement is ongoing or has ceased. Inappropriate repairs may have been made in the past, and inappropriate materials introduced. All these interventions must be understood and their structural implications assessed before conservation policies are determined.

Trials and testing

At this stage in the proceedings, after comprehensive recording and analytical work has been completed and before firm conservation policy decisions are taken, trials may be informative. These can range from

Figure 3.7 Bishop Brithwold, after conservation trials to establish the appropriate degree of mortar repair modelling (as opposed to the capping of friable stone for strictly conservation purposes) and to formulate a policy for the sheltercoating of statuary. Here the bishop's outer garment is sheltercoated, but the remainder of the figure is not. As a result of these trials it was decided to treat all statuary completely for conservation reasons, the colour selected being very slightly paler than the stone background to improve legibility.

Figure 3.8 Discussions with the client group resulted in trials, again undertaken on Bishop Brithwold, concerning the reintroduction of missing attributes to make the figures more readily recognizable. In Brithwold's case, this entailed the modelling of his hand, raised in blessing, and his bishop's staff. It was possible to do this from earlier photographs, but the trial resulted in a policy to conserve as found.

relatively simple sample areas of cleaning or pointing to more sophisticated and specialized work on particular elements. Samples of proposed replacement stone may be subjected to petrographic analysis, crushing tests, accelerated freeze/thaw cycles and carving tests for tractability.

Sometimes, alternative options may need to be tested to inform decision-making on policy proposals. At Salisbury Cathedral, for example, trials were undertaken on the nineteenth-century statue of Bishop Brithwold to clarify conservation issues for the remainder of the West Front figures.

Conclusions and policy-making

Policies for conservation and repair will ideally follow from investigations such as those outlined above. Such policies will vary for each masonry conservation project, but it may be of interest to consider the policies developed at Salisbury Cathedral for the work on the West Front, carried out between 1995 and 2000 as an example (see the case study below). These policies were formulated and approved prior to commencement of scheduling and contract documentation. The document itself covered all aspects of the West Front programme, including polychrome decoration, the conservation of glass and window assemblies, recording procedures and archaeological protocol. In some instances, such as those of stone consolidation and statuary conservation, the works as carried out departed from the original policy, but this does not invalidate the policy-making process, for it is not the policy itself that is of value but the thinking from which it develops (and from which, of course, the ongoing process grows).

Within this policy-making process, be it at a great cathedral or the smallest masonry structure, there is an inherent consideration of stone renewal and conservation that stems directly from the restoration/conservation debate. Within the overriding principles of the established conservation policy, those charged with decision-making will consider several, often conflicting issues when deciding the future of an individual stone. Those issues may be summarized as follows:

- Significance
- Authenticity
- Structural integrity
- Weathering capability
- Durability
- Location/accessibility
- Prominence

The decisions that result from the consideration of these issues must only be taken at the appropriate time within the project's development. For example, a detailed assessment cannot be made of a stone's condition until access is available. But by the time a scaffold is in place, it is too late to undertake photogrammetric recording. Generally the process might be as follows:

- Recording
- Scaffolding
- (Cleaning) – in parentheses because cleaning is not always part of the process but if it is, scheduling is more accurate after cleaning than before
- Archaeological/Geological/Condition surveying and mark-up, trials and policy-making
- First scheduling (provisional mark-up for renewal/conservation)
- Approvals
- Tendering
- Contract commencement
- Rescheduling with contracting mason/conservator (final mark-up)
- Undertaking renewal and primary conservation work
- Adjustment after intervention to balance conservation needs with presentation, if necessary.

By following a planned process along these lines, considering the merits of individual stones within the parameters of a predetermined policy, and bearing in mind all the relevant issues that might affect decision-making, the renewal or repair of masonry becomes part of an overarching conservation process. No longer should the conservator feel that stone replacement is an admission of defeat; conversely, nor should the stonemason think that the conservator's work is merely a token short-term stopgap measure. Both are integral parts of a properly conceived programme of conservation and repair. No longer is there room for argument about the relative merits of restoration and conservation.

CASE STUDY

The following is an extract from another paper by the author based on the abovementioned work he was involved with on the West Front of Salisbury Cathedral.[11] It describes the policy document that was prepared in that case by Nicholas Durnan, Consultant Conservator to Salisbury Cathedral, in conjunction with the author as Cathedral Architect, and the extracts below provide a fitting conclusion to this chapter.

SALISBURY CATHEDRAL, WEST FRONT

At Salisbury the aim is to preserve as much of the existing stonework as possible with special emphasis on the stone surfaces which hold valuable archaeological information and artistic content, and to do this without creating problems for those who will care for the building later. It is accepted that severely decayed architectural stonework will need to be replaced for either structural or visual reasons but every effort will be made to conserve sculpture and ornament and retain it *in situ*. The intention is to preserve the feeling of age that the West Front conveys whilst clarifying the original design through sensitive cleaning and repair. For example, worn or lichen-covered surfaces are acceptable if the stone is sound, whereas black soot crusts, which are thought to be disfiguring and potentially harmful, are to be reduced.

The original intention of the architects, builders and sculptors will be respected by ensuring meticulous replication of the original design where stone replacement is the only option. Dr Richard Morris of Warwick University is providing full-size copies of the medieval moulding profiles to assist the masons when templating work stones. The masons are encouraged to develop their own creative ability, the Works Department having run stone-carving courses under John Green to develop their skills. The masons are encouraged to model first in clay to allow their designs to develop. This gives the architect an opportunity to become involved in the process too, trying to inject life into the piece and to give it its place on the building. A specialist carver has recently been appointed to lead the team on the programme of carved replacements on the West Front.

The lime treatments used during previous decades on the limestone west fronts of Wells, Exeter and Rochester Cathedrals and Bath Abbey have been broadly similar; cleaning to remove pollutants and their

Figure 3.9   Salisbury Cathedral West Front in 1994, before conservation and repair.

Figure 3.10   Salisbury Cathedral West Front in 1994. Detail of statuary before conservation.

products; undoing past inappropriate repair techniques; filling voids and protecting and consolidating fragile surfaces with lime mortar, lime-water and sheltercoat, along with minimum stone replacement. The emphasis has been on using techniques that are, as far as is possible, reversible and re-treatable, believed to behave in a similar way or in harmony with the stone being treated, and are sacrificial (i.e. they are designed to deteriorate before and in preference to the stone). The conservation work is invariably supported by an archaeological investigation and detailed documentation.

It is important to remember that lime treatments were seen at Wells and Exeter Cathedrals as a holding operation until better treatments were devised, rather than as a really long-term remedy for stone decay problems. Therefore, regular maintenance and inspection are an essential part of this treatment to ensure the continued well being of the stone. However, it is understood that post-treatment surveys at Wells have on the whole shown the conservation work to be slowing down the rate of weathering and decay as well as or better than expected, and have also suggested ways of improving the effectiveness of the treatment. Re-treatment of lime-treated stonework has been successfully carried out at both these sites.

However the processes whereby lime treatments reduce the rate of stone decay are not fully understood and further work is needed in quantifying how each different aspect of the treatment works in relation to the overall conservation approach. English Heritage, active in continuing assessment of lime treatments, agree that lime treatments in their present form are the most appropriate current method for conserving exterior limestone at the Cathedral. Conservation experience elsewhere on the Cathedral in recent years using lime treatments has been good but the concern of others about the lack of scientific evidence for the beneficial effects of limewater and sheltercoat treatment is shared. As with any conservation treatment, the aim is to prescribe the appropriate remedy for each particular problem. To this end decay mechanisms continue to be assessed, as do the effects of the proposed conservation treatments, as the programme progresses. Techniques are thus fine-tuned or adjusted accordingly in the light of experience.

The stone conservation policy was proposed in the light of results from trial conservation and repair work in conjunction with a detailed survey of the central scaffolded area (below the great west window) and experience gained from recent major repair projects elsewhere on the cathedral. The policy differs depending on the architectural function performed by the stone in question and these functions are divided, for the purposes of this policy, into:

- architectural framework;
- ornament;
- statuary;
- polychromed stonework.

Each is dealt with separately in the policy document but as space does not permit a full exposition here, only those aspects common to all can be looked at on this occasion. As far as cleaning is concerned the general policy is to reduce surface deposits rather than remove them. Generally a 50% cleaning policy is found appropriate as the surface colorations of algae and lichen are seen to be an inherent part of the visual appeal of the stonework. Although this policy varies on differing elements of the West Front, it appears that little physical harm is caused to the stonework by algae and lichens and this is supported by a report from the Natural History Museum. As a variety of cleaning techniques are being employed according to the type of deposit, the result will be carefully monitored to achieve a balanced result. Loose algae and lichen are removed by dry brushing followed by localized poulticing and reduction of soot crusts using the Jos vortex piccolo (water/calcite abrasive) system.

As a general rule only cement mortar placed over medieval lime joints is to be removed and then only if the joint width is wide enough to allow removal without damage. Cement mortar pointing to 1860s rebuilding, bedded in cement mortar, is to be cut out only to re-pointing depth and only if it can be removed without damage to the stone arises. If damage to the stone is unavoidable cement mortar is left in place unless there is a good case for its removal.

Laminating stone is held together using threaded stainless-steel dowels set in lime mortar. Hydraulic and non-hydraulic limes are used as appropriate. It is not known whether or how quickly laminations will occur, although each statue will be carefully inspected in an attempt to anticipate where future laminations may occur. Regular future inspection of the statues is especially important so as to monitor and repair as necessary further laminating.

The figure of Bishop Brithwold was selected for trial conservation during the twelve-month period of trials and analysis [see Figures 3.7 and 3.8]. Lessons learned here suggest that careful dentistry repairs can fill cracks and voids while blistering skins may be packed from behind.

Friable substrate should be removed wherever possible before applying repairs. Small loose pieces may be re-adhered with fine lime mortar or pure putty. As a general rule small areas of lost form (say up to 24 mm) are remodelled to the original surface, large areas of loss (over 24 mm) are capped to suggest lost form. Mortar is designed to be slightly weaker than stone and both more porous and more permeable.

The statuary is very absorbent (perhaps because it is face-bedded) and therefore takes in more limewater than other stonework. Limewatering of Chilmark stone suggests a beneficial effect and is to be undertaken in selected areas. It is thought likely that the beneficial effect on face-bedded stone may be greater due to the relative absorption rate. 40–50 applications of limewater are to be applied to each statue. [In fact limewatering was abandoned on the West Front programme soon after the policy was formulated, its benefit being questionable. Most conservation proved achievable without a consolidant but, in a handful of instances, a synthetic consolidant (ethyl silicate) was used on a 'use it or loose it' basis.] The effect of sheltercoating in 1982 on the north buttress appears to be beneficial in that much has survived for 14 years. The surfaces are generally sound both where it survives and where it has been washed away. Sheltercoat application is proposed on the statuary for the following reasons:

- the statuary surfaces are open and water-permeable which makes them vulnerable to future decay especially since they are all face-bedded; sheltercoat is intended to control the surface permeability.
- The rate of decay since the 1860s on some of the Victoriana and all of the medieval statues has been quite dramatic; sheltercoat should slow down the rate of surface sulphation;
- The statues are inadequately protected from direct rainfall; the north buttress trial in 1982 seems to indicate that sheltercoat will protect rain-washed surfaces in the short-term.

Sheltercoat will be applied as a single application to each statue ensuring that there is no obscuration of fine detail by careful brushing away of excess both during and after application.

A policy for conservation and repair of statuary

It is proposed that all surviving medieval and Victorian statuary should remain on the West Front and that every effort should be made to solve all conservation problems *in situ*, the nineteenth-century sculpture being

Figure 3.11 Salisbury Cathedral West Front: a figure in the topmost tier, in an advanced state of decay. The damage relates not only to the medieval torso but also to the nineteenth-century additions of the head and right arm; the restraining bands are thought to be from the mid-twentieth century. Later analysis revealed that this figure, initially re-attributed as an angel at the foot of Christ in Majesty in the high gable above, was actually a bishop vested for mass in the original medieval iconography.

treated from the same ethical standpoint as the medieval. This policy is based upon the following observations:

- both the medieval and Victorian statues were designed to be situated in niches and viewed from the ground at their various heights; no museum could adequately simulate these conditions;
- the decayed medieval statues are barely worthy of exhibition in a museum as their worn forms look so much better when viewed from a distance;
- the fragility of the decayed statues is such that the physical process of moving them from the West Front to a place of 'safe keeping' could cause further damage;
- many people would rather see the authentic article on the West Front, no matter how decayed, than look at a replica;
- to create something of equal or better quality than the removed statues is a task that requires enormous skill and sensitivity, as experience at other cathedrals will testify.

It is, however, important to face up to the fact that although it is thought that hopefully nearly all medieval and Victorian statuary can be retained, as part of this programme of conservation and repair, there will come a time in the future when the condition of the statuary will necessitate removal and replacement. [In fact two figures, that shown in Figure 3.11 and its partner on the other side of the high gable, were found to be in such poor condition that they had to be taken down for the safety of those passing below. They were re-housed in the nave roof space nearby, new figures being carved by Jason Battle and set in that place.]

The author

Michael Drury RIBA, DipArch, GradDiplConsAA, AABC

Michael Drury is an architect, involved in the care of historic buildings belonging to the National Trust as well as Salisbury, Portsmouth and Westminster Cathedrals. His writings on building conservation and on the architecture of the Arts and Crafts Movement have been widely published.

References

1   Ruskin, J., *The Seven Lamps of Architecture*, Smith, Elder and Co., London, 1849, reprinted Noonday Press, New York, 1961.
2   *British Standard BS7913: 1998 Guide to the Principles of Conservation of Historic Buildings*, British Standards Institute, 1998.

3   Brereton, C., *The Repair of Historic Buildings: Advice on Principles and Methods*. English Heritage, London, 2nd edn, 1995.

4   Letter from Octavia Hill to Sydney Cockerell in 1895, in the SPAB's file on Alfriston Clergy House, SPAB archive, London.

5   Waterson, M., *The National Trust: The First Hundred Years*, The National Trust, London, 1994, p. 265.

6   *British Standard BS7913: 1998 Guide to the Principles of Conservation of Historic Buildings*, British Standards Institution, 1998.

7   Ruskin, J., 'The Lamp of Memory' in *The Seven Lamps of Architecture, op. cit.*

8   Ibid.

9   See Miele, C. (ed.), *From William Morris: Building Conservation and the Cult of Authenticity, 1877–1939*, Paul Mellon, London, Yale, 2005.

10   Drury, M., 'The West Front of Salisbury Cathedral: The Development of a Policy for its Repair and Conservation', *ASCHB Transactions*, Vol. 20, 1995, pp. 49–58.

11   Ibid.

Chapter Four

The Role of Archaeology

Jerry Sampson

At a time when public interest in archaeology has perhaps never been greater, that branch of the discipline which is concerned with the analysis and recording of standing buildings is still little known. This means, for example, that most parishes will understand that there is an archaeological dimension to the work if large holes are to be excavated in the floor of their parish church for a new heating system. However, they may not appreciate the existence of this dimension if similar interventions in the standing fabric have to be carried out in the church tower to install a new telephone system.[1] Even amongst professional archaeologists, the below-ground aspects of a building conservation project are more likely to be addressed than those pertaining to the standing fabric. In part, this is because the below-ground deposits are obviously destroyed by earth-moving, whereas the standing fabric usually appears to remain substantially unaltered in all but the most intrusive programmes of works. However, the mere provision of scaffolding enables close examination of parts of a building to which access may not have been available for a century or more. Such examination often shows that even the apparently harmless process of repointing a wall may diminish or even destroy the historical information encoded in the building, which a skilled building archaeologist may be able to read.

In general, the task of the building archaeologist is to record the standing fabric of historic buildings, seeking to understand how such a building was erected, how it functioned and how it appeared when it was completed, and what alterations and repairs it has undergone from that time to the present. The erection of scaffolding during modern repair programmes assists immeasurably in the achievement of these objectives by allowing close examination of otherwise inaccessible parts of the fabric. Increasingly, the building archaeologist has become a key contributor to stonework conservation projects in particular. By properly integrating archaeological recording into a repair programme, both the archaeologist and the conservator can benefit greatly. While archaeological investigation has a clear agenda of its own, the detailed assessment of the significance of the fabric which it yields can be utilized by the stone conservator in determining what must be retained and what can be safely renewed without diminishing that significance.

Over the last 25 years, the archaeological monitoring of standing fabric during conservation projects in our greater buildings has become standard practice. All of the English and Welsh cathedrals have their own archaeological consultants, and English Heritage and Cadw generally require an archaeological survey as an integral part of repair programmes for buildings in their own guardianship, or for those receiving grants. However, repairs to smaller buildings – particularly those that, for a variety of reasons, do not apply for or do not receive grants – are less likely to form the subject of an archaeological survey or watching brief.

THE ROLE OF ARCHAEOLOGY IN STONE CONSERVATION

In any conservation project, the archaeological examination of the building should form an essential preliminary, only through a full understanding of the structure can the nature, extent and programme of works be responsibly specified. Such an understanding should lie at the heart of the decision-making process, both in the overall design of the project and in the detail of the subsequent decisions. This can be illustrated by the approach undertaken in the conservation of the West Front at Salisbury Cathedral,[2] where, between 1995 and 2000, each season of the cleaning, repair and conservation programme was preceded by an archaeological survey using hand-enhanced photogrammetric drawings as base-maps to record the fabric in detail.

In this instance, two main sets of base-maps were marked up; one was coded to record the stonework itself, and the other annotated to mark the position of surviving traces of medieval or later decorative finishes. The first coded record drawing had two aspects. It colour-coded each block of the structure to indicate the date of its emplacement in the building – whether it was original, whether it belonged to one of the earlier restorations identifiable from the documentary records, or whether it was part of an undocumented restoration. It also provided annotated codes defining each block's geological origin, the presence of any original tooling, original hot mastic repairs, or other significant details. These drawings, as well as forming the basis for the analysis of the historical repair of the façade, were also used to inform the detailed decisions on stone replacement during the modern repair, since the completed drawings were passed to the architect and consultant conservator for use on the scaffolding during the process of marking-up the proposed areas for repair. This meant that as each individual block was specified for replacement or repair, the architect and conservator were aware of the significance of that stone in terms of its date and whether it bore surviving tooling or other significant finishes.

In determining whether to repair or replace a stone within a complex building such as the west façade of a cathedral, a major factor will always be the extent to which that block can still perform its architectural function. Granting this, greater efforts towards preservation will always be made in borderline decisions if the stone in question is known to possess features that enhance its significance. In general, there will be a greater reluctance to renew a medieval stone (particularly if it bears decorative carvings or mouldings) than a Victorian restoration, but there is also a more subtle hierarchy of significance in the context of the medieval fabric. For instance, the delicate hot mastic repairs used by medieval masons to mend accidental breaks from the early thirteenth century onwards are often difficult to see and are still little known.[3,4,5] But the early identification of more than eighty such repairs, and notification of their presence to the Salisbury conservators, ensured the preservation of a considerably higher number than would otherwise have been the case.

The preliminary archaeological survey at Salisbury also proved to be of particular importance with regard to the survival of the external medieval polychromy of the façade and the west porch. As part of the initial survey, the building archaeologist recorded those areas where paint could be identified with certainty, together with those areas where (given the discoloured nature of the stone in its uncleaned state) it was suspected to have survived but could not be clearly isolated. These areas having been identified during the initial survey, they could then be further appraised and analysed by the specialist polychromy consultant, Eddie Sinclair. The cleaning and treatment of the stonework could then be adapted as necessary to respect the presence of the paint and to ensure its survival. With the exception of its extensive survival in the west porch, paint on the façade proved to be particularly rare. The preliminary survey showed that it occurred only on those niches where medieval sculptures had been installed in what was evidently a severely restricted campaign of figure carving in the second quarter of the fourteenth century. As a result of this finding, extra vigilance was exercised by the conservators in cleaning the

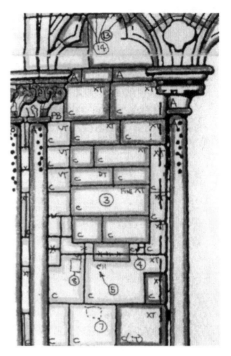

Figure 4.1   Close analysis of standing fabric can result in the stone-by-stone analysis of a building into phases of building and restoration, as here in the West Front of Bath Abbey.

Figure 4.2   Phase drawing for part of the west porch of Salisbury Cathedral. No re-pointing was done here, but there would have been a case for re-pointing the rectangular scar of the blocked niche in the wall beneath the canopies in the slightly orange-coloured mortar of the blocking in order to allow it to be seen more clearly.

stonework around known and suspected sites of lost and surviving medieval figures, and a number of new paint traces were discovered in this way, incidentally enabling the extent of the medieval sculptural campaign to be accurately reconstructed.

Indeed, in a wider context the work at Salisbury shows how extensively archaeological surveying can underwrite a conservation project. The findings of the archaeological survey did feed back into the conservation of stone and polychromy as intended, but they also formed the foundation for technical aspects of the art historical analysis. They did this by providing the means of identification for the position of lost medieval sculptures, and of those few surviving examples of medieval foliate carving. Also, by defining the technical characteristics of the nineteenth-century workshop that produced the restored figure sculptures, it was possible to refine our understanding of the order of execution of the carvings and to isolate those figures that were not part of its *oeuvre*.

Although the West Front of Salisbury cathedral is an example of 'high conservation', benefiting greatly from the provision of photogrammetry and a budget capable of supporting detailed survey work, it should not be assumed that humbler buildings with lesser financial resources could not benefit from an archaeological survey. While it may not be possible to provide stone-by-stone analysis and recording of the fabric, even a brief survey can provide insights that might significantly affect conservation decisions. Even merely alerting a conservation team to the possibility of the existence of some feature of a building – as with the expectation of paint survivals on niches with original sculptures at Salisbury – could result in discoveries that might otherwise have passed unnoticed. Indeed, recent discoveries of medieval pigment surviving on the quatrefoil band on the west tower of Beaminster church in Dorset show that external polychromy was applied to medieval parish churches as well as the great cathedrals.

PRELIMINARY SURVEY

Ideally, prior to the erection of the scaffolding, a preliminary archaeological survey, using documentation (the so-called 'desk-top survey') and examination of the structure from the ground, should provide the basis for an initial understanding of the building. It is at this stage also (in projects where accurate drawings are unlikely to be available) that photographs for rectification or use as base-maps for acetate overlays should be taken. It is important, however, that 'received wisdom' about a building should not be allowed to lead to any hasty assumptions about the status of the fabric.

Isle Abbots possesses one of the classical Somerset towers for which the county is famous, its significance greatly enhanced by the survival of ten of the twelve figure sculptures with which it was originally adorned. However, the archaeological desk-top survey located documentary evidence that the upper parts of the tower had been entirely rebuilt around 1870. A preliminary survey of the interior of the tower and its stair turret showed that at the level of the apex of the west window, the stonework changes, from random rubble in a white lime mortar, to crisp blue Lias block laid in courses and fixed with cement. Thus the tower has evidently been taken down to the top of the ground floor chamber and rebuilt. It would have been tempting, on this basis, to assume that the upper fabric of the tower had been wholly renewed, and that the upper stonework was therefore of less intrinsic importance. However, on the exterior the carved freestone elements appear consistent with a fifteenth-century date in their surface morphology and the extent of the lichen growth on their surfaces, both now and in photographs taken around 1900. Evidently, then, when the tower was taken down c.1870, the worked medieval stonework must have been carefully set aside and subsequently built back into the renewed structure. The care with which this was done was illustrated by the discovery of the slots for two of the pre-restoration cramps set in the ringing-chamber window sills (to resist the movement that was the cause of the rebuilding of the tower), reset by the rebuilders in perfect register.

Indeed, even what appears at first to be the least promising of sites should not be automatically assumed to be archaeologically barren. The West Front of St David's Cathedral in Pembrokeshire has been rebuilt twice in a century, the medieval façade having come close to collapse in the 1790s when it was already 2 ft 11 in. (89 cm) out of true and moving at the rate of ½ in. (1.3 cm) per annum. John Nash built an early Gothic Revival West Front (incorporating massive western buttresses) in 1793–4, which, by the 1850s was so ill regarded that the best the contemporary historians of the cathedral could find to say of it was that it did not spoil the view of the building by moonlight.[6] Its mongrel Gothicism led to its replacement by Sir George Gilbert Scott's practice in 1880–2. However, even two apparent campaigns of total reconstruction left the lower part of the internal west wall largely intact, and careful inspection of the exterior northwest corner in 1999 proved that the lower half of the early thirteenth-century stair turret had survived both rebuildings (and a subsequent mid-twentieth-century repair campaign). Evidently, Scott must have recognized that Nash had left this fragment of the original fabric intact, and he incorporated it into his own rebuilding. Not only did he retain the medieval fabric that he found, but he also encased parts of the Nash structure itself; this became evident when some of the moulded stonework of Nash's west door was exposed when parts of the 1880s ashlar were removed from the west porch in the course of repairs in 1999.

In either of these instances, any hasty assumption that rebuilding had destroyed or severely reduced the significance of the fabric could have led to quite different conservation philosophies being employed in the programme of repair, and in turn to the actual diminution of the significance of the building.

CLOSER INSPECTION

Once scaffolding has been erected, the beginning of the conservation programme should be preceded by a close-range archaeological investigation of the fabric, giving sufficient opportunity for any discoveries made in the course of the survey to be integrated into the programme of work.

Occasionally the archaeological survey is directed towards addressing a specific conservation proposal, as with the 1998 survey of the Abbots' Fish House at Meare in Somerset for English Heritage. Here, in a fourteenth-century first-floor hall dwelling (traditionally associated with the official of Glastonbury Abbey charged with the use and maintenance of the lake that the abbey used for its fish supplies), the blue Lias walling of the exterior had decayed to such an extent that it was proposed to render the exterior as a way of protecting it from further weathering. A watercolour drawing from the 1820s by J.C. Buckler, apparently showing the building rendered, supported the contention that the building would have been covered with plaster in the middle ages. However, the survey analysis of the building showed that the primary fabric had originally consisted of beautifully finished Lias ashlars, laid in alternating deep and narrow courses of such precision that it seemed highly likely that they were intended to be seen, rather than to be hidden beneath a plaster finish. Furthermore, other contemporary Lias construction in the same style was identified in the parish church of Meare and in the precinct wall of the Abbey in Glastonbury. The findings suggested that this was a hallmark of the building style of the abbey's masons' yard during the abbacy of Adam of Sodbury, and therefore, given the existence of substantial doubts about the form of the original finish of the building, the proposal to render the walls was placed in abeyance.

More usually, the close-range survey serves to inform the conservation process by identifying significant elements of the fabric and providing a detailed analysis, which will assist in minimizing the impact of the repairs. It should seek to assist the conservator by highlighting the most significant survivals and those elements most at risk (such as the last examples of original mouldings which might be rendered extinct by injudicious replacement, or traces of original finishes or pigments which might be erased in cleaning), and enabling the proper recording or salvaging of those elements which cannot otherwise be preserved. Thus, in some cases it has to be accepted that an archaeological record made at this time may have to substitute for the thing itself.

Figure 4.3   The decorated arch of the west doorway from the 1794 West
Front of St David's Cathedral was discovered during cutting-out of stonework
in the Scott West Front of 1880. Scott also preserved a fragment of the
medieval West Front that survived the 1794 rebuilding.

Figure 4.4   Removal of ironwork can destroy the evidence for the fixing of statues in the middle ages, with colour-matched mortar repairs leaving little or no trace of their former presence.

This last is most often the case where the retention of a fitting – such as a metal cramp set in stonework – threatens the survival of the fabric itself. Prior to the mid-nineteenth century, restorers (and in many instances, medieval builders and sculptors themselves) incorporated metal reinforcements into the fabric, while figure sculptures were often fixed into their niches with iron cramps, which may represent in some instances the only current evidence of the previous existence of statues. Intrinsically important for their evidence of building practice or the extent of sculptural decoration on a building, such ironwork is routinely removed during conservation of stonework, and it is essential that a proper record of it exists, preferably with the retention and safe storage of the ironwork itself.

Because part of the discipline of archaeological recording consists in a drawn and/or photographic record, the archaeologist can often assist the conservator by providing a recording pro-forma, onto which areas of repair or other conservation treatments can be plotted. Drawings of the sculptures prepared by the recording archaeologist were used in this way at Wells and Salisbury West Fronts and on the tower of Beaminster parish church in Dorset, and collages of full-figure photographs from front and sides were recently employed in the same way for maintaining the conservation records of the figure sculptures at Isle Abbots in Somerset.

It is entirely possible that some aspects of the findings of the archaeological survey will not be completely understood at the time. Apparently random metal or wooden fixings may be located in a wall, and no clear explanation for them may be identified; however, it should not be assumed, as a result, that they lack significance. Two instances may serve to illustrate this point, both of which may have a more general application. As these examples eloquently demonstrate, at the very least, all such fittings should be adequately recorded prior to removal, against a time when their significance may become apparent.

On the south-eastern crossing pier at Glastonbury Abbey in Somerset, a group of small wooden wedges were found during the survey in 2005 – they were clearly of some antiquity, since their expansion had caused spalling of the surrounding stone. It was only after they had been removed that their significance was realized. In 1189, the Abbey's finances had dried up following the death of Henry II; this monetary crisis was recorded by the Abbey's chronicler, Adam of Domerham in the 1270s. Adam stated that 'the work stopped, because no funds were forthcoming to pay the wages of the workmen'.[7] The effects of the stoppage can be seen in the south door of the Lady Chapel, where the carving of the biblical scenes on the voussoirs ceases abruptly with two panels nearly completed and the outlines of the next two merely set out. It seems likely that the fixer masons working at the top of the rising masonry of the crossing in the summer of 1189 had set wedges in the joints to prevent the mortar being squeezed out by the weight of the stonework above. When the masons were laid off, these were probably untouched until the mortar had set hard, and as a result remained in place when work started again and were left there. It is possible that at other sites where a similar forced termination to a building programme took place, particularly in a tower or other area where there would have been no particular aesthetic incentive to remove them, fixers' wedges may also survive to record the event.

Another example comes from Chewton Mendip in Somerset in 2002. While recording a sculpture of the Resurrection, a series of pintles for supporting external shutters were noted in the jambs of the west window. At the time, no reason could be identified why a window whose apex lay more than 10 metres above the ground should be shuttered. The pintles were removed, and the holes were neatly filled with colour-matched mortar. In 2003, a routine survey in advance of conservation of the south nave aisle of Compton Martin Church, also in Somerset, again identified pintles for external shuttering on both windows of the west bay adjacent to the tower. This time, it was realized that the shuttering of the windows occurred next to the blind wall of the south side of the tower, and that the corners of an adjacent aisle buttress had been cut away to form a series of footholds for climbing. Clearly, the shutters were intended to protect the window glass from an external threat. The obvious candidate was the game of fives (handball), known to have been popular in west country churchyards in the seventeenth and eighteenth centuries. Presumably the footholds had been cut in the buttresses in order to allow the players to climb up to the lead roof to retrieve lost balls from the parapet. In order to check this conclusion, several churches where documentary evidence exists to connect the tower with fives play were surveyed, and these were found to have corroborative evidence of the impact of the game on the fabric – together with signs of the hooks required to hold the shutters open, of railings to keep the players away, and even of local worthies choosing to be buried in the fives place in order to finally banish the game from the churchyard.

Once these signs of the game, fossilized in the church fabric, were established, a pilot survey in the Wells area of Somerset visited 100 churches and found that 56 of them retained physical evidence for one or more fives courts. Of the remainder, a number had documentary evidence for the game having been played even though no signs remained in the

Figure 4.5 The stub of an iron pintle (and associated cracking) is a natural target for repair during conservation. However, this represents almost the only tangible trace of the shutters that Mr Bower would have closed to protect the window on 22 July 1764 before the gentlemen played fives in the churchyard at Babcary, and Parson Woodford (as he recorded in his diary) lost 1/6d betting on the game.

Figure 4.6 The window of the north aisle next to the west tower of East Pennard (Somerset) shows the classic signs of having borne shutters to protect the glass from fives playing in the churchyard: four iron pintles to support the shutters, and sections of the arch moulding cut away to allow them to open, as well as small rings to hold the hooks for securing the shutters open.

stonework. A total of eighteen diagnostic signs of fives play have now been identified, but unfortunately, where the significance of these traces is not understood, repair continues to remove the surviving evidence. Also, since the expansion of iron fittings is a major cause of disruption to stonework, its removal is often specified as a matter of course during conservation. Furthermore, where the usual carefully colour-matched repair mortars are inserted into the holes left by the withdrawal of the pintles, this almost certainly renders the evidence invisible for the foreseeable future. The problem is even greater where lighter lattices were used to protect the glazing: since these were fixed with small pins driven into the joints of the window jambs, and their removal usually leaves no trace.

At Compton Martin, the pintles were carefully preserved during the conservation of the south-aisle stonework.[8]

MONITORING WORK IN PROGRESS

Following the close survey from the scaffolding, it is relatively rare that the opportunity arises for the archaeologist to be present on site throughout a conservation programme. During the course of the works, the conservator is usually the person best placed to make the primary observations. The conservation team are continually present on the project site, and, given the painstaking nature of their work, are usually left with the time to think deeply about the problems of the building. They are intimately involved in the opening up of fabric, having the hands-on 'feel' of the materials – for example, in cutting-out they will be able to tell whether mortar is harder or softer in particular areas, or whether some mortars which appear superficially similar are in fact different mixes. And they are the ones who will make the discoveries in cleaning or cutting-out that will test or confirm the working hypotheses.

The willingness of conservators and archaeologists to work closely together is essential to the success of any recording project. The building archaeologist should always strive to form the same sort of relationship with all of the people working on the fabric (conservators, builders and labourers) that exists in archaeological excavation, where they act as the project archaeologist's eyes, constantly alerting him or her to the questions and answers that the fabric poses and provides. Indeed, it is often the case that there is an entirely reciprocal arrangement, where stone conservation is found in the service of building archaeology.

One phase of the work that is essential for the archaeologist to monitor, however, often seriously neglected in the specification of archaeological involvement with stone conservation, is the one when the building is in its state of maximum undress during a programme of de-pointing. The stripping-out of pointing is unfortunately seldom perceived as an opportunity for archaeological investigation: not only does it represent the best occasion for understanding the phasing of a building, but once the pointing is replaced the opportunity may be lost for the foreseeable future. In 1996, the parish church of Welsh St Donats (Glamorgan) was stripped

Figure 4.7   Ottery St Mary parish church before re-pointing.

Figure 4.8   Ottery St Mary parish church after re-pointing.

Figures 4.7 and 4.8   During de-pointing of the west bay of the south aisle of Ottery St Mary parish church, traces of the west cloister were revealed, which have been incorporated into the re-pointing – the sloping roofline of the fourteenth-century pentice can be seen running up to the white security camera on the western buttress.

of its hard late nineteenth-century plaster, the raking-out of the joints exposing the early mortars throughout the church. All the existing datable features in the building are of later fifteenth- or early sixteenth-century construction, and the presumption had been that the whole fabric was of a similar age; however, once the mortars had been be examined, it became apparent that every door and window in the nave and chancel had been inserted into pre-existing walls; in the chancel, the scars of two lancet windows in the south wall showed that this part of the building, at least, was of thirteenth-century construction. At the same time, the rood-loft door was revealed, and significant traces of the seating for the rood screen and its loft (probably inserted in the early sixteenth century) were identified. Had the archaeological survey not been undertaken, the true history of the standing fabric would have been lost, and that loss would very likely have been permanent. Unless repointing is done badly, there is rarely any need to repeat it on the interior of a building. Also, since most specifications require the mortar to be raked out to a depth of at least 5 cm, it is unlikely that the historic mortars will ever be revealed to such a degree in the future. A similar exercise on the tower of St Sannan, Bedwellty, in Gwent, for example, failed to penetrate the 1980s repointing.

Such discoveries made during a programme of repointing are unlikely to have a direct bearing on the outcome of the conservation itself, since attempting to reinstate pointing which imitate the phase changes within the walling would be both prohibitively time-consuming and aesthetically unacceptable. However, there are occasions when discoveries made in this way should be perpetuated in the re-pointing, as in the following example.[9]

At the collegiate church of Ottery St Mary (Devon), de-pointing of the south nave aisle in 2005 confirmed the findings of the preliminary archaeological survey that a cloister had adjoined the south side of the church when it was built in the mid-fourteenth century. Two irregular areas of geologically different stonework had been identified that appeared to correspond to the positions of the original doorways leading from aisle to cloister. As a result, the conservators were alerted to the possibility that signs of the scars of the cloister walls and pentice roof might exist beneath the nineteenth-century pointing. Taking off the dark pointing in these areas quickly identified both the wall scars and the flashing line of the sloping pentice roofs above the scars of the doorways, while de-pointing around the putative western door confirmed its existence by identifying the first two voussoirs of its relieving arch, and the positions of its robbed-out ashlar jamb stones.

The more open jointing of the blocking of the doorways meant that the modern re-pointing in a brighter lime mortar than the previous grey-brown cement has rendered these areas naturally more visible. A decision was also taken to point the wall scars and flashing lines of the fourteenth-century cloister in such a way as to render them visible, but without dominating the finished elevation. This careful perpetuation of the historic form of the elevation allows the evidence of the building to be read by the interested observer, without risking the disfigurement of what remains one of the finest parish churches of Devon.

The interplay between archaeologist and stone conservator during the repair of historic stonework remains a richly reciprocal arrangement, which should be mutually beneficial. The archaeologist must take advantage of the presence of the repair scaffolding to record what is significant, and to incorporate into that primary record what has been learnt during the course of the intrusive programme of conservation. This can ensure that as much as possible can be placed on record of the manner of the creation, the original appearance, the history and present condition of the structure under repair. But his or her work must also be capable of performing other functions, and in particular to feed into the decision-making processes of the architect and the consultant conservator. The archaeologist also has a responsibility to provide basic information to the builders, masons and conservators working on the building (thereby also opening up a two-way flow of information that provides further raw material to the archaeologist), enabling them to implement the requirements transmitted to them by the architect in as constructive and intelligent a manner as possible.

It may be necessary for the archaeologist to fulfil certain duties that are normally the province of the conservator or architect in instances where these would otherwise remain derelict, as in general repair programmes where no report is normally generated. In this respect, it may fall to the archaeologist to provide an archive record of the building and its previous repair and conservation history, and a record should also be made (no matter who assembles it) of its treatment during the project. This would ensure that those in charge of future conservation of the building can be as fully briefed as we ourselves might have wished to have been; and so that the methods used in our own repair and conservation programme, as well as those of past repairs, can be subjected to long-term monitoring (the only reliable form of testing); and so that this record can also serve to inform the ongoing research into conservation practice.

The author

Jerry Sampson FSA

Jerry Sampson is the archaeological consultant to the conservation architects Caroe and Partners and to the Dean and Chapter of St David's Cathedral. He has worked as a building archaeologist on conservation projects since 1979 when he became the recording archaeologist for the west front conservation programme at Wells Cathedral; he is the author of *Wells Cathedral West Front* and a major contributor to *Salisbury Cathedral West Front*, both projects being based on archaeological recording closely integrated with conservation.

References

1   Thus, the installers of a phone relay system in a major church tower were aware that they would need to monitor service trenches in the churchyard, but failed to see an archaeological dimension in the installation of a new floor in the ringing chamber, or to notice the implications of the concealment of much of the interior fabric by the erection of their equipment.

2   Ayers, T. (ed.) *Salisbury Cathedral – The West Front: A History and Study in Conservation*, Philimore, Chichester, 2000.

3   Ibid., pp. 28, 32–3.

4   Sampson, J., *Wells Cathedral West Front: Construction, Sculpture and Conservation*, Alan Sutton, Stroud, (1998), pp. 103–7.

5   Salzman, L. F., *Building in England Down to 1540*, Oxford University Press, Oxford, 2nd edn, 1967, pp. 153–4.

6   Evans, J. W., 'Foreword to the 1998 edition' in Jones, W. B. and Freeman, E. A., *The History and Antiquities of St David's*, Cyngor Sir Penfro/Pembrokeshire County Council, 1998, p. ii. As Jones and Freeman say (p. 50), 'night throws its pall over the technical deficiencies even of Nash himself, and brings out the real grandeur and solidity of outline which cannot be denied to his otherwise hideous composition.'

7   Adam of Domerham, quoted in Willis, Rev. R., *The Architectural History of Glastonbury Abbey*, Parker, London, 1866, p. 22.

8   For a brief consideration of the evidence left in church fabric by fives playing, see Sampson, J., 'Churchyard Fives', *Wells History and Archaeological Society Report* 2004/5, pp. 8–20. A PDF document is available at the website of Caroe and Partners Architects, www.caroe.co.uk, which presently forms the home of the *Somerset Fives Project*.

9   Watkin, D. A., 'Presidential Address', *Proceedings of the Somerset Archaeological and Natural History Society 1969*, p. 12. Dom Aelred Watkin drew attention to an overlooked aspect of repointing programmes when he noted the existence of plaster pads at head-height as the sites for the painted external consecration crosses on Somerset churches. He observed that 'the modern taste for repointing church walls' had often swept these away unnoticed.

Chapter Five

Principles and Practice

Nicholas Durnan and Colin Muir

INSPECTION, ANALYSIS AND METHODOLOGY

The development of a well defined philosophy is fundamental to the preparation of a conservation and repair policy. The approach to and aim of a given project, be it a major undertaking like the west front of a cathedral or a small project like a church wall monument, need to be thought out before the work starts. For a small project, an examination and short report may be all that is necessary, and previous experience of similar projects or similar stone types will inform intervention decisions. An important part of a conservator's training is learning how to prepare a conservator's report, which is essentially an information gathering exercise, and using the information gathered to propose, and then carry out, conservation treatment.

For a major project, detailed study, analysis and discussion are essential to ensure that policy decisions are based on a thorough knowledge of the materials, their conditions and their rates of decay. An investigation of the causes and patterns of decay and weathering by studying the stone and referring to past photographs will provide a holistic understanding of the behaviour of the stone be it architectural or sculptural. A draft policy can then be drawn up, trials carried out, and a proposed methodology and detailed specification prepared that allows for any fine-tuning as the work progresses. This may include geological analysis, mortar analysis, salt analysis, measuring rates of decay using past photographs, or laser recording and mapping of the stone surface at regular time intervals (typically annual) for a five-year period, and carrying out and assessing well documented trial work using a range of appropriate techniques.

Even on a small project, much of this kind of work can be carried out. Obtaining early photographs from the National Monument Record at

Figure 5.1   The statues and architectural stonework of the Image Screen at Exeter Cathedral are inspected by cherry picker every five years by the cathedral architect and consultant conservator. A major repair and conservation programme was carried out in 1978–85, and the subsequent inspections have informed a regular maintenance programme.

Swindon or the Conway Library at Burlington House in London can often be very illuminating in relation to rates of decay and for appreciating detail now lost.

Inspection

Inspection of stonework is best carried out as close to the subject as possible. When the area is at height, ideally this should involve temporary scaffolding or a hydraulic personnel lift (i.e. a 'cherry-picker'), though rope-access is sometimes necessary. In some forms of stone decay, the surface can appear sound until it separates from the substrate; tapping the surface may be the only way of determining the soundness of the substrate and finding out which areas are affected by hollowness or detachment. Assessing the condition of previous repairs and conservation treatments can also be difficult from a distance. An inspection that affords a low level of hand-contact will compromise the thoroughness of the evaluation. Physical contact with the stone surface should always be a priority during assessment, and condition surveys should be organized around this proviso. In some circumstances, much more specific non-visual investigation may be required prior to the devising of conservation proposals. This may require the contracting of non-destructive testing equipment and specialist operators. These systems can be grouped into three categories as follows:

- electromagnetic: impulse radar, free electro-magnetic radiation (FEMR), thermography
- nuclear: radiography
- accoustic: ultrasonic pulse velocity (UPV), impact-echo

These methods allow for the detection of various hidden features, such as internal metal fixings, wall voids, cracks, areas of damp and even old repairs.

Recording and monitoring stone decay

The most basic tools for recording stone decay are a pencil, notebook, tape measure and camera. These enable the taking of comprehensive notes, field sketches and photographs. Photography is a core element of recording, and careful photographic surveys should be conducted before, during and after any conservation treatment. Where pertinent, black-and-white scales should be included in shot, as should inventory numbers if a large number of elements are being dealt with. Where visual comparison of particular areas over time is required, photographs should be taken from the same viewpoint, and with the same angle and strength of lighting. Where detailed measured drawings exist, these can be invaluable as the basis for decay mapping. Mapping the various types of decay present in different colours onto photocopies of the survey drawings enables an overview of the scale of the problems, and can also start to point to causes of decay not immediately evident.

Condition assessment and analysis

Before attempting to assess the causes of stone decay, it is helpful to observe the surface of the stone *in situ* and attempt, if possible, to discern its original characteristics, and how consistent they are. Are there different bands of colour or grain-size evident? Is there evidence of pronounced bedding structures? Is the stone easily scratched? A stone's colour, bedding-orientation, hardness, porosity, and the size, sorting and angularity of its grain, can all help to identify its geology and possible decay mechanisms. Having ascertained a 'norm' for the stone's appearance, what form(s) of decay are visible? Are some areas decaying faster than others? Can the decay be explained by evident geological causes or differences, or might there be an external cause? These should all be carefully noted and photographed; highly unstable surfaces can change rapidly through surface loss. Hollows and blistered areas should be investigated for evidence of efflorescence, usually visible as a loose white powder forming on the surface. Samples of these deposits should be bagged, numbered and annotated with site, date and sample location details, for later laboratory analysis. Salt-testing strips (e.g. Merck) for the main salt types, such as sulphates, carbonates, and nitrates are a useful field tool, though more qualitative than quantitative in their results.

The original architect, mason or sculptor may have chosen particular stones for reasons of appearance, workability or locality. The conservation architect and conservator, however, need to know a lot more than this to formulate and guide the appropriate conservation and repair strategy. Seeking the advice of a geologist with local knowledge and the skill to undertake mineralogical analysis is essential for establishing the provenance of a particular stone. Furthermore, identifying and comparing the physical and chemical characteristics of different stone types and the more subtle differences between beds and individual blocks of stone from the same quarry provides information that can help define the causes of decay and weathering, and may help determine how the stone will respond to particular conservation treatments.

REPAIR AND CONSERVATION

Skills

Practical stone repair and conservation requires the synthesis of three domains: masonry, stone carving and practical conservation. These are three distinct disciplines, yet all of great importance in the conservation and repair of historic buildings. Each discipline itself combines many skills. Masonry involves the setting-out skills of technical drawing, geometry and mould-making, all requiring very precise measurement; the banker-work skills of applying templates and accurately cutting the stone into the vast range and scale of mouldings for doorways, windows, vaults, columns, weatherings and parapets; and the fixer-mason's skills of cutting away perished stone, and lifting, handling, aligning and setting the new stone.

Carving involves historical knowledge of carving styles; drawing and clay-modelling ability; an understanding of anatomy and drapery; and an ability to gather clues from damaged and deteriorated carvings to provide the basis for the replacement piece.

Conservation involves recognition of the chemical and physical characteristics of each particular stone; understanding the rates and types of decay and deterioration; finding the safest way to remove unwanted material like soot, salts, rusting iron, inappropriate past repairs in cement or synthetic resin; making decisions about which adhesive, support, filler, consolidant and coating to use; and making careful records of the condition and treatment of the stonework.

Protection and removal

The concept of physically protecting vulnerable stonework is common to all types of stone, though those that can decay rapidly, such as sandstones, benefit all the more from such measures. The scale of protection and its visibility can vary, from the fitting of a lead weathering fillet over a broken sill or moulding to redirect water flow, to the construction of an encapsulating glass and steel structure over a monument in order to modify its environment. Such measures tend to only be used where carved or sculpted stonework that is historically or artistically significant, and therefore 'irreplaceable', is under threat. In such cases, a balance should be sought between retaining a subject *in situ* for as long as possible, but not so long that important sculptural details are lost forever. This is where ongoing recording and monitoring provide crucial data to finally make the decision that removal of the item is necessary and justifiable. When the latter course of action is selected, the process usually entails the removal of the original to a controlled, internal environment, preferably as near to the original location as possible. A replica of the item may be inserted into the building to retain the visual appearance and context of the original. Effective replicas have been created in carved stone, or cast from moulds of the original in ordinary Portland cement (OPC) mortars or glass reinforced plastics (GRP). Three-dimensional laser scanning now offers the possibility of non-contact recording of surfaces, and the translation of such data into physical facsimiles. These can be produced through

Figure 5.2a The eleventh-century limestone Romsey Rood on the exterior wall of the south transept at Romsey Abbey is protected by a purpose-built roof to prevent rainwater flowing over the carved surfaces.

Figure 5.2b The Sueno's Stone, a sandstone Pictish sculpture, is protected *in situ* by a bespoke glass-and-steel enclosure.

rapid-prototyping equipment, 3-D printers and computer-controlled milling machines. The latter offers the option to recreate in the original stone type, and to match broken surfaces perfectly.

Alternatively, removal of an original carving, particularly one that is severely eroded, may create an opportunity for the commissioning of a new work of art rather than a replica. On the West Front at Salisbury Cathedral, two new statues were commissioned to replace the originals, which had lost much of their form and structural integrity. The new statues respected the overall form of the original sculptures, but allowed the carver the opportunity to express his creativity of design.

Pointing and bedding mortars

Many stone buildings have suffered greatly from the widespread use of OPC-based mortars. These materials may be impermeable, overly hard and often, salt laden. Traditionally, lime mortars were used for bedding and pointing of stone buildings. However, Portland cement's rapidity of set and ease of use have led to it being the norm in many locations. The use of cement-based mortars on historic stonework has usually been for re-pointing purposes. However, in stone buildings built within the last

Figure 5.3 Using a tungsten-tipped chisel to remove hard cement pointing from narrow joints.

Figure 5.4a   The deeply eroded carved detail of the seventeenth-century Chilmark limestone surround to the foundation inscription at the College of Matrons in the Close at Salisbury.

Figure 5.4b   During the 2004 conservation programme the surviving original surface detail was conserved and missing areas were reinstated using pozzolanic lime putty mortars, with the remodelling based on careful examination of the original design.

hundred years it has, more worryingly, been used as the bedding mortar as well. Raking out of cement pointing becomes a slow and painstaking process if further damage to vulnerable and possibly eroded masonry is to be avoided. Power tools and grinders should not be used to clear joints, due to the risk of vibration damage and of running over onto the stone itself. Instead, fine tungsten-headed chisels (of 3 mm width) should be used to clear the cement to a depth of at least 25 mm. This can then be re-pointed with a lime-based mortar using an appropriate aggregate. The choice of lime binder, whether lime-putty or hydraulic lime, will depend on the hardness and rapidity of set required, and the level of weather exposure expected.

Plastic repairs

Rather than replace an entire piece of masonry, it has often been preferable to repair a small area of damage using a 'plastic repair'. Such a repair can be defined as an amorphous material (such as a mortar) that solidifies to create a mass that closely resembles the lost area of stone. There are examples of plastic repairs dating back to antiquity. Sometimes, these were used to repair transit-damaged masonry during building, or even to correct spelling mistakes made during inscription carving. Over the last one hundred and fifty years, such repairs have predominantly been used to address issues of decay or damage of historic fabric where cost or ethics have negated masonry replacement. Many such repairs, including commercially coloured mixes, were based on OPC, and have proven damaging in their own right. These types of repairs often lost their dye-based colour, contained damaging soluble salts, and were harder than the surrounding stone (resulting in preferential erosion of the stone). Cracking or separation of the repair from the substrate could also occur, negating the treatment and causing a risk to public safety.

Ideal characteristics for a plastic-repair medium are considered to be integral colour and grain-matching, usually derived from a calculated mix of selected, graded sands. Its binder should be inert and resilient to external weather conditions. The final product should have a similar vapour permeability to the stone itself, but be slightly softer (and therefore sacrificial). Ideally. it would also be reversible. The most widely used plastic repairs are lime-based mortars, but acrylic resin-bound mortars are occasionally used.

Structural repair techniques

For over a century, the predominant method of structurally repairing stonework was to assemble the parts using neat OPC as an adhesive. Any voids were filled with cement-based mortar, often with rough aggregate to bulk out the lost area. Where greater strength was required, internal dowels might also have been used, again fixed with neat cement. When such internal fixings were of ferrous metals, problems relating to oxidation and 'rust-jacking' often occurred. Cement-based products have often proved to be particularly harmful to the main building stone types, and are thus often removed by conservators to halt their ongoing impact. In the last thirty years, most structural repairs to stone have involved the use of synthetic resin adhesives, mainly polyester-based, though acrylic- and epoxy-based products have also been used. Internal fixings are now usually of non-oxidizing metals such as phosphor bronze and type-316 stainless steel, though synthetic rods such as glass or carbon-reinforced resin, are also sometimes used.

The problem with both OPC and resins as structural adhesives is that they are impermeable, and thus prevent moisture transfer across a bond interface. With resins, this is normally countered by applying the adhesive in the form of dots or a lattice to ensure some parts of the interface are 'dry', thereby allowing some moisture passage. Another method is to rely only on internal dowels to hold a joint together, with no adhesive at the joint interface, and then to point the external edge of the joint with a very fine mortar to limit moisture ingress. A vapour permeable adhesive based on ethyl silicate is in development by Wacker specifically for use with sandstone; whilst it is strong it doesn't appear readily reversible (but this is also true of OPC and epoxy resins).

Where internal dowels are introduced as fixings, the bedding of the stone should be considered, so that dowels don't create leverage stress along a bedding plane. Face-bedded panels at risk of delamination can be pinned through the bedding planes to ensure that the layers remain attached. Metal dowels are usually bonded with a polyester or epoxy resin, and the holes filled and hidden with a repair mortar. This technique requires considerable intervention to the subject, both in terms of drilling and introducing the resin deep into the stone, and as such is only recommended as a final measure. Disaggregating stone is particularly difficult to adhere, and the various parts may need to be consolidated individually before their surfaces are sound enough to enable the adhesive to achieve an effective bond.

STONE REPLACEMENT

Perhaps the best way of making a decision about replacement of architectural stonework on a working building is for the inspection and scheduling process (specifying conservation treatment and stone replacement) to be done on the scaffold by a team, comprising the conservation architect, conservator and mason. As well as focussing on individual stones and the advantages and disadvantages of conservation versus replacement in each case, it is important to step back and assess the overall pattern of conservation repairs and replacements on a given section of the building. Aspects such as historic importance, uniqueness, quality of stone, position on building, visibility, condition of adjacent stone and availability of geologically similar stone all need to be taken into account, plus, of course, an assessment of possible future loss of surface detail and mouldings.

Stone must also be judged on its ability to fulfil its function within the greater structure. Is it capable of supporting the masonry above it? Is it able to shed water as it was designed to do, or is it causing damage elsewhere due to deficiency in this area? Or even worse, is it channelling water into the building?

Figure 5.5   The severely decayed upper half of this thirteenth-century capital on the West Front of Salisbury Cathedral was pieced-in with newly carved Chicksgrove stone after careful study of the form and stylistic qualities of the original mediaeval work (1995–2000 repair and conservation programme).

In terms of established conservation ethics, replacement of historic stone masonry is ideally to be avoided in order to retain as much of the original material, for as long as possible. Protective measures include hoods or shelters, chemical consolidation, mechanical fixings and plastic repairs. However, given that buildings, and some monuments, are external by nature and will continue to deteriorate despite even the best conservation treatments, replacement does eventually become an inescapable necessity. It is also necessary to realize that there is an appropriate time period within which to effectively replace stone; too early, and original material is needlessly removed from context; too late and a stone's failure can endanger the public, surrounding masonry, and even the structure as whole.

Where a stone is to be replaced, meticulous replication of the original moulding or carved detail is essential. Where a missing section of carved work is to be replaced, such as a carved label stop or capital, the making of drawings and clay models of similar carvings of comparable date from the same building is the best preparation for executing such work.

It is always preferable to replace stone 'like with like', both in terms of prevalent conservation ethics and in terms of retaining a homogenous functionality across a façade. This means the replacement will not only look like the original, but will behave similarly as well. Unfortunately it is not always possible to secure a supply of the same stone as was originally used. This may be because the original quarry is unknown or worked-out, or, if it is still functioning, the stone now being quarried there may have different attributes (colour, density, bed height, etc.) due to a different geological horizon now being worked.

Observation of a stone's surface, and its constituent aggregate when broken up, can give clues to its geological make-up in terms of its possible age and deposition environment. However determining its exact chemical/mineral components and their ratios requires specialist laboratory equipment and analysis. To produce this data usually requires sacrificial core-samples of the original material to be provided for analysis. The results will not only be able to give a more precise breakdown of the stone's chemistry, but will also enable a likely site of origin to be proposed. These data will facilitate matching the material as closely as possible to currently available stones. Further advice on sourcing and selection of stone for replacement is described by Ewan Hyslop in Chapter 6.

Face bedding, where the bedding planes of a stone are orientated vertically and parallel to the elevation's surface, is generally to be avoided in construction, since it speeds bedding erosion and failure. However, stone was used historically in this orientation to execute a number of common features, such as vertical tracery elements and carved decorative panels. The reasons for this usually related to the limited bed height of stone available, so that to get a large vertical element, it had to be used 'on end'. Additionally it is easier to cut slabs along the bedding plane, and the resultant panel is stronger this way than it would be if cut across the bedding. Unfortunately, these advantages are lost when the stone is then used 'on end', relief-carved elements can shear off, and inscribed features can channel water behind the surface and down into the internal bedding planes. Despite these design and performance issues, it is customary to replace new stone in the same orientation as the original element, even where this is known to be problematic. To do otherwise may unduly change the character of the building, and such a course should be taken only after careful thought and justification. To reduce the risk of the problem recurring, it may be considered prudent to install low-visibility measures such as plastic or lead weathering fillets above such features to protect their exposed bedding structure.

Stone indents, or 'Dutchmen' as they are known in the States, are partial stone replacements in which only the decayed or damaged area of the stone is cut out, not the entire masonry block. Indents offer long-term repairs in material compatible with the original, and help to retain historic material. A full indent consists in the removal and replacement of the entire face of an ashlar unit, whilst a part-indent addresses a small damaged area of a stone. Such part-indents should not span joints between masonry blocks, as this would distort the historic jointing-pattern of a façade. Unless extremely well executed, part-indents may be aesthetically distracting, and they increase the number of joints and their associated problems. However they may be considered appropriate for the repair of certain sculptural and moulded elements, as well as spalls resulting from rusting ferrous fixings.

CONSERVATION RECORDS

Documentation of conservation and repair work is essential for several reasons. Firstly it provides practical and historical information for those who inspect or re-treat the stonework in the future. Referring back to the conservator's report and treatment records will aid assessment of the effect of a given treatment and may guide on how to re-treat the architectural and sculptural stonework. It is important the recorded information is accessible both in terms of how the information is presented and where the information is stored. A precise description of the techniques, materials and formulations used and the prevailing conditions is essential, as is ensuring copies of the reports and records are kept in a safe and accessible place.

Secondly and equally important, for the conservator, the process of compiling written, drawn and photographic records ensures the gaining of a detailed knowledge of the object through observation and touch before the work starts and as the work proceeds. This personal experience and knowledge is invaluable to the conservator when discussion is required with fellow professionals. Furthermore, the dissemination of such information to the conservation profession and the general public is enhanced by exemplary documentation. The recording and understanding of an object be it sculptural or architectural through inspection, analysis, discussion and through the process of the actual practical conservation work not only benefits the object and those who care for it now but provides the framework for the continued care and appreciation of historic stonework into the future.

The authors

Nicholas Durnan DiplCons

Nicholas Durnan has over 30 years experience working on the conservation and repair of stonework on cathedrals, churches and historic buildings. After a masonry apprenticeship at Canterbury Cathedral and a diploma in carving at the City and Guilds of London Art School he trained as a sculpture conservator at Wells Cathedral. For most of his career he has worked as a sculpture conservator and conservation consultant. He has been involved in both these roles for the major repair and conservation programmes of the West Fronts of Wells, Exeter and Salisbury Cathedrals.

Colin Muir BA(Hons) MSc, ACR, FSA Scot

Colin Muir graduated from Grays School of Art, Aberdeen in 1988 with a BA(Hons) in Sculpture. He obtained an MSc in Architectural Stone Conservation from Bournemouth University, and went on to work for Cliveden Conservation. For the last ten years he has worked throughout Scotland as a Stone Conservator for Historic Scotland. His current role involves the provision of specialist advice and the conservation treatment of sculptural and decorative stonework.

Chapter Six

Sourcing and Selection of Stone for Repair

Ewan Hyslop

INTRODUCTION

Careful selection of appropriate stone is often crucial for the success of a repairs project, and to ensure the future health of a stone building or monument. In many cases, however, stone selection is not given enough consideration. There may be insufficient effort to characterize the nature of the original stone and to identify a replacement stone with compatible characteristics. Yet, the use of inappropriate stone may not only impair the appearance of a building or monument, it may also cause physical damage to the remaining original materials, resulting in wasted time and money. The process of selection and sourcing of stone for repair should be built into a project, and carried out at an early stage. In comparison to the overall timescale and cost of a typical project, the involvement of a stone specialist is generally a very small proportion. A thoughtful and sensible approach to stone selection can avoid poor decision-making and the need for compromise, which is all too common when the selection of stone is left to a late stage in a project.

THE DECISION TO REPLACE STONE

The case for replacing stone needs to be clearly made. The importance and significance of the existing stone should be considered, in terms of its historical, artistic and/or architectural value. Decayed stone can have a value of its own if it provides a connection with the past, and this possibility should not be overlooked. The ability of the existing stone to continue to perform its structural and functional role in a building or monument is important in deciding whether to replace stone. For example, repairs to a damaged cornice or moulded string course which is designed to prevent water running down the face of a building may be considered essential, in order to prevent further damage to the original masonry. In short, the decision to replace stone should form part of an overall repairs philosophy or conservation plan for a particular project, where both the value and functional role of stone is thoroughly understood.

Alternatives to stone replacement should also be considered. In some cases, the introduction of protective materials, such as discreet lead flashings, may allow the retention of valued historic stonework. The use of chemical treatments, such as water repellents and consolidants, should be viewed with caution and only sanctioned once their effects on the stone and its surroundings are thoroughly understood. In some cases, it may be appropriate to undertake a 'plastic repair', which may avoid the need for replacement of more stone than is necessary. Again, the effect of introducing such material must be investigated, and in general restricted to the use of lime-based conservation materials, which are less durable than, and sacrificial to, the original stone. Although alternatives such as chemical treatment and plastic repair may be initially less costly, they are likely to have a limited life (typically a few decades at best) compared to replacing stone, and may therefore not be cost-effective in the long term. In addition, the introduction of alternative materials to stone can result in increased damage to any remaining original stone. The effects of the new material on the stone, and on the structure as a whole, should be thoroughly understood.

If stone replacement is to be undertaken, it should be carried out to the highest standards. Poor stone repairs, using inappropriate materials or poor quality craftsmanship, can cause further damage to the building or monument. Unless one is confident that a repair will be properly executed, it may be best not to replace the stone at all.

The value and problems of previous repairs should be recognized. There are many examples where selection of incompatible stone has resulted in increased damage to the remaining original stone, as well as examples of repairs that have proved successful over the long term. Previous repairs provide a valuable record, and we should be willing to learn from them.

THE CHOICE OF STONE

Once the decision to use a replacement stone has been made, the type of stone required needs to be selected carefully. Selection should initially be driven by the repair philosophy adopted: for example, is a 'like-for-like' replacement required, or should the new stone be intentionally distinguishable from the original? In some cases, it may be desirable to select a replacement stone that will protect the remaining original stone in a sacrificial way by, for example, allowing more moisture to pass through it. In contrast, on particularly exposed or structurally important parts of a building, a harder-wearing or less permeable replacement stone may be required, if the original type of stone has proved inadequate in such a position. It has long been known that certain stone types are incompatible when placed in close proximity; for example, the preferential decay of sandstone adjacent to limestone, and limestone adjacent to magnesian limestone. In some cases, it may be necessary to contemplate loss of historical accuracy in order to prevent further decay from occurring in the future. However, in most cases, it is likely to be best to select the closest possible matching stone, in order both to retain the visual appearance and ensure compatibility with the surviving original stone over the long term.

The first task in the selection of a replacement stone is to characterize the original material. This is best done in consultation with a stone specialist, ideally a petrographer or geologist, who can determine the exact mineral and textural characteristics of the stone. In most cases, it is necessary to obtain a sample of the existing stone, which needs to be representative of all of the stone that is to be replaced. For a basic petrographic (i.e. microscopic) analysis, only a small amount of stone is usually required, but the sample should be as fresh as possible, as it can be difficult to characterize the original properties of a stone that has been altered by weathering and decay. A small-diameter diamond core drill (for example 30–40 mm) is an ideal tool for obtaining samples, as fresh stone is usually encountered only tens of millimetres below the surface. Modern portable equipment makes coring an easy and quick option in many cases. If required, the weathered outer part of the core can be used to cap the hole to minimize the visual effect.

The choice of sample is important, and it is worth involving the specialist at this stage. Many historic buildings contain several varieties of stone, which may not be obvious without a detailed inspection. It is not uncommon for different stone types to have been used for different elements of a building: for example, a harder or more durable stone for a

Figure 6.1 Examples of stone repairs showing replacement sandstone (pale colours), which has different compositional and porosity characteristics to the original masonry. The juxtaposition of incompatible stone-types can lead to the accelerated decay of the original stone. In these examples, the replacement sandstone is less porous, leading to enhanced moisture retention in the original stone and causing it to decay more rapidly.

base course or copestones, and a softer stone for carved details. Rubble walling may be constructed of local stone from a nearby quarry (or a mixture of local stone types), whilst in the same building, the higher quality dressed stone could have been brought in from a greater distance. As buildings have been extended, adapted and repaired over time, different stone types may have been used, reflecting the availability of stone at particular times. In order to ensure that the sample is representative and correctly characterizes the stone type(s) present, it may be necessary to take a range of samples.

If documentary records exist of the original stone types used, efforts should be made to identify and consult such sources of information. However, the existence of a documentary reference to a particular stone type does not necessarily mean that it was actually used. In addition the nature of stone from a quarry can change over time, so stone produced today from a quarry may differ from that produced in the past. The fact that the majority of historical quarries are no longer in operation means that testing and characterization of samples of the existing stone type is essential.

TESTING OF STONE

Testing of stone is a complex business, and a large number of standard tests for building stone have been developed. Most available stone types are accompanied by a portfolio of standard test results, but many of these are designed for new-build construction, and thus the data may not be relevant for repair and conservation. Over-reliance on certain test results can result in the selection of inappropriate stone, which can in turn lead to damage to the remaining original stone. For example, selection of stone types on the basis of high values of durability, strength and resistance to salt and frost action may be ideal for new-build purposes, but could be too 'dense' or 'hard' for a repairs project, where the stone is to be placed alongside vulnerable historic masonry. Test results need to be viewed in a critical way, keeping in mind how they relate to particular properties and the overall performance of the stone, and most importantly which are relevant to the particular repairs project. It is worth remembering that most historic building stones were not subjected to extensive testing before use.

A large number of standard tests exist for natural building stone, most now published in the United Kingdom as European 'BS EN' Standards, formerly produced as Building Research Establishment (BRE) Reports and American Society for Testing and Materials (ASTM International) Standards. These range from mechanical tests, such as ones for flexural and compressive strength, and physical and chemical tests for 'durability', such as acid immersion, salt crystallization, saturation coefficient, and porosity tests. Other tests, such as abrasion and slip resistance, water absorption, density and frost resistance, provide specific information for particular uses.

One of the most useful tests when identification of a matching or compatible stone type is required for repair purposes, is BS EN 12407:2000

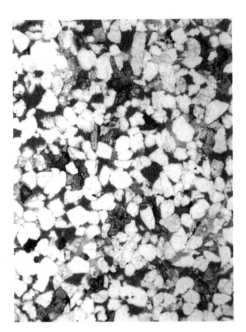

Figure 6.2 Microscopic images of two sandstone types showing differences in grain size, mineral composition and porosity. Figure 6.2a (right) shows a sandstone used in Victorian Glasgow, which is now unavailable. Figure 6.2b (left) is a replacement sandstone from northern England currently used for repairs in Glasgow. The differences between the two stone types suggest that they may not be compatible, resulting in a different appearance over time with possible damage to the remaining historical stone if placed together. Both images are 3 mm across.

'Petrographic Description'. This involves the systematic description and characterisation of a stone at both macroscopic (hand specimen) and microscopic (thin section) scales. The test uses a series of internationally recognized standard criteria for the description of different aspects, such as the colour, mineral composition, and size, shape and distribution of grains, effectively producing a 'fingerprint' for a particular stone type. Thin sections can be impregnated with coloured resin in order to highlight porosity and to allow visual estimation of the connectivity of the pore spaces (permeability). Used in conjunction with specific tests, such as those for porosity and water absorption, petrographic description is one of the best methods for characterizing a stone type for the selection of a replacement stone.

Once a sample of the original stone has been characterized in this way, it can be compared to currently available stone types in order to identify the most similar (or most appropriate) stone type for repairs.

The thin section method of stone matching is a relatively rapid and cost-effective technique for assessing the original stone and identifying potential replacement stone types. Examination of factors such as mineral composition and porosity characteristics can provide an insight into the future weathering behaviour of a particular stone type. For example, although two stone types may appear superficially similar, clues to their longer-term behaviour, and issues of compatibility, may be determined from their internal microscopic characteristics.

In addition to the stone-matching procedures described above, the selection of stone type should also take into account the views and requirements of others involved in the project. For example, the mason or sculptor will be able to advise on whether a stone type is capable of being worked in the required way, such as being able to take detailed carving, or a particular style of surface finish or tooling.

Figure 6.3a   Sample of historical masonry sandstone from the sixteenth-century King's Fountain, Linlithgow Palace.

Figure 6.3b   Thin section of closest matching sandstone from Yorkshire.

Figure 6.3c   Detail of part of the King's Fountain, Edinburgh, showing indents of new stone with old. Because the new stone has similar characteristics of composition, texture and porosity, it is compatible with the original stone, and will blend in over time to give a similar appearance.

Figure 6.3   Examples of diagnosis of stone-type in thin section.

SOURCING OF STONE FROM QUARRIES

If the original quarry source is known, and a like-for-like repair strategy is proposed, then it should be established whether or not the quarry is still active. Information on working quarries and current sources of stone in the United Kingdom can be obtained from various sources, including the British Geological Survey, Building Research Establishment, British Stone, Stone Federation Great Britain, and from the *Natural Stone Directory*.

In some cases, it may be possible to re-open a former quarry on a temporary basis to obtain a limited supply of stone. This method, sometimes termed 'snatch' quarrying, has been used in a number of cases where a specific stone type was required for the repair of important buildings or monuments that could not be obtained from alternative sources. For example, the former Binny quarry near Edinburgh was re-opened on a temporary basis in 1997 to allow extraction of a limited quantity of the original sandstone for repairs to the Scott Monument. The site was subsequently reinstated to its current use (part of a golf course) with no remains of the recent quarrying activity in evidence. Former quarries may be located using local maps and other historical records, as well as published and archive information from organisations such as the British Geological Survey and Building Research Establishment.

The re-opening of former quarries is undoubtedly necessary for the long-term preservation of many historic stone buildings and monuments. In particular, the ability to obtain local stone is important if the character and distinctiveness of the built heritage is to be maintained. However, in the United Kingdom at least, the ability to re-open a quarry, even on a temporary basis for such purposes, has become increasingly difficult due to constraints resulting from unsympathetic planning legislation. Fortunately, such issues are being increasingly recognized by mineral planning legislation, and it seems likely that future guidance will at least acknowledge the importance of mineral planning in order to safeguard sources of building and roofing stone for historic buildings.

If an original quarry source cannot be identified, or if suitable stone cannot be obtained from a particular quarry, then an alternative stone type must be found. Such an alternative must match the characteristics of the original stone, as defined by the petrographic analysis, or otherwise satisfy the conservation requirements of the project as closely as possible.

Once a particular quarry source has been identified, it must be established whether it can supply sufficient stone of the correct type, block size and consistency, and within the desired timescale. Factors such as bed height and joint spacing need to be assessed in order to ensure sufficient block size for the project. Because stone is a natural material, it will always display some degree of variability, and the nature of stone extracted from a quarry can vary over time. A visit to the quarry may be the best way of ensuring the specific requirements can be met, either by identifying the particular beds from which the stone should be extracted, or by inspecting the stockpiles of blocks that some quarries hold, and which can be reserved for a particular project.

Reclaimed stone from demolition or other sources is generally under-valued, but can provide a good source of stone, particularly if the amount

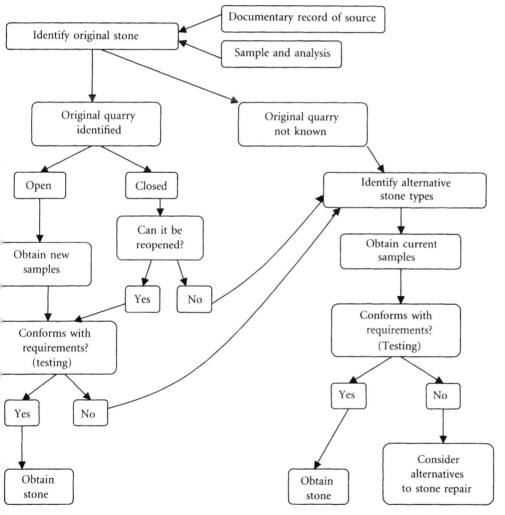

Figure 6.4 Flow diagram illustrating the procedure for selection of stone for repairs.

required is small. This has the advantage of obtaining historic stone, sometimes from a known source, when new supplies of that stone type may be unavailable. In addition, reclaimed stone has already been 'aged', with a proven ability to withstand weathering. The disadvantage of reclaimed stone is that supplies may be limited, and it is commonly necessary to redress the material, leading to a loss of block size during the process.

CONCLUSION

Stone for repair should be selected on the basis of a number of criteria, not just colour and appearance. Detailed analysis of the mineralogy, chemistry, physical and textural characteristics of a stone will provide information on its long-term behaviour. Stone selected as replacement material should not be considered in isolation, but in the context of the building as a whole, and its functional suitability and relationship to adjacent stonework must be taken into account. The use of specialist advice and analysis is recommended, and should be built in at an early stage in any project. Test results for stone must be viewed critically, and must be relevant to a particular project. Use of stone with unsuitable or incompatible characteristics can lead to the decay of remaining historic stone, damaging the original fabric and raising costs in the long term.

The author

Ewan Hyslop BSc, MSc, PhD, FGS

Dr Ewan Hyslop is a building stones expert with the British Geological Survey, Edinburgh. He graduated with a geological PhD from Hull University and gained an MSc in architectural conservation from Edinburgh College of Art. As well as working in numerous building stones projects, he is also keen to communicate his work to others.

Bibliography

Ashurst, J. and Ashurst, N., *Practical Building Conservation Volume 1: Stone Masonry*, Gower Technical Press, Aldershot, 1988.

Ashurst, N. and Kelly, J., 'The analytical approach to stone, its cleaning, repair and treatment, Appendix 4', in Ashurst J. and Dimes F. (eds), *Conservation of Building and Decorative Stone*, Volume 2, Butterworth-Heinemann, London, 1980.

Brereton, C. *The Repair of Historic Buildings: Advice on Principles and Methods*, second edition, English Heritage, London, 1995.

British Geological Survey, *Building Stone Resources Map of Britain*, British Geological Survey, Nottingham, 2001.

British Geological Survey, *Directory of Mines and Quarries*, British Geological Survey, Nottingham, 2005.

British Standard BS 7913, *Guide to the Principles of the Conservation of Historic Buildings*, British Standards Institution, London, 1998.

British Standard BS 8221:2, *Code of Practice for Cleaning and Surface Repair of Buildings*, British Standards Institution, London, 2000, Section 8: Stone masonry repair.

English Heritage, *Identifying and Sourcing Stone for Historic Building Repair: An approach to determining and obtaining compatible stone*, Technical Advice Note, English Heritage, London, 2006.

Historic Scotland, *The Memorandum of Guidance on Listed Buildings and Conservation Areas*, Historic Scotland, Edinburgh, 1998.

Honeyborne, D. B. 'The selection of stone for repairs', in Ashurst J. and Dimes F. (eds), *Conservation of Building and Decorative Stone*, Volume 2, Butterworth-Heinemann, London, 1980.

Knight, J. (ed.), *The Repair of Historic Buildings in Scotland: Advice on Principles and Method*, Historic Scotland, Edinburgh, 1995.

Natural Stone Directory, QMJ Publishing Ltd, Nottingham, 2006/2007.

Stone Federation Great Britain, *Stone Specifiers Guide*, Excel Publishing Ltd, Manchester, 2006.

Stone Roof Working Group, *Stone-Slate Quarries or Delphs: A Guide to Making a Mineral Planning Application for a Stone-Slate Production*, Institute of Historic Building Conservation, 2005.

Chapter Seven

Consolidation

Clifford A. Price

INTRODUCTION

Few people who have looked closely at historic stone buildings can have failed to be dismayed by the condition of the stone they have sometimes seen. While some stones weather well, the majority of limestones and sandstones are susceptible to severe weathering over long periods. Some-times, the stone erodes away leaving a sound surface behind; at other times, it blisters, crumbles, powders and flakes, leaving the remaining stone so weakened that it seems to be held together by little more than habit. Such damage is particularly disturbing in carved work, for the loss of just 1–2 cm from the surface can result in the complete loss of the carver's original concept. The faceless, featureless figures that peer blindly at us from so many buildings and monuments attest powerfully to such damage. It is no wonder that we want to 'do something about it', by applying a treatment that will strengthen and preserve the stone.

This chapter is concerned primarily with carved stonework that is exposed outdoors, where it is usually difficult or impossible to isolate the stone from the building, or to modify the environment to protect it. Outdoor stone that is not carved is usually dealt with by mortar repair, or indent or stone replacement; it is only carved work that is normally considered a candidate for consolidation, given its particular historical and aesthetic importance.

Interest in techniques of consolidation reached its most recent apogee around twenty-five years ago. Since then, much has been learned about the dynamics and complexity of stone decay and its relation to the ambient environment. Simultaneously, as we shall see, the performance and longevity of consolidant treatments have been assessed in real-time. This, in turn, has lead to a marked downgrade of expectations, as well as a loss of some of the mystique and mistrust surrounding the use of synthetic treatments.

From the point of view of those directly concerned with the specification of treatments for historic stonework, the topic of consolidation can seem formidable nevertheless, and it is hoped that this chapter may present a more realistic perspective.

Foremost in this regard, it must be stressed that consolidants are no substitute for common sense or good housekeeping. Most decay processes involve water, so regular maintenance should be carried out wherever practicable: re-pointing, filling cracks, securing loose flakes and using mortar fillets to protect any points at which surface water might otherwise enter the body of the stone. Protective features such as string courses, canopies, cornices and hood moulds must be kept in good condition in order for them to function as intended, or a new canopy or shelter might be provided. Control of temperature and humidity may help to slow down decay, and in some instances it may be appropriate to remove a sculpture to a more sheltered or indoor environment. For some types of stone, periodic cleaning may help to slow down decay.

It is important to draw a distinction between consolidation and preservation, which, although closely intertwined, are essentially quite different. Consolidation is the process of strengthening and reinforcing,

Figure 7.1 Consolidation with a silane, at Dorchester Abbey, Oxfordshire.

and it attempts to rectify what has gone wrong in the past. Preservation, on the other hand, looks more to the future, and aims to prevent any further decay from taking place. Consolidation will often be a component of an attempt at preservation, but need not necessarily be so. Few authors draw this distinction, although Félix and Furlan,[1] and Alonso et al.,[2] for example, reported damage to certain stones after consolidation with ethyl silicate unless the stones were also given a water repellent coating.

The term 'surface consolidation' is sometimes used, and may in some circumstances appear to be illogical: how can one strengthen weakened stone by strengthening only its surface? This is a valid concern if the stone has been weakened to a considerable depth, but it is less of a concern if only the surface is powdering, and the intention is to stop the powdering, or to secure any surviving polychromy, for example.

HISTORICAL PERSPECTIVE

The history of stone consolidation and preservation is long and disappointing. Numerous materials have, in turn, been advocated and then deprecated. Materials that looked very promising for a period of a few years have turned out, in the long run, to have little or no effect. In some cases, they have proved positively harmful.

Most past treatments have entailed the application of a shallow surface coating, aimed primarily, but over-optimistically, at preservation by preventing the ingress of water. It was not until the 1970s that a concerted effort was made to develop deeply penetrating treatments that, it was hoped, would both consolidate and protect the stone, and which would not be bedevilled by the problems that had been the downfall of surface treatments. The interface between treated and untreated stone would lie at a much greater depth (perhaps 25–50 mm from the surface), where temperature and moisture fluctuations would be less pronounced. Much stress was placed at the time on the possibility of 'encapsulating' harmful salts that might otherwise crystallize within the stone, thereby causing damage. However, subsequent work showed that some consolidants actually increased the mobility of salts,[3] to the point that this could be put to good use in the desalination of museum objects. Nonetheless, the general desirability of deep impregnation has since gone unquestioned, despite the difficulties of achieving it.

PROPERTIES AND PERFORMANCE REQUIREMENTS

What properties should one be looking for in a consolidant? The most important criterion is that it should work, but there are many other criteria. Some relate specifically to the moment of application and others are more concerned with long-term performance.

Properties such as cost, health and safety hazard, environmental impact, ease of application, time required for application and sensitivity to temperature and humidity during application may influence the choice of consolidant.

A consolidant should be able to penetrate deeply into the stone in a reasonable period of time, and then to solidify. The ability of a consolidant to penetrate is governed by two factors: first, the consolidant must wet the stone readily and not bead up on the surface;[4] second, the consolidant must have a very low viscosity (i.e. it must be very runny). Once in the stone, solidification is usually achieved by means of a chemical reaction or by the evaporation of a solvent.

Solidification of the consolidant should reinstate the internal cohesion of the stone destroyed through decay, thus increasing its compressive strength, abrasion resistance and resistance to chemical weathering, and thereby slowing down the rate of future decay. The consolidant must be compatible with the specific substrate to which it is applied in terms of its thermo-dimensional properties. It should not block the pores of the stone or inhibit moisture movement through the stone. The difficulties of determining the effectiveness of a consolidant will be considered later.

Significant changes in the appearance of the stone, such as in its colour, texture and reflectivity are seldom acceptable: the consolidant must effectively be invisible. It should also be resistant to visible and ultra-violet light and to chemical breakdown, and must not darken or become brittle with age. It should not encourage bacterial, algal or other biological growth on the stone surface.

Wherever possible, conservators prefer to use procedures that are reversible; in other words, work that can be undone should it prove unsuccessful or better procedures become available.[5] Nonetheless, reversibility is an ideal that is honoured more in word than in practice, for many conservation procedures, such as cleaning, are necessarily irreversible, and extraction of a consolidant from life-sized figure sculpture on the exterior of a building may be quite impracticable. In this context, the ideal of re-treatability may be more appropriate: treatments should not be used that may prejudice the subsequent application of the same or another material.[6,7] Those who argue that reversibility should not be sacrificed or compromised at any cost should note that neglect is not reversible either.

CONSOLIDANT TYPES

It is convenient to group consolidants used today into two broad categories: organic and inorganic. Organic consolidants include silanes and acrylic polymers. The inorganic consolidants are primarily calcium and barium hydroxides.

Organic consolidants

Three different approaches have been adopted, with varying degrees of success, in order to ensure a sufficiently low viscosity. Some early treatments centred around waxes with a relatively low melting point that could be made to penetrate the stone by warming. The approach was used for some years by the British Museum during the 1950s and 1960s for consolidating limestone with polyethylene glycol, but was less used for exterior stonework because of the difficulty of heating the stone. It was used, nonetheless, for the treatment of Cleopatra's Needle in London in 1949, the stone being 'very gently heated with a blowlamp'.[8] A further drawback of the approach, as with all wax treatments, is that the treated stone remains somewhat tacky, particularly when the weather is warm, and it is inclined to become rather dirty. The only 'waxes' used as stone consolidants today are volatile solids such as cyclododecane, which are useful for temporary consolidation and tissue facings. Applied in solution in a non-polar solvent, the deposited solid evaporates almost completely after a few weeks.

A second approach has been to dissolve the consolidant in a low-viscosity solvent to aid penetration. This approach was adopted for naturally occurring resins such as shellac and linseed oil as bottled solvents became available in the later nineteenth century, and also, more recently, for synthetic resins such as epoxies and acrylics. But there are several drawbacks to such an approach. Although the solution may appear to penetrate deeply into the stone, there is no guarantee that the resin itself will not be selectively absorbed at the surface and so may not penetrate at all. Even if it does penetrate, there is a danger that it will be drawn back to the surface as the solvent evaporates. The use of large quantities of solvents is also undesirable on health, safety and environmental grounds.

Nonetheless, the approach has been widely adopted, and some researchers have gone to great lengths to find appropriate combinations of consolidant and solvent.[9] Today this form of consolidation is the most widely used in all branches of conservation, not least stone conservation. Acrylics are most commonly used (see below), but some conservators, especially in Eastern Europe, favour the use of animal glues such as isinglass (sturgeon glue). These display remarkable consolidant properties even at low concentrations. The use of epoxy resins as consolidants has never been widely adopted by the profession because of the insolubility of the resultant polymer (and the consequent irreversibility of any process using it), the inflexibility of its application, the difficulty of avoiding immediate darkening, and uncertainties regarding the longevity of such treatments. The most famous ensemble of sculpture consolidated with epoxy resin is perhaps the Portail Royal of Chartres Cathedral.[10]

A third approach is also widely favoured today. It consists of impregnating the stone with a monomer, and then inducing polymerization *in situ*. Monomers are relatively small molecules that can react together to make a much larger molecule, a polymer. The reaction is referred to as polymerization. Monomers are frequently low viscosity liquids, whereas polymers are often solids. So the treatment is introduced to the stone in the form of a liquid monomer, following which the reaction is triggered, and the resulting solid polymer provides the required consolidation. Acrylic monomers have been used in this way, with polymerization being achieved by the use of heat, γ-radiation or room-temperature accelerators. Although some success has been claimed, applications have been limited, and far more attention has been paid to the use of alkoxysilanes, or silanes for short (see below).

Acrylic polymers

Acrylic resins. Acrylic resins consist of small molecules (monomers), linked together to form long chain-like polymers. Unlike silanes, these chains do not cross-link to one another and it is possible to dissolve acrylic resin in organic solvents, imparting a degree of reversibility to these consolidants.

Acrylic resins have been used in stone conservation since the late 1960s. Many types have been tested for conservation, and some have been found to have very useful properties of stability, longevity, low toxicity, reversibility and flexibility of use. The majority of acrylic polymers used in stone conservation come from two families of monomers: acrylates and methacrylates. At the time of writing, the acrylic resin most commonly used by conservators is Paraloid B72 (a co-polymer of methylethacrylate and ethylmethacrylate).

Acrylic resins are dissolved in an organic solvent such as acetone, industrial methylated spirits, toluene or xylene. Typical concentrations are between 2–5% of consolidant in solvent by weight/volume. The type of solvent and the concentration of the solution are varied according to the type of stone being treated and the degree and depth of consolidation required.

Hardening of the consolidant is due to evaporation of the solvent. If a volatile solvent, such as acetone, is used there may be good initial penetration of the consolidant, but rapid evaporation of the solvent will simply draw the resin back to the surface of the stone, resulting in consolidation to a depth of only a few millimetres. This can be overcome by employing a less volatile solvent such as xylene. To achieve appreciable consolidation, several applications are usually required, but darkening of the stone may occur as a result. Stone consolidated with acrylic resin can be cleaned using organic solvents, although care must be taken to ensure that the solvent does not dissolve some of the acrylic; if this occurs further application of consolidant may be required.

Acrylic resins are capable of bridging (in microscopic terms) very large gaps. They provide a good increase in strength in decayed stone, and they are extremely resistant to degradation by oxygen and ultra-violet light. They are particularly useful for the consolidation of superficially laminated structures where interlaminar decohesion is a problem, and for consolidating friable and powdery surface layers, rather than for deep impregnation. They are also useful for consolidating painted stone. Flakes of hardened consolidant can be slipped behind the detached paint layer and the paint then pressed gently into position using a heated spatula; because acrylic resins are thermoplastic, the heat softens the resin, which adheres to the paint layer and to the stone substrate. Concentrated solutions of acrylic resin form the basis of various proprietary conservation adhesives, which can be used to secure flakes of stone. They can also be mixed with fine stone dust and other fillers for surface repairs, grouting and crack fills. For the consolidation of paint flakes and other forms of gross detachment, the other consolidant types here described are unsuitable.

The disadvantages of acrylic resins for stone in outdoor locations are plain. The resins tend to block the pores of stone, and are quite hydrophobic. They tend to be deposited superficially when used with a volatile solvent. They are adversely affected by moisture and are best suited to consolidating objects in an internal or sheltered external environment. Where moisture movements within stone are pronounced, or where salt contamination is a problem, acrylics should be used with the greatest circumspection, even if the working concentration is kept very low (<2%, for example). Whilst the ability of acrylics to strengthen grossly decayed laminated structures makes them potentially very desirable for exterior work, one crucial limitation must always be borne in mind: some of them soften dramatically at temperatures that can readily be experienced by stone that is exposed to direct sunlight.

Acrylic dispersions. These are typically copolymers of methylmethacrylate and ethylacrylate, dispersed in water. As the water evaporates, or is absorbed by the stone, the small polymer particles coalesce to form a film, which can bind disaggregated stone particles. Penetration can be impeded if this happens too fast. The excellent film-forming capability of acrylic dispersions is one of their attractions as commercial paint media.

Acrylic dispersions have been used in conservation since the 1950s. The most widely used product in stone conservation in the past two decades has been Primal AC33, though this is no longer available (replaced by Primal (Rhoplex) B60A). Diluted in de-ionized water to 10% w/w or lower, they are commonly used for surface consolidation of stone and for re-adhering detached flakes of paint. They can also be used for temporary facing up and are sometimes added to lime-based grouts, to improve adhesion. Some acrylic dispersions are more resistant to degradation by moisture than acrylic resins, and can be used in damp locations or in humid conditions. Because acrylic dispersions are diluted with water, they do not pose the health hazards associated with resins dissolved in volatile organic solvents.

Silanes

Because of their chemical compatibilities with sandstone and their low molecular weights, silanes remain a very important class of consolidant. They are particularly useful for the treatment of powdering stone suffering intermediate decay. In such cases, their deployment may retard further decay. They are also used as treatments of last resort against extreme decay, where the use of alternative consolidants is unfeasible because of their mode of application (e.g. through a poultice as with barium hydroxide treatments), or because of their heightened propensity to inhibit porosity (e.g. acrylic solutions or dispersions). Nonetheless, they are relatively ineffective in cases where gross disaggregation or detachments and discontinuities within the stone are a strong feature of the decay, since they are incapable of bridging large (in molecular terms) gaps. There have been some problems with their use in the past, but an understanding of their chemical and physical properties will help to identify appropriate circumstances in which they can be used safely.

There are two principal types of silane consolidant – alkoxysilanes and silicon esters – that have been used during the past 30 years, and which differ only in the extent of initial polymerization. Silanes react with water (hydrolysis) to form polymers that are derivatives of silicon dioxide, the basic constituent of sand and sandstones. The water needed for this reaction may be added deliberately to the monomer, or it may be derived from moisture already present in the stone or in the atmosphere. An alcohol is given off during the reaction, and this is lost by evaporation. As a result, the polymer does not fill the whole of the available pore space within the stone, and the treated stone remains permeable to water vapour.

Once formed, the chemical bond linking the polymers cannot be broken by solvents, which means that treatments that use these consolidants are irreversible. Some alkoxysilane polymers have water repellent properties, due to the presence of methyl (CH_3) or ethyl (C_2H_5) groups attached to the silicon.

A number of different silane monomers have been tried, with methyltrimethoxysilane (MTMOS), ethyltriethoxysilane (ETEOS) and tetraethoxysilane (TEOS)[11] being predominant. A wide variety of silane formulations exist, both as commercial products and as experimental systems. They may contain more than one silane, and may also contain catalysts, water, and solvents to ensure miscibility. Acrylic resins can be added to silanes to increase the yield of the silane, and to provide a harder surface finish.

Uncatalysed silanes are suitable only for consolidating sculpture and small items; on large areas of a building façade they penetrate the stonework uncontrollably and do not build up into sufficient concentrations to provide adequate consolidation.

The most widely used catalysed MTMOS in the UK was Brethane, developed in the early 1980s by the Building Research Establishment, but no longer commercially available. Catalysed MTMOS comprises MTMOS, a catalyst and solvents, mixed immediately prior to application. Initial viscosity is low so it penetrates well, but due to the action of the catalyst, gelling takes place quickly (within 2–4 hours), arresting further movement of the liquid consolidant, preventing both evaporation and uncontrolled penetration, and thus helping to ensure that the majority of the consolidant is deposited in the outer 25 mm or more of the stone. Full polymerization occurs over a matter of weeks.

Catalysed ETEOS (such as Wacker H) achieves good consolidation, but its hydrophobic properties reduce the adhesion of lime-based mortars, so pointing, grouting and mortar repairs must be carried out before application of ETEOS. It will also seriously impede aqueous cleaning techniques and desalination. ETEOS is not often used on exterior stonework, and is the least frequently encountered of the silane classes here described.

TEOS is the same chemically as ethyl silicate, which has been used as a stone consolidant for a long time. For example it was used at Bath Abbey in the 1950s. Commercial TEOS consolidants, such as Wacker OH, usually comprise TEOS, a catalyst and solvents. TEOS achieves good consolidation, and since it does not have water repellent properties, lime-based grouts, pointing mortars and repair mortars can be used after consolidation. If a water repellent finish is required, ETEOS can be applied after all cleaning, grouting and filling operations have been completed. Desalination, cleaning and re-treatment are possible after treatment with TEOS, albeit not entirely unaffected.

TEOS consolidants are very effective for the consolidation of sandstones and have been used throughout Europe for about 30 years. In continental Europe in particular their use is very common on limestones, too.

From a chemical point of view, silanes (especially TEOS) can be loosely seen as putting sand back into sandstones, and it might well be expected that any silane would perform better on sandstones than on calcareous stones. However, at least one formulation has proved to be no less effective on limestones.[12] This could suggest that bonding between consolidant and substrate is not of primary importance, and that the consolidant may function simply by providing internal 'scaffolding' that permeates the pore structure. This tentatively recommends silanes for the consolidation of stones such as granite, and even decorative stones such as marble, alabaster and polishable limestones (e.g. Purbeck 'marble'). Further analysis and alternative interpretations are provided in Wheeler's comprehensive review of alkoxysilanes.[13]

Weiss has suggested the use of tartaric acid to act as a 'go-between' between limestones and silane consolidants,[14] in what he describes as a hydroxylating conversion treatment (HCT). The tartaric acid bonds with the limestone to produce a layer of calcium tartrate tetrahydrate (CTT), which should in turn bond more readily with the silane. However, even the formation of CTT alone appears to offer some protection to the stone, and its use is being explored further.

Advantages and disadvantages of silane consolidants. Silanes have been widely adopted in some countries, whilst other countries (notably the UK) have taken a much more cautious approach. There was initial concern, based on laboratory experiments, that catalysed systems in particular might not meet the criterion of re-treatability,[15] but this concern has largely subsided in the light of practical experience. There has also been understandable concern about the use of formulations containing water on stone with a high clay content, or stone with abnormally high levels of salts (because of the problems associated with swelling of these substances through hydration). In such instances, the conservator might consider the use of a consolidant in solution in a non-polar solvent. Silanes also pose health and safety risks and should be used only in a well ventilated area or with fume extraction, and appropriate protective clothing and respiratory equipment must be worn.

However, silanes also offer potential advantages: no removal of unsound stone is required prior to application; they can penetrate deeply and polymerize *in situ*, resulting in good consolidation of friable stone; they remain chemically stable over time and do not significantly discolour treated stone; as well as increasing the physical strength and cohesion of the stone they can also increase its resistance to chemical weathering; and they do not necessarily preclude related treatments such as cleaning and surface repair. Nonetheless, silanes should only be used as a last resort, after consideration of all other options, on stone that would otherwise be lost to decay.

Other organic consolidants

Perfluoropolyethers have been marketed for some time. Commonly used in Italy, they display very interesting properties of water repellency and breathability. They are available as elastomers (for example, Akeogard CO), and are particularly useful for the consolidation of very badly disaggregated stone.

Inorganic consolidants

Inorganic consolidants are of mineral origin, and include solutions of calcium hydroxide and barium hydroxide. Under certain conditions, they react to form insoluble calcium or barium carbonate, which can bind together disaggregated particles of deteriorated stone. The cases in which they may be useful will be similar to those for silanes (see above), and, in the case of barium hydroxide, particularly where there is sulphate contamination. However, their effect is not deep-penetrating, and their utility is limited by this.

Calcium hydroxide

A four-stage conservation treatment based on lime (calcium hydroxide) was proposed by Baker in the early 1960s, and first tried on figure sculpture at Merton College, Oxford.[16] It consisted of a hot poultice of slaked lime, followed by multiple applications of limewater (a saturated solution of calcium hydroxide). The stone, thus consolidated,[17] was then repaired as necessary with carefully selected lime mortars, and the entire surface was finally given a protective, sacrificial coating (sheltercoat) based on lime. The procedure, which is intended only for limestones, is fully described in Ashurst[18] and in Fidler.[19] None of the stages was novel in itself, but the package as a whole had not been promulgated before.

The treatment soon attracted vigorous proponents ('What could be more natural than putting back lime into a limestone?'), and equally vigorous opponents, who argued that there was no evidence that the first two stages had any consolidating effect at all. Calcium hydroxide is sparingly soluble in water (with maximum solubility at low temperatures), and one litre of saturated calcium hydroxide solution contains only approximately 1.7 g of calcium hydroxide, which would carbonate to yield 2.3 g of calcium carbonate. Multiple applications of limewater are required in order to deposit significant amounts of calcium carbonate. Nevertheless, many practitioners claimed significant improvements following lime-watering. It is likely that some consolidation may be due to redistribution and re-crystallization of calcium sulphate (gypsum) and other soluble minerals within sulphated limestone. Whether in the long term this is beneficial or harmful is not known.

Baker himself was opposed to any form of experimental evaluation, and it was not until he retired that Price et al were able to undertake any systematic investigation.[20,21] Radioactive lime was used to track the depth of penetration of the limewater, and to monitor conclusively the final deposition of the lime. Price's team showed that more than half the lime was deposited in the outer 2 mm of the stone, and that so little was deposited at greater depths that no consolidating effect could reasonably be expected. They concluded that the success of the lime process was probably attributable not to the chemical properties of the lime poultice or the limewater, but more to the skills of the conservator in placing the repair mortars, which enhanced the stone's ability to resist further weathering.

Figure 7.2   Wells Cathedral, Somerset. The figure on the right has been treated by the lime method; the figure on the left is untreated.

The technique was adopted for the conservation of nearly 300 figures on the West Front of Wells Cathedral in England between 1974 and 1986, and has since been widely adopted elsewhere in England and in Europe. At Wells, it has proved more effective than anyone dared to hope at the time, with only minor maintenance having been needed so far. Nonetheless, the lime poultice is seldom used today, with most practitioners preferring instead to clean the stone with air abrasives, lasers or with other types of poultice, before continuing to the remaining stages.

Severely decayed stone cannot be consolidated using limewater, and must be removed prior to lime mortar repairs being carried out. This may result in unacceptable loss of carved detail in some circumstances. For stone in a less advanced state of decay, lime techniques can provide improved strength and consolidation, and have the advantage of being stable and chemically compatible with limestone. However, limewater must not be used on non-calcareous sandstones. The introduction of calcium carbonate into sandstones can result in the secondary formation of gypsum due to reaction with acid rain, and this can initiate forms of decay that would not otherwise have occurred (limewater does not significantly add to the reservoir of calcium carbonate available for sulphation in limestones).

Attention has recently been given to the use of calcite-forming bacteria as an alternative method of depositing calcium carbonate in decayed limestone, and several buildings in France have been so treated.[22] One possible drawback noted by Hansen et al. is the limited depth of penetration, but this is equally true of the more conventional means of deposition.

Barium hydroxide

From a chemical standpoint, barium and calcium have much in common, and it is not surprising that the use of calcium hydroxide should have led to an interest in barium hydroxide also. Barium hydroxide may convert calcium sulphate to barium sulphate. Unlike calcium sulphate, barium sulphate is insoluble in water so this reaction stabilizes sulphates, thereby reducing the risk of further salt crystallization damage. Barium hydroxide, when applied to stone in solution in water, also carbonates in a manner analogous to calcium hydroxide. The resultant deposit of barium carbonate may further react with atmospheric sulphur dioxide, forming insoluble barium sulphate, and making the stone more resistant to decay due to atmospheric pollutants.

Barium hydroxide, or 'Baryta water', was first used in the nineteenth century for consolidating marble and limestone. However, it was found that the treatment resulted in the formation of crusts on the surface of the stone, which de-laminated during weathering, and as early as 1932, Schaffer wrote that 'in practice the method proved a failure'.[23] Although it was not widely used in the first half of the twentieth century, it continued to attract interest, and in the mid-1960s attention focused on using it in combination with other treatments.[24] Techniques of treating limestone by immersion in a solution of barium hydroxide, glycerol and urea were developed in the 1960s, though now these have largely been abandoned. More recently, barium hydroxide has been extensively used as part of a two-stage process, in conjunction with the application of ammonium carbonate, for the conservation of wall paintings in Italy.[25] It provides an excellent means of neutralizing sulphate salt species in carbonate substrates. Its use must be carefully controlled, not least from the point of view of health and safety. Early exposure to the air results in the formation of an insoluble bloom upon the surface of the object (the principal problem with the early patented 'Baryta Process'). The solution is therefore usually applied to the surface mixed to a pulp with cellulose; this allows the solution to penetrate without exposure to the air. Following the removal of this poultice, care must be taken to rinse away any superficial deposits of barium hydroxide solution. This can be done through a layer of tissue paper to obviate disruption of fragile surfaces.

Due to uneven deposition of the barium carbonate, this method could be considered for consolidation problems that are essentially superficial, particularly those associated with stones for which the maintenance of free porosity is less of an issue (for example, sulphate contaminated Purbeck 'marble'). The consolidant effect is physically analogous to that imparted by silanes.

The use of barium hydroxide can be hazardous, both to operatives and to some other construction materials.

A thorough review of inorganic consolidants for calcareous materials is provided by Hansen et al.[26] They examine the use of both calcium and barium compounds, including the relatively novel use of calcium oxalate and tartrate.

APPLICATION OF CONSOLIDANTS

The method by which a consolidant is applied will depend to some extent on the condition of the stone and on the area to be treated. Most consolidants are applied by spray, or by flooding the surface using a brush or a pipette. For deep penetration, application has to continue over a long period. This will usually entail multiple applications, over several hours. More elaborate methods have been described for large-scale operations, but have not found widespread application in practice: Schoonbrood,[27] for example, describes the use of a low pressure application technique that is claimed to maximize capillary absorption, and Balfour-Beatty experimented for a time with vacuum application.[28] Whatever method is used, care should be taken to prevent any run-off onto areas that are not to be treated. To avoid discolouration caused by saturation of the immediate surface of the stone, it is common practice to rinse the stone with a compatible solvent following impregnation.

If cleaning is necessary, this should normally take place before the application of the consolidant. This is particularly important where black crusts or biological growths are present, which would prevent penetration of the consolidant. Non-contact cleaning regimes such as Nd:YAG laser can be very useful in such cases. But it is also important that the stone should be reasonably dry when the consolidant is applied, or else the water in the stone may prevent penetration. This will need careful planning, especially if water-based methods are used for cleaning. It will often be necessary to erect some sort of temporary shelter over the stonework to protect it from rainfall in the days preceding treatment, and space heaters may sometimes be used to dry the stone. Treatment should not take place under extremes of temperature or of relative humidity.

If a water-repellent consolidant is to be applied, thought must be given to the timing of any grouting, pointing or mortar repairs. These should normally precede treatment, with sufficient time being allowed for drying and hardening. This avoids the possibility that the mortar or grout will be unable to wet, and thus bond to, the water-repellent surface.

Sometimes, it may be appropriate to consider 'preconsolidation', the prior stabilization of a particularly vulnerable surface to enable it to withstand the full-scale application of the consolidant. Such stabilization may also reduce the risk of damage during cleaning or the removal of salts. A wide range of materials have been used for preconsolidation, often in conjunction with facing tissue that is subsequently removed.[29] The

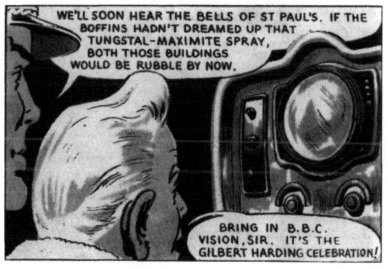

Figure 7.3   Fictional space-traveller, Dan Dare, alludes to the development of successful stone consolidant, *Tungstal Maximite*. Unfortunately, the composition of *Tungstal Maximite* is unknown. (*Eagle Annual 5*, Hulton).

preconsolidant itself is left in place, and may be dissolved and carried further into the stone by the subsequent application of the main consolidant.

Due attention must always be paid to health and safety. Protective clothing will always be necessary and, in poorly ventilated conditions, respirators will be essential when applying organic consolidants. Eye protection is also important, particularly with lime and with some silanes.

Finally, it cannot be over-stressed that no treatment will be effective if it is not applied with skill and understanding. Success is not just a matter of specifying a suitable material. The expertise and knowledge of the conservator who applies the material is equally important.

EVALUATING THE EFFECTIVENESS OF CONSOLIDANTS

Article 10 of the *Venice Charter* reads:[30]

> Where traditional techniques prove inadequate, the consolidation of a monument can be achieved by the use of any modern technique for conservation and construction, the efficacy of which has been shown by scientific data and proved by experience.

If only it were so easy. How does one demonstrate the efficacy of a consolidant? What scientific data, and what experience, are required? How does one know when enough of each has been amassed?

The problem can be divided into two parts. First, does the consolidant work? In other words, does it strengthen the stone? Second, and much harder to demonstrate, does it keep on working?

A number of tests have been devised for evaluating the short-term effectiveness of consolidants. They are intended to demonstrate only the extent to which the treatment has strengthened the stone, and include direct tensile tests, three-point bending, resistance to air abrasives, and direct abrasion resistance. Wheeler describes the application of such tests and examines their relevance.[31] The ability of a consolidant to bind sand or crushed stone has also been an important and emotionally satisfying test. Despite a large number of published papers, relatively little attention has been given to the magnitude of the strength increase that is desirable, or to related issues such as the change in Young's modulus (coefficient of elasticity), or to changes in porosity of the stone after treatment. Most authors have been satisfied simply to demonstrate that a treatment has had a significant consolidating effect.

Demonstrating the long-term effectiveness of a consolidant is more problematic. How long will the consolidant remain effective? Will it have any undesirable side effects? What are the risks that it may even do positive harm over a period of years? There are essentially two approaches, which are further elaborated by Price.[32,33] The first is to use laboratory tests in an attempt to speed up the passage of time. Some of these tests, such as exposure to ultra-violet radiation, are focused on the consolidant itself: is it resistant to chemical, photochemical, physical and biological degradation? Others are focused on the stone/consolidant composite: is it resistant to salt crystallization, to thermal cycling, or to changes in moisture content, for example? Some caution is required in the interpretation of results. A common error is to use a salt crystallization test on water-repellent samples, the water repellency preventing any solution from ever entering the samples.

Laboratory tests undoubtedly have a part to play in evaluating the long-term effectiveness of consolidants, but they can provide only part of the picture. No matter how sophisticated the test, or how elaborate the accelerated ageing chamber, one can never be entirely certain that they have properly simulated natural weathering, or by what factor they have speeded up time. There is no substitute for natural exposure tests, in which treated samples or panels are exposed to the weather over a period of years. But even here, there are difficulties: such tests can give information only about the consolidant's performance on a particular type of stone under particular environmental conditions. There is no guarantee that the consolidant will perform in the same way on a different stone under different conditions. And who wants to wait twenty or thirty years for an answer? By that time, new treatments will have come along, and one will have to start all over again. Nonetheless, there have been some commendable attempts to monitor the long-term performance of certain consolidants,[34,35,36] and Wheeler[37] attempts to correlate field and laboratory data relating to alkoxysilane consolidants.

Whatever the testing protocol, very little work has been done on the problem of multiple treatments. Researchers almost always assume that consolidants will be applied to stone that has never been treated before, but this assumption may not be justified where historic stonework is concerned. Over a long period of time, the stone may acquire a cocktail of different treatments that may behave in a very unpredictable way. This intractable problem has yet to be addressed. A good example of this is the Temple Church doorway in London, treated with linseed oil in the nineteenth century, 'Hemingway's Patent Chemical' circa 1900, and then Brethane and acrylic silane in the 1980s.

WHEN ARE CONSOLIDANTS USED?

Given the difficulty of evaluating the long-term effectiveness of any consolidant, there is inevitably some risk associated with its use. This is not to say that consolidants should never be used. Rather, it is necessary to weigh up the potential benefits against the potential losses, and arrive at a reasoned judgement. One will be more cautious about applying a consolidant to important medieval figure sculpture, for example, than in applying it to more recent stonework of less architectural or historic interest.

It may be helpful to consider those instances in which a consolidant should not be used. Situations of high salt contamination have already been mentioned, and one would be equally wary of applying a consolidant in situations where water could readily enter the stone from the back, for example where rising damp is present. Certainly, consolidants should never be used as a substitute for regular maintenance, for common sense, or for preventive conservation when practicable. They should not be used to restore structural stability to stone masonry. Nor should they be used unless there are reasonable grounds for believing that they will be effective in the situation in question.

This may sometimes entail setting up trial panels, although it is unrealistic to insist that this should always be done. Moreover, consolidants should not be used unless there is objective evidence that the stone is decaying at an unacceptably fast rate; this takes time and careful monitoring. Stone decay is usually quite a slow process, and one must not be panicked into the unnecessary use of consolidants. The causes of decay should be fully explored, evaluated and, if possible, eliminated before any consideration of consolidation. The trauma of any eventual re-treatment following the inevitable breakdown of the consolidant selected should be taken into account (this will normally include a campaign of cleaning).

If, after all such caveats have been dismissed, and the surface is very weak and friable, consolidation may be indicated without further delay.

The best way for conservators to familiarize themselves with the various consolidants available is for them to buy some samples to experiment with. They can learn more about the properties of a particular consolidant by allowing it to harden in a dish, attempting to bind stone dust with it, or by simply feeling it than ever they might through reading scientific papers alone. It is not necessary to spend a fortune on samples of every conceivable product since, in practice, the more unusual options for consolidation should be pursued only in particularly important or intractable cases.

In 1980, the Society for the Protection of Ancient Buildings (SPAB), based in London, called for a moratorium on the use of silanes. SPAB was concerned that there was insufficient experience of the long-term behaviour of silanes to justify their widespread use. The moratorium came at a time when a silane formulation had been used to consolidate the two Saxon crosses at Sandbach, Cheshire – a treatment that was controversial at the time, and that would probably be controversial today, given the importance of the crosses. SPAB's moratorium has never been repealed, although it was discussed at a meeting called by the Society in 1998. Interestingly, the consensus of the meeting appeared to be that the moratorium was of little significance, since there was now relatively little call for the use of silanes in the UK. This does not necessarily mean that there is little need.

Another *cause celèbre* was the Great West Doorway of York Minster, dating from the fourteenth century, and built in magnesian limestone. In the early 1970s, the doorway was exhibiting the floury, cavernous decay typical of magnesian limestones. Field trials were set up to compare the performance of a range of silane formulations, the decay being considered too grave to be addressed by any other method. It was concluded that no treatment was going to be capable of arresting decay indefinitely, but that it would be possible to achieve sufficient consolidation in the short term to allow moulds to be taken (note again the distinction between consolidation and preservation). Treatment with Brethane went ahead on this understanding.[38] In the event, moulds were never taken, and by 1998 the doorway had been removed and replaced.

The case of York Minster leads on to the issue of recording. We have to accept that we may never be able to arrest the decay of stone permanently. Recording the stone in its existing condition thus becomes the most enduring means of passing the stone on to future generations. Photography, drawing and photogrammetry each have their place, but laser scanning and digital recording are becoming the predominant recording methods. We would be failing in our duty as stewards of the past, if we were not to hand on to future generations the best possible records of the stonework that is presently in our care.

THE FUTURE

New consolidants are always appearing over the horizon. For example, biomineralization as a means of consolidating limestone is likely to spawn a variety of new treatments, and Weiss[39] is reporting promising results in the use of tartaric acid, either on its own or as a pre-treatment for alkoxysilanes. However, given the long and disappointing history of stone consolidants, the sceptical may be tempted to think, '*Plus ça change.* ...'[40] On the other hand, we must always be open to the possibility that future treatments may prove more successful than their predecessors. An eminent cathedral architect, the late Emil Godfrey, when confronted with the assertion that no stone preservative had ever proved successful, wryly replied, 'They said that of aeroplanes when I was a boy'.

What is likely to change is our expectations of consolidants. For too long, we have been hoping for treatments that would last forever, or at least for the century or so that might elapse between successive scaffolded accesses to the more inaccessible parts of major historic buildings. However, we are gradually becoming more sensible in our expectations and are realising that a ten or twenty year life-cycle may be the best we can hope for. At the same time, the increasing availability of mobile access platforms ('cherry pickers') is facilitating more frequent access.

Another likely change lies in our ability to select particular consolidants or formulations for specific purposes. In the past, there has been a tendency to look for universal consolidants that would hopefully work equally well on all types of stone in all possible environments. Wheeler's careful analysis of the influence of stone type on the behaviour of alkoxysilanes, and of the varying ability of alkoxysilanes to deal with different types of deterioration,[41] highlights the absurdity of the 'one size fits all' approach. It is to be hoped that further research, both in the field and in the laboratory, will lead to a much better ability to match the consolidant to the particular need.

Finally, it may be appropriate to conclude on a philosophical note. The current fashion, at least in the western world, is very much centred on the preservation of material culture. However, as Lowenthal notes:[42]

> ... the concept of conservation ... goes far beyond the acts of material preservation on which Western societies concentrate their efforts.

In focusing our attention on the consolidation and preservation of historic stonework, we should not ignore the function of the buildings we seek to conserve, or the maintenance of the skills that went into their creation.

These deserve just as much consideration as the stone itself and, if we are led to conclude that stone cannot always be made to last for perpetuity, we may be better able to redress the balance.

Acknowledgments

The author wishes to acknowledge the contributions to this chapter from Seamus Hanna and Christopher Weeks. Some of the text that has been included is based upon material supplied by English Heritage from two of their forthcoming publications: *Practical Building Conservation* second edition, volume on *Stone* and the Technical Advice Note: *The Use of Stone Consolidants.*

The author

Clifford Price MA, PhD, CChem, FRSC, FIIC, FSA

Clifford Price is Professor of Archaeological Conservation at the Institute of Archaeology, University College London. He received his PhD in chemistry from the University of Cambridge. He first became involved in stone conservation during his employment at the Building Research Establishment, where he led the development of the consolidant Brethane. He was Head of the Ancient Monuments Laboratory, English Heritage, from 1983 to 1990.

References

1   Félix, C. and Furlan, V., 'Variations dimensionelles de grès et calcaires liées à leur consolidation avec un silicate d'éthyle' in Fassina V., Ott H. and Zezza F. (eds), *La conservazione dei monumenti nel bacino del Mediterraneo*, Soprintendenza ai Beni Artistici e Storici di Venezia, Venice, 1994, pp. 855–9.

2   Alonso, F. J., Esbert, R. M., Alonso, J. and Ordaz, J., 'Saline spray action on a treated dolomitic stone', in Fassina, V., Ott H. and Zezza F. (eds.), *La conservazione dei monumenti nel bacino del Mediterraneo*, Soprintendenza ai Beni Artistici e Storici di Venezia, Venice, 1994, pp. 867–70.

3   Bradley, S. M. and Hanna, S. B., 'The effect of soluble salt movements on the conservation of an Egyptian limestone standing figure', in Bromelle, N. S. and Smith, P. (eds.), *Case Studies in the Conservation of Stone and Wallpaintings*, International Institute for Conservation, London, 1986, pp. 132–8.

4   A consolidant will penetrate if the solid/liquid surface energy is lower than the solid/air surface energy. It is too facile to refer simply to the surface tension of the consolidant (the liquid/air surface energy). Note, for example, the conflicting statements of two well-respected texts:

> 'To achieve good penetration ... a liquid of high surface tension is desirable'. Crafts Council, *Science for Conservators, 3, Adhesives and Coatings*, Crafts Council, London(1983).

> 'Much the best penetration is achieved by dissolving a polymer in a low surface tension organic solvent'. Cronyn, J. M., *The Elements of Archaeological Conservation*, Routledge, London (1990).

5   Oddy, W. A. and Carroll, S., *Reversibility – does it exist?*, British Museum Occasional Paper 135. British Museum, London (1999).

6   Price, C. A., *Brethane Stone Preservative*, Building Research Establishment Current Paper 1/81, Building Research Establishment, Watford (1981).

7   Applebaum, B., 'Criteria for treatment: reversibility', *Journal of the American Institute for Conservation*, vol. 26 (1987), pp. 65–73.

8   Burgess, S. G. and Schaffer, R. J., 'Cleopatra's Needle', *Chemistry and Industry*, 18 October 1952, pp. 1026–9.

9   Selwitz, C. M., *Research in conservation, 7: Epoxy resins in stone conservation*, Getty Conservation Institute, Los Angeles (1992).

10   Nonfarmale, O. and Rossi Manaresi, R., 'Il restauro del "Portail Royal" della cattedrale di Chartres', in *Arte Medievale* (1987), pp. 259–75.

11   Under a former system of nomenclature, tetraethoxysilane was known as tetraethyl orthosilicate, conveniently having the same acronym.

12   Martin, B., Mason, D., Teutonico, J. M., Chapman, S., Butlin, R. and Yates, T., 'Stone consolidants: Brethane. Report of an 18-year review of Brethane-treated sites', in Fidler, J. (ed.), *English Heritage Research Transactions: Stone*, James and James, London (2002), pp. 3–18.

13   Wheeler, G., *Alkoxysilanes and the Consolidation of Stone*, Getty Conservation Institute, Los Angeles (2005).

14   Hansen, E., Doehne, E., Fidler, J., Larson, J., Martin, B., Matteini, M., Rodríguez-Navarro, C., Sebastián Pardo, E., Price, C., de Tagle, A., Teutonico, J. M. and Weiss, N., 'A review of selected inorganic consolidants and protective treatments for porous calcareous materials', *Reviews in Conservation*, 2003, pp. 13–25.

15   Larson, J., 'A museum approach to the techniques of stone conservation', in *Proceedings of the 4th International Congress on the Deterioration and Preservation of Stone*, University of Louisville, Louisville (1982), pp. 219–37.

16   Oakeshott, W. F. (ed.), *Oxford Stone Restored*, Trustees of the Oxford Historic Buildings Fund, Oxford (1975), p. 81.

17   Consolidation was presumed to be due to the conversion of calcium hydroxide to calcium carbonate through reaction with atmospheric carbon dioxide, in a manner comparable to the hardening of lime mortars.

18 Ashurst, J., 'The cleaning and treatment of limestone by the lime method', in Ashurst, J. and Dimes, F. (eds), *Conservation of Building and Decorative Stone*, Butterworth-Heinemann, London (1990), pp. 169–176.

19 Fidler, J., 'Lime treatments: An overview of lime watering and shelter coating of friable historic limestone masonry', in Fidler, J. (ed.) *English Heritage Research Transactions: Stone*, James and James, London (2002), pp. 19–28.

20 Price, C. A., Ross, K. D., and White, G., 'A further appraisal of the "lime technique" for limestone consolidation, using a radioactive tracer', *Studies in Conservation*, No. 33, 1988, pp. 178–86.

21 Price, C. A. and Ross, K., 'Technical appraisal of stone conservation techniques at Wells Cathedral', in Ashurst J. and Dimes F. (eds.), *The Conservation of Building and Decorative Stone*, Butterworths, Guildford (1990), pp. 176–84.

22 Hansen, *et al., op. cit.*

23 Schaffer, R. J., *The Weathering of Natural Building Stones*, (reprint of 1932 edition), Donhead, Shaftesbury (2004), p. 84.

24 Hansen, *et al., op. cit.*

25 Matteini, M., 'In review: an assessment of Florentine methods of wall painting conservation based on the use of mineral treatments', in Cather, S. (ed.), *The Conservation of Wall Paintings*, Getty Conservation Institute, Los Angeles (1991), pp. 137–48.

26 Hansen *et al., op. cit.*

27 Schoonbrood, J. W. M., 'Low pressure application technique for stone preservatives', Thiel, M.-J. (ed.), *Conservation of Stone and Other Materials*, E & FN Spon, London (1993), pp. 512–18.

28 Antonelli, V., 'Il restauro della Porta della Carta in Venezia', *Deterioramento e conservazione della pietra: atti del 3 Congresso internazionale*, Università degli Studi di Padova, Padova (1979), pp. 629–44.

29 Wheeler, *op. cit.*

30 ICOMOS, *International Charter for the Conservation and Restoration of Monuments and Sites (Venice Charter)*, 1964.

31 Wheeler, *op. cit.*

32 Price, C. A., 'The evaluation of stone preservatives', in *Conservation of Historic Stone Buildings and Monuments*, National Academy Press, Washington DC (1982), pp. 329–40.

33 Price, C. A., 'Methods of evaluating products for the conservation of porous building materials in monuments. VI: Weathering', *Science and Technology for Cultural Heritage*, 5 (1), 1996, pp. 105–9.

34 Rossi Manaresi, R., Rattazzi, A. and Toniolo, L., 'Long term effectiveness of treatments of sandstone', in *Methods of Evaluating Products for the Conservation of Porous Building Materials in Monuments*, ICCROM, Rome (1995), pp. 225–4.

35 Martin, *et al., op. cit.*

36   Woolfitt, C., 'Lime method evaluation: a survey of sites where lime-based conservation techniques have been employed to treat decaying limestone', in Fidler, J. (ed.), *English Heritage Research Transactions: Stone*, James and James, London (2002), pp. 29–44.

37   Wheeler, *op. cit.*

38   Leary, E., *Report of the Brethane Treatment of the Great West Doorway at York Minster*, Internal note N66/81, Building Research Establishment, Watford, (1981).

39   Hansen, *et al.*, *op. cit.*

39   'Plus ça change, plus c'est la même chose'. (The more things change, the more they are the same.) Karr A., *Les Guêpes* (1849).

40   Wheeler, *op. cit.*

41   Lowenthal, D., *The Past is a Foreign Country*, Cambridge University Press, Cambridge (1985), p. 385.

Chapter Eight

Cleaning Techniques

Kyle C. Normandin and Deborah Slaton

INTRODUCTION

The intention of this chapter is to provide an overview of the different cleaning technologies currently available for cleaning stone monuments and façades, including an assessment of which techniques are appropriate for different stone substrates.

The cleaning of stone monuments and building façades is not only necessary for aesthetic reasons, but often promotes conservation and is also undertaken as part of maintenance. Most cleaning of moderately soiled stone on buildings is performed primarily for aesthetic reasons, as soiling may obscure the colour and details of the façade. In many cases, however, severe soiling may affect the long-term conservation of a building or monument by concealing open joints and structural deficiencies, such as cracks and incipient spalls. Some types of soiling, for example ones involving the development of gypsum crusts or acid-secreting biological growths, may actively contribute to deterioration of stone substrates. However, it has also been argued that soiling accretions combined with interrelated patterns of surface erosion are part of the historic appearance of a structure; in some cases, it may be a challenge to differentiate harmful layers of atmospheric build-up and soiling from benign patinas that contribute to the character of a historic structure.

Although the primary reasons for cleaning a stone façade may vary, it is good conservation practice to select the gentlest effective cleaning method. In establishing criteria for a stone façade-cleaning project, a careful consideration of the nature and composition of the stone substrate is always a key factor in the selection of an appropriate cleaning method.

The United Kingdom has developed codes of practice that reflect sensitive cleaning methods and provide guidance for the removal of soiling and dirt from building substrates. The *British Standard BS 8221–1:2000 Code of Practice for cleaning and surface repair of buildings, Part I: Cleaning of natural stones, brick, terracotta and concrete*, was prepared and came into effect on 15 April 2000, updating a previous standard adopted in 1982. This code of practice represents an updated set of guidelines and recommendations on the selection and application of cleaning methods for building façades. This guidance is meant to be used in conjunction with the *British Standard BS 8221–2 Code of Practice for cleaning and surface repair of buildings, Part II: Surface repair of natural stones, brick and terracotta*, which provides guidelines for surface repairs of masonry. The former is not a specification on how cleaning should be performed; rather, it outlines a range of practices that includes identification of characteristics of soiling deposits and evaluation of the susceptibility of substrates to different cleaning processes. It was prepared by the British Standards Institution Technical Committee B/560(B/209/07), and adopted by organizations such as English Heritage, Historic Scotland, the Royal Institute of British Architects and other councils, associations, research institutions and producers throughout the UK.

CAUSES AND IDENTIFICATION OF SOILING

Contaminants are deposited on the surface of masonry structures over time as a result of various chemical reactions between atmospheric gases, particulates deposited from the atmosphere, and/or constituents of the substrate. Organic growth, bird droppings and human actions can also soil masonry substrates. The nature and magnitude of any soiling is related to several factors including the composition of stone soiled, previous treatments it has been given, the composition of adjacent façade elements, the type and concentration of pollutants in the atmosphere and the degree of exposure of the building.

The environment in which a building or monument is located has a direct effect on the soiling composition and patterns it faces. Many stone buildings within urban environments are affected by pollution caused by vehicles. Microclimates around the building may also contribute to the types, patterns and extent of soiling. Protection from rainfall that might be provided by adjacent buildings can also affect the type of soiling that may be encountered on masonry substrates. Natural sheeting of water on certain portions of a structure can increase their rate of erosion, but may also keep dirt from accumulating. On parts of the façade protected from water runoff, including surfaces directly below water tables, areas around dentils, and other projecting elements, crusts may form.

The identification of dirt and contaminants on stone is a critical factor in assessing their role in the deterioration of stone in building façades. Following is a brief synopsis of the causes, appearance and characteristics of soiling and stain types commonly found on stone.

Gypsum crusts and black carbon coatings

When atmospheric pollutants contain sulphur dioxide (SO_2) and sulphur trioxide (SO_3), these contaminants combine with water to form sulphurous and sulphuric acids (acid rain). This can react with the calcium carbonate contained in limestone, marble, calcareous sandstones and even lime mortar to form soluble calcium sulphate dihydrate (gypsum). As the water evaporates, the gypsum crystallizes. On rainwashed parts of a building, any such gypsum is regularly dissolved and washed away, but in sheltered areas, dissolved matter can redeposit on the surface during subsequent wetting and drying cycles, forming a gypsum crust, which may range in thicknesses from 20 to 600 μm. A pure gypsum crust is transparent, but in polluted areas, gypsum crusts are often black due to the encapsulation of atmospheric fly ash and carbon particulates (Figure 8.1). In a heavily polluted environment, thick layers of soiling may form on building façades. When a black gypsum crust is examined microscopically, it has the appearance of a micro-concrete; the gypsum serves as the binder and the fly ash and carbon particulates serve as a micro-aggregate.

Gypsum crusts may retain water and cause damage to the stone substrate.[1] The selection of a cleaning technique or other treatments has to address the issue of whether a gypsum crust, if present, needs to be removed.

Soiling patterns in sandstone are numerous and can be formed both in areas which are protected and unprotected from rainwash. In polluted urban environments, atmospheric particulates can accumulate on the rainwashed parts of sandstone buildings. The porous texture of the exposed stone retains moisture longer than more sheltered parts of the building, increasing the adhesion of soot, fly ash and other debris. Soiling may also be cemented by minerals contained in sandstone that can be solubilized and subsequently migrate to the surface; natural cement can potentially be re-deposited in this manner, and serve to bind particulates onto a sandstone surface. Common possible 'cementing' agents include calcium carbonate, soluble silica (which is less likely), iron oxide (which also has

Figure 8.1 Decorative limestone with some soiling and gypsum crust accumulation at interior crevice. (Wiss, Janney, Elstner Associates, Inc.)

colour itself), and gypsum, which can form from reaction between sulphuric acid from the atmosphere (acid rain) and calcium contained in calcite cements or lime mortars.

A useful discussion of different types of sulphuric acid and carbon compounds found as contaminants on building stone is presented in the paper 'Environmental Pollution in Relation to Stone Decay'.[2]

Figure 8.2   Mineral alteration of granite stone. The peeling granite substrate shows areas of surface alteration. (Wiss, Janney, Elstner Associates, Inc.)

Alteration crusts

Alteration crusts typically form on granite and related stone types. They consist of surface accumulations of altered stone, formed by reaction of the stone with certain chemicals, such as strong acids used in some cleaning products. Alteration crusts typically appear grey to white in colour and are hard, but porous (Figure 8.2).

Metallic stains

Staining can be defined as the penetration of a coloured material into the masonry pores. Even a small amount of a metallic mineral can result in strong stains. Metallic stains may be orange, red, brown, green, or blue-green in colour, depending on the minerals present. Metallic stains can result from corrosion of mineral inclusions in the stone, corrosion of embedded metals (such as unprotected steel fixings), or waterborne run-off from metallic materials elsewhere on the building (such as copper ornamental or cladding elements). They are typically salts of iron, copper and manganese, and are often the result of a reaction with a strong acid, either acid rain or an inappropriate chemical cleaner, although corrosion of some mineral components in stone can also occur in the presence of normal rainwater.

Biological growth

Living organisms present in the environment sometimes adhere to stone masonry façades, especially along horizontal surfaces including water tables, sills, and on small ledges. Biological growth includes, but is not limited to, fungi, algae, and moss. It typically occurs in areas where moisture is retained on the stone surface or within the pore structure of the stone, such as on shaded or north-facing walls, at low levels on masonry in contact with damp ground, and on horizontal surfaces where water can accumulate. Some sandstones are particularly susceptible to biological growth because their porous textures retain moisture, even on vertical rainwashed façades.

STONE PROPERTIES AND CHOICE OF CLEANING METHOD

Stone is a natural material that is characterized by a wide range of mineral compositions and textures. Each type has unique physical and chemical properties that may influence the choice of cleaning method. Petrographic examination using a microscope is an effective method for identifying mineral composition, porosity, structure, grain size and grain interlocking, as well as for detecting the presence of flaws or veins. Observations based on such methods can contribute to a preliminary evaluation of the potential effects of any cleaning systems proposed. Physical testing can be used to identify other properties of the stone, although characteristics such as compressive and flexural strength are typically less significant in selection of cleaning systems than mineral composition, porosity and internal structure.

Mineral composition

The various building stones used in construction – most commonly limestone, marble, sandstone, and granite – contain a variety of minerals, and the mineralogy of a stone type is important in evaluating the suitability of cleaning systems. Diurnal temperature changes cause expansions and contractions that vary according to mineral type and

Figure 8.3 This microphotograph shows horizontal cracking in microcline (10× magnification). (Wiss, Janney, Elstner Associates, Inc.)

crystal size. Microcline, a silicate mineral sometimes found in granite, expands significantly more in the 'a' crystallographic direction than in the 'b' or 'c' directions, causing tightly packed individual crystals to separate along grain boundaries (Figure 8.3). This may eventually allow entrance of liquids such as cleaning solutions and water, or solid airborne substances.

Some clay minerals expand when water enters their crystal lattices, and repeated wetting and drying of such clay minerals will result in cycles of expansion and contraction, which can lead to weakening of the stone; this might preclude the use of water based cleaning systems.

Some stones contain minerals that are susceptible to reaction with acids; this may have implications for the use of suitable chemical cleaning methods for them. For example, the calcite in limestones and calcareous sandstones can be dissolved by hydrochloric acid, and plagioclase, a calcium silicate mineral that often occurs in granite, can be broken down by hydrofluoric acid. Biotite and pyrite are both iron bearing minerals that may be present in igneous, sedimentary and metamorphic rock types (Figure 8.4). They can cause brown iron oxide stains when they react with acidic rainwater, and they also react with acids such as the hydrochloric

Figure 8.4   This microphotograph shows plagioclase inclusions (black minerals) in granite (10× magnification). (Wiss, Janney, Elstner Associates, Inc.)

and hydrofluoric acids used in some cleaning solutions, resulting in staining of the stone.

Calcareous sandstones are similar to a micro-concrete, with individual sand grains bound in a natural matrix such as calcite. Removal of natural calcite cement in the near-surface region of such sandstones by an acid-based chemical cleaning system can increase the stone's surface area and result in an increase in the rate of subsequent soiling.

Structure

The structure of a stone consists of physical features, such as jointing, parting planes within the rock, fracture patterns, bedding and cross-bedding, and folding features that result from its formation. They may be difficult to observe on a small scale. The structure of a stone type may affect the selection of a cleaning system when considering how the cleaner will act on the stone surface. For example, it may be difficult to remove chemical cleaners from granite, which contains many microfractures into which chemicals can penetrate. Arkosic sandstone (brownstone) is sometimes cross-bedded and it may exhibit wide variation in grain size of adjacent layers within a single stone. It would thus be susceptible to differential surface loss during abrasive cleaning. Biotite and Muscovite are two very soft minerals that are sometimes concentrated along foliation planes in some metamorphic stones, and they would be easily eroded if such stones were treated with abrasive cleaning methods. This type of structural concentration of biotite has also been known to lead to thin bands of iron staining when the iron contained in it is leached out during application of mineral acids during cleaning.

Hardness

The hardness of a stone refers to its resistance to scratching, indentation, bending, breaking, abrasion, cleavage, or fracture. Moh's scale of hardness is commonly used to define hardness based on how well a substance will resist scratching, and it may be applied to individual mineral grains. Hardness of a stone is somewhat more difficult to define if the stone is composed of more than one mineral species. However, hardness of stone is relevant to the cleaning system used: for example, in the choice of medium for use with a microabrasive cleaning system. Wide variations in hardness occur in some stone types, which in turn results in variable effects even from a single cleaning application. Thus, a limestone may contain softer clay layers that are more readily eroded by abrasives as well as by natural weathering. In general, abrasive cleaning techniques as well as pressurized water cannot differentiate between the varying hardnesses that might exist within a single block of stone. The mineral in a stone that has the lowest hardness should be considered when evaluating abrasive cleaning and pressure washing.

Porosity

For a very porous stone, the use of cleaning systems containing chemicals may not be appropriate, as the chemicals are likely to penetrate into the stone. In addition, it is difficult to rinse off chemicals that have penetrated into the pores of the stone.

Texture

Texture is the geometric aspect of the mineral particles, which includes the shape and size of minerals and their overall arrangement within the stone. Some cleaning systems may affect the texture of the stone. For example, normal weathering of a coarse-grained marble will loosen the bonds between interlocking mineral grains and cause the surface to have a 'sugary' texture. Abrasive techniques and water applications, even when carefully controlled in terms of pressure may dislodge a significant number of loosely bonded mineral grains from such a sugared marble surface. High-pressure water or abrasive cleaning can actually roughen the surface of a smooth stone. Even chemical cleaning systems used with very low water pressure rinsing can cause material loss and increase surface relief. For example, acid cleaners can etch the surface of polished stone, resulting in an altered texture.

Colour

Stone colour refers to the distribution and uniformity of colour throughout the stone and is related to mineralogy. A cleaning system should be selected that will not affect the inherent colour and reflectivity of the stone surface. If, for example, a strong acid cleaner is used on white marble containing ferrous minerals, the minerals will oxidize and give the marble a yellow or orange-brown hue. Experience has shown that even trace amounts of oxidation of pyrite (iron sulphide) can result in formation of significant red-brown staining. As another example, if an abrasive cleaning technique is used on polished stone, the surface reflectivity is likely to be altered.

SELECTION OF CLEANING TECHNIQUES FOR STONE

Stone cleaning techniques available today include traditional methods such as water and steam as well as new techniques – for example microabrasive systems – that have come into use in the past two decades. In addition, systems initially designed either for use in other industries (such as pelletized carbon dioxide developed for cleaning metal industrial equipment), or for use with other objects and sculpture (such as laser cleaning), are increasingly being applied to the cleaning of building façades.[3] Current cleaning systems used on stone façades can be grouped

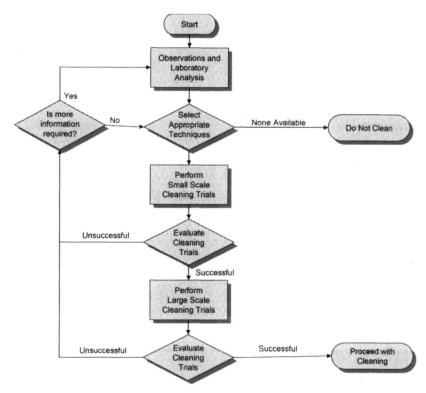

Figure 8.5 This flow chart shows a typical approach to a façade cleaning project. Extensive cleaning should only be performed following successful field trials. (J. Freedland and L. Chan, Wiss, Janney, Elstner Associates Inc.)

into four categories: water, abrasive, laser and chemical techniques. Depending on the nature and condition of the substrate, and on the character of the soiling to be removed, one or a combination of systems may be appropriate for a specific cleaning campaign. Other criteria to be considered include protection requirements, environmental constraints, special application requirements, and cost.

The level of cleanliness desired may be an important factor in identifying the cleaning systems that should be used in a particular application. For example, if reducing the amount of soiling rather than removing it completely would be acceptable, then it may be possible to use a gentler cleaning system than if more thorough removal of soiling were required. It is often useful to consider the approach illustrated in Figure 8.5 at an early stage in developing a cleaning programme for which cleaning results may be variable; it is not always possible to obtain a consistently clean appearance, even with a substrate composed entirely of one stone type, given the natural variations that exist even in a single block of stone.

Selection of Appropriate Cleaning Technique

Types of Soiling and Stains	Calcareous Stone Substrate (e.g. marble, limestone, travertine)		Siliceous Stone Substrate (e.g. granite, sandstone)	
	Heavy soiling	Light to moderate soiling	Heavy soiling	Light to moderate soilin
Soil, soot, oils	Water Microabrasive Chemical	Water Chemical	Microabrasive Chemical	Water Chemical
Gypsum crusts	Water Microabrasive Chemical	Water Chemical	Microabrasive Chemical	Water Chemical
Alteration crusts[1]	Water Microabrasive Chemical	Water Microabrasive Chemical	Microabrasive Chemical	Microabrasive Chemical
Metallic stains	Water Microabrasive Chemical	Water Microabrasive Chemical	Microabrasive Chemical	Microabrasive Chemical
Organic stains	Microabrasive Chemical	Microabrasive Chemical	Microabrasive Chemical	Microabrasive Chemical
Biological growth	Water Microabrasive Chemical	Water Microabrasive Chemical	Microabrasive Chemical	Microabrasive Chemical

Notes

1 Typically, different types of alteration crusts may form depending on the mineral composition of the stone substrate. Petrographic and microscopic examination of all types of substrates to be cleaned is recommended in order to determine what type of cleaning system is appropriate for gentle removal of soiling and whether or not the alteration crust should be removed.

Figure 8.6 Cleaning programme goals and selection criteria chart.

Figures 8.6 and 8.7 illustrate a methodology for selecting a cleaning technique. Variables in cleaning systems include formulations, concentrations, and dwell times for chemical methods; size, shape and hardness of abrasives and air pressure for abrasive techniques; and application pressures and water temperatures for water used in pre-wetting, cleaning, and rinsing.

Water and steam systems

In water and steam cleaning techniques, loosely bonded atmospheric dust and dirt, soot, and other deposits can be softened or dissolved by brushing,

A Guide to Selection of Methods for Cleaning of Stone

Method	Types of Calcareous Stones (e.g. marble, limestone, travertine)		Types of Siliceous Stones (e.g. granite, sandstone)	
	Heavy soiling	Moderate soiling	Heavy soiling	Moderate soiling
Water soiling				
Low Pressure Water Misting	Yes	Yes	No	Yes
Steam Cleaning	Yes	Yes	No	Yes
Abrasive Cleaning Systems				
Microabrasive Systems	Yes	Yes	No	Yes
Sponge-Jet	Yes	Yes	Yes	Yes
Laser Cleaning System				
Q-switched Nd:YAG laser	Yes	Yes	Yes	Yes
Chemical Cleaning				
Detergents	No	Yes	No	Yes
Chemical (alkaline)	Yes[1]	Yes[1]	No	Yes[1]
Chemical (acid)	No[2]	No	No[3]	No
Poultice[4] (Clay, Latex)	Yes	Yes	Yes	Yes

Notes

1 Although water and microabrasive cleaning techniques are usually effective on limestone, alkaline cleaners are sometimes needed to remove localized severe stains that cannot be removed by other methods. Alkaline cleaners require pre-wetting of the substrate before application and are followed by use of a mild acid after-wash to neutralize the alkaline pre-wash.
2 Acid cleaners should be avoided, as they can dissolve calcareous stones. Also, other methods such as water systems are typically successful. Note that acids may be needed as an after-wash to neutralize alkaline cleaners.
3 Weak acids may be acceptable as cleaners. Note that acids may be needed as an after-wash to neutralize alkaline cleaners.
4 Selection of poultices for cleaning depends primarily on the chemicals included in the medium.

Figure 8.7   A guide to selection of methods for cleaning of stone.

soaking, or mist spraying, and the surface then rinsed to remove the residue. For water cleaning to be effective, the soiling must be capable of being dissolved or loosened by water. Surface dirt and some gypsum deposits can be removed from soft stones by water washing. Any water used in cleaning should be checked to confirm that it is free from impurities that could stain the substrate. For example, even a small amount of iron present in the water source used for cleaning can result in staining of a light-coloured substrate such as white marble.

Water cleaning

An important factor to consider in the use of water systems is the pressure at which the water is applied to the wall. Depending on the substrate, the definition of low, medium, and high pressures varies widely. Gentle water cleaning methods based upon intermittent misting or continuous soaking use very low pressures (less than 100 psi), followed by a low (100 to 200 psi) or medium (200 to 400 psi) pressure water rinse. Moderate to high pressure water washing (400 to 800 psi) is generally safe for use on stone such as granite.[4] However, water washing at these higher pressures can potentially erode soft or fragile stone surfaces.[5]

The effect of the water spray or stream on the substrate is also related to the volume of water, the aperture of the nozzle, and the distance of the nozzle from the wall surface. Low pressure water cleaning techniques often involve the use of multiple fan-spray nozzles attached to a spray rack suspended adjacent to the surface being cleaned. Specialized rack systems can be built to clean complex surface profiles, and low pressure sprays may be continuous or intermittent. The use of intermittent sprays is desirable in that less water is needed for cleaning. This is helpful when cleaning porous substrates, or where environmental constraints require that a lower volume of water be used overall.

In contrast, high pressure water cleaning is typically performed using a single nozzle with a very narrow fan spray. A narrow aperture or a higher water volume at a given application pressure will generally result in higher pressure as water reaches the wall.

Low pressure water soak and misting systems are typically most successful on calcareous materials such as limestone and marble, because the soiling on these substrates is often bound by gypsum, which is water soluble (Figure 8.8 and Figure 8.9). These systems are often less successful in cleaning siliceous substrates such as sandstones or granites. Although a somewhat higher pressure may typically be used on granite, for example,

Figure 8.8 Water mist cleaning in progress on a limestone façade. This system uses spray racks with multiple nozzles to lightly soak the stone and loosen soiling on the surface. The substrate can then be rinsed with a very low pressure for improved results. (Wiss, Janney, Elstner Associates, Inc.)

Figure 8.9   For fine mist cleaning, adjustable mist spray nozzles are conformed to reach small crevices of ornate sculpture work. Each nozzle is adjustable and equipped with an arm that can be preset to different angles where soot and carbon can accumulate. (Wiss, Janney, Elstner Associates, Inc.)

than on marble without damage to the stone, high pressures are not recommended for cleaning any type of stone. Pressures that are too high can damage the stone and drive the water into the masonry.

Successful water cleaning depends on appropriate selection of application techniques and pressures, proper protection for any adjacent materials not being cleaned, and the skill of the operative in maintaining a controlled application. In addition to issues related to water pressure, problems associated with improper water cleaning include water ingress through open joints or cracks, or through the face of porous masonry materials such as sandstone and certain oolitic limestones. Damage can occur due to cyclic freezing and thawing of entrapped moisture if water cleaning is performed in cold climates during winter weather. Other concerns include risk of corrosion of embedded iron elements, or mobilization of salts, if the masonry becomes saturated; metallic staining from corrosion of ferrous minerals; and the need to control water run-off. Although these issues need to be considered with water cleaning, they are of lesser concern with water alone than if chemical cleaners are used.

Steam cleaning

Steam cleaning systems use either a large scale apparatus such as the DOFF high temperature steam cleaning system,[6] or a small scale pencil steam cleaner for carved work, especially marble. Steam cleaning offers the advantage of using less water than most water cleaning techniques, and is therefore a good alternative if the volume of water used in the cleaning process needs to be limited because of the nature of the substrate or site constraints. In addition, steam cleaning can sometimes enhance the effectiveness of other cleaning techniques. For example, steam may be used as part of the rinse process after detergent or chemical cleaning to treat organic growth, or on oily or bituminous stains. Steam cleaning was not used for some time because of the hazard it posed to workers, but has become available during the past decade through improved equipment that provides better control and safety.

Abrasive systems

Abrasive systems clean by abrading, roughening, or eroding the dirt, and, perhaps to some extent, the stone surface; however, the extent to which this abrasion may damage the substrate depends upon the nature of the substrate and the aggressiveness of the system used. High pressure sand or grit blasting should not be used on stone substrates because of damage caused to the substrate by such cleaning. In contrast to this type of abrasive technique, gentler abrasive systems have come into use during the past few decades. These clean by directing fine particles (usually less than 90 μm in diameter) of abrasive, such as finely ground dolomite, at the wall at very low pressures, typically between 25 psi and 75 psi.[7] Both wet[8] and a dry[9] proprietary low pressure cleaning systems are available, each using specialized nozzles.[10] Systems employing a small nozzle (less than 5 mm diameter) are termed 'microabrasive' systems. Unlike the older methods, these newer, gentler techniques, when used with proper controls, can remove contaminants from delicate surfaces without significantly damaging the underlying material. Abrasive and microabrasive systems vary in the type of materials and specialized nozzles or other equipment used, and in whether the system involves water for cleaning and rinsing (Figure 8.10). As these systems depend on compressed air, other variables that affect the cleaning process include the air pressure and flow rate employed.

Abrasive techniques have been found to be effective on a wide range of stone substrates, if used with care and following proper trials. They have been particularly effective on limestones and sandstones, but are not appropriate for polished substrates because they will alter the

Figure 8.10 Gentle abrasive techniques, used with care, can successfully clean a wide variety of soiling from a range of stone substrates. (Stonehealth Ltd)

texture and reflectivity of the surface. Abrasive cleaning is effective on light to moderate soiling, but is less effective on severe soiling or on deep-set stains.

A proprietary abrasive system, originally developed in the United Kingdom as a cleaning system for selective industrial uses, employs an open-cell water-based polyurethane sponge, to which various types of abrasives of varying sizes are bonded. The sponge is then applied to the stone surface at very low pressures (typically 35 to 60 psi).[11] The particles of abrasive-covered sponge are larger than in the systems described above. Although this system is considered a gentle abrasive cleaning technique, it can also be used at higher pressures (and with special grits) to provide a more forceful cleaning process.[12] For example, this system can be used to remove alteration crust from granite and also to provide limited redressing of an altered stone surface (Figures 8.11a and 8.11b).

Another medium used in microabrasive cleaning, sodium bicarbonate (baking soda), is problematic in that is difficult to remove after application and rinsing. In addition, sodium bicarbonate is a salt, and if it is not thoroughly removed by rinsing, it can be damaging to the stone substrate. Frozen carbon dioxide (CO_2, or 'dry ice') pellets, applied at high velocity, have been used effectively to clean metal substrates, but appear to have had limited success so far on cleaning stone substrates.

During recent years, there has been increasing concern over some of the more conventional methods of abrasive cleaning that have been used on sculpture and decorative elements on historic buildings. Inappropriate use of these techniques has certainly lead to various types of damage to the substrate. For example, loss of surface detail due to overcleaning can impair the visual appearance of a stone surface, and in some documented cases has also been shown to lead to accelerated decay of the substrate. Even if cleaning is carried out in a most careful manner, air-abrasive techniques can result in the loss of historic surface material. In particular, loss of historic material can occur when the stone surface is crumbling or decayed, as it is very difficult for abrasive systems (and their users) to discriminate between the soiling and the actual stone surface in such cases. It is important that operators of these types of mechanical cleaning systems should be trained, and ideally have documented experience in the use of the equipment. In addition, abrasive and micro-abrasive systems typically require breathing protection for workers, and dust control for operatives, the general public, and surrounding areas. Most proprietary systems incorporate methods of protection to address these concerns, as well as means for collection of spent abrasives and debris.

Figure 8.11a   A detail view of Figur
8.11b before removal of alteration
crust showing the build-up of altered
minerals on the granite surface. The
surface crust traps moisture, leading t
accelerated deterioration of the stone
(Wiss, Janney, Elstner Associates, Inc

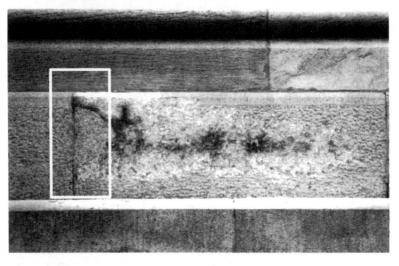

Figure 8.11b   The same area after removal of altered minerals which
should extend the life of the stone. Note the black organic growth at
areas of trapped moisture beneath the substrate. (Wiss, Janney, Elstner
Associates, Inc.)

Even microabrasive systems can damage stone, and should only be implemented after a thorough review, including laboratory and *in situ* trials and evaluation.

Laser cleaning

Laser-based cleaning systems, initially used for cleaning monuments and artwork, have gained increasing recognition over the last two decades following their successful use in building cleaning. These systems operate by emitting rapid short pulses of light at a specific wavelength (near-infrared wavelengths of around 1.064 mm are common). As a laser beam interacts with a surface, some of the energy in the beam is reflected and some is absorbed by the surface. The fraction of energy absorbed by a surface depends on its physical and chemical properties. Most types of dirt absorb energy very strongly at such wavelengths, whereas most stones absorb relatively little. As a dirt layer on a stone substrate absorbs the laser energy, it is rapidly heated and this causes the dirt to expand and lift away from the surface of the stone. Because the pulses of energy are so short, very little heat is conducted into the stone substrate. Once the dirt has been removed, additional laser pulses will have no effect on the cleaned stone surface, because insufficient energy is absorbed by the stone. So cleaning stops and there is no danger of over-cleaning.

The laser beam is directed at the stone surface using a hand-held device that can focus the laser beam to a fine point, thereby adjusting the intensity of the laser over the surface (Figure 8.12). Over the last decade, several commercial laser cleaning systems have been available throughout Europe, and they are being used by numerous conservation laboratories. The most commonly used laser in conservation is the Q-switched Nd:YAG laser.

One of the main advantages of laser cleaning is that it can selectively remove layers of dirt without harming the stone substrate, and without the 'over-cleaning' that is noted in many other types of cleaning systems. As the laser energy is delivered in the form of light it does not make a mechanical contact with the surface of the stone substrate, so it allows extremely fragile or decayed surfaces to be cleaned without damage to, or removal or dissolution of, the substrate that might occur through the use of other types of cleaning systems.

Laser cleaning generates very small quantities of waste material; the only waste generated is the dirt removed from the surface, which is manifested as visible small particles. Because there is no use of hazardous chemicals or solvents, laser cleaning is considered to be a clean technique, and one that

Figure 8.12   Laser cleaning of the architectural details of the façade.
(Giancarlo Calgano, Ltech Srl, Italy)

also produces very little noise. The operator of the equipment, who should be trained to use the laser properly, is only required to wear protective clothing and a face mask as a safety precaution against possible airborne dust particles. Health and safety legislation also lays down guidelines limiting the time for which any one operative can use a laser continuously. Training courses are available which will teach the conservator when and how to use a laser.

Given the fineness of the laser point, it is often time consuming to achieve an even appearance with laser cleaning, particularly on large surface areas. Although its application to objects and monuments has shown promise, its use in large scale applications has to date been very limited.[13] The relatively high cost of purchasing a laser system has sometimes been viewed by conservators and other professionals as a disadvantage. However, this initial set-up cost should be compared with the low cost of maintenance of cleaned stone, and the savings that can be obtained over the long-term life of a building. Purchasing a laser cleaning system should be viewed as a long-term investment.

Over the past twelve years, the interest in lasers for cleaning has increased through the research and work presented in the conference series undertaken by Lasers in Conservation of Artworks (LACONA), the first international organization dedicated to research and development of lasers for conservation. In addition, extensive research in the use of laser technology has been undertaken by the European Cooperation in the Field of Scientific and Technical Research (COST) under cultural heritage groups like Artwork Conservation by Laser (Action G7), to monitor the development of new instrumentation, accumulating validation of laser based techniques and extending the use of laser for conservation throughout Europe.[14] The most recent conference was held in October 2005 in Vienna, Austria. The conference brought together scientists, engineers and conservators to discuss current work (which includes the use of many different types of laser) and future developments in this rapidly expanding field.

Chemical systems

Chemical cleaners react directly with dirt, or with the substrate, to dissolve soiling and stains so that they can be rinsed off the stone. Because many chemical cleaners are used with water, the same concerns about appropriate water pressures and the need to prevent leakage through open joints in the masonry apply. In addition, many chemical cleaners contain strong alkalis or acids that are very hazardous to humans and animals. They can also cause damage to the stone being cleaned as well as to other building elements, site features, plants, the environment, and even to adjacent vehicles and buildings. Special collection and disposal procedures may be required to control run-off from chemical cleaning.

Chemical cleaning compounds include alkalis, acids, detergents, surfactants, and organic solvents, in liquid, gel, or poultice form. In addition to the composition of the cleaning compound, other factors in their application include dilution, application technique, and dwell time.[15] While product literature or the Material Safety Data Sheet (MSDS) or Control of Substances Hazardous to Health (COSHH) data may provide a description of the cleaning product and information on how to use it, it is necessary to obtain detailed information about the product's composition to understand fully the specific safety and protection issues.

Detergents

A detergent is a compound, or a mixture of compounds, intended to assist in the removal of dirt by acting on oily films that trap dirt particles. The detergent disrupts the oil film, allowing the dirt particles to become miscible (capable of being mixed) with water, so that they can be removed by rinsing. Detergents may contain various other components to assist in cleaning, such as surfactants, abrasives, and compounds for bleaching, removing deposits, and otherwise modifying the performance of the cleaner. Detergent-based cleaners may be strongly alkaline or acidic, and in some cases proprietary products marketed as detergents in fact contain strong acids of concern in façade cleaning. Also, phosphate-containing detergents are no longer used in many areas because of concerns about problems with waterways. A variety of proprietary detergents are marketed specifically as cleaners for masonry, many of which contain surfactants as discussed below. In the UK, a proprietary detergent using a mild soap solution has recently been used with success in the conservation and cleaning of Cleopatra's Needle at the Victoria Embankment in London.[16]

Surfactants (or surface active agents) are important detergent components that, when used in very low concentrations, can greatly reduce the surface tension of water. For a detergent to be effective, the surface to be cleaned and the soiling to be removed must initially be wet, and the loosened soils must then be suspended, dissolved, or separated from the substrate so that they can be rinsed away, and not redeposited on the surface. The surfactant assists the detergent in achieving this goal. There are several types of surfactants, of which non-ionic surfactants are typically non-reactive with the substrate and effective in stone cleaning. Detergents containing non-ionic surfactants are effective in cleaning light accumulations of surface dirt from limestone or marble that cannot be effectively cleaned by low pressure water washing alone.

Detergents are generally effective on lightly to moderately soiled stone but are typically not effective on severe soiling, such as heavy carbon deposits, or on deep stains. Detergents are also effective for removal of organic growth from stone when used in combination with sodium hypochlorite (household bleach), although these compounds may not be as effective in long-term deterrence of organic growth as some proprietary biocides. Several proprietary biocides are marketed for removal of organic growth from masonry, some of which are specially formulated to avoid the use of chlorides and thus eliminate the possibility of introducing harmful soluble salts into the stone. Biocides are further discussed below.

Acids and alkalis

Two alkaline compounds occasionally used in masonry cleaning are tri-sodium phosphate (TSP) and sodium hydroxide solution. These cleaners may be used alone or as a pre-wash in combination with a mildly acidic after-wash. In this case, the alkaline pre-wash reacts with the soiling, and the acidic after-wash neutralizes the pre-wash. Two-part systems of this type are particularly effective in removing severe soiling from hard, dense stones such as granite, although care must be taken to pre-wet the masonry to help prevent the chemical from being absorbed into the natural microfractures of the granite. Alkaline pre-wash/acidic after-wash systems generally are found to remove soiling or stains that cannot be removed by water, detergents, or mild acids alone. The alkaline pre-wash should not be used alone, because the wall surface will remain alkaline rather than neutral after cleaning without the neutralizing after-wash. In contrast, mildly acidic cleaners can be used alone on some stone substrates because the natural alkalinity of the stone helps to neutralize the cleaner.

Many cleaning products contain acids. Some acids may safely remove soiling from some stone substrates, but cause damage to others, while strong acids can damage all types of stone and other masonry. Examples of acids contained in some proprietary cleaners that can cause damage to stone (and other) substrates include hydrofluoric acid, which dissolves siliceous components found in many types of stone, ammonium bifluoride or sodium bifluoride, which can etch glass[17] and hydrochloric (also known as muriatic) acid. Use of hydrofluoric acid has been associated with damage to most types of stone masonry surfaces, including discolouration and surface etching, and it can also cause severe injury to the worker. On this basis its use is rarely, if ever, justified. Chlorides contributed by application of hydrochloric (muriatic) acid can cause further degradation of the masonry over time due to these salts being carried into the pores of the stone. Chlorides can also cause corrosion of embedded steel fixings.

Visual effects of improper chemical cleaning include areas of yellow or orange staining from the reaction of strong acid cleaners with iron minerals in the stone, or with metal fixings within the structure. Chemicals absorbed by masonry components can migrate and form stains after the water evaporates, and can also be visible in the form of efflorescence, which may potentially damage the masonry substrate over time. Absorption of chemicals can be reduced by pre-wetting the stone with water, but cannot be altogether prevented. Any acid or alkali cleaning system brings the risk of subsequent salt formation.

A shift from the use of extremely aggressive acids to less harmful ones has occurred in the cleaning industry in recent years. The problems associated with the use of cleaners containing hydrofluoric acid has led to the development of products that are more environmentally and user friendly. Some of these new proprietary chemical cleaners contain what is referred to by the manufacturers as 'less harmful' ammonium bifluoride. However, these 'gentler' chemicals should still be considered potentially dangerous, and the user should be aware of problems that can arise with their use. Some products are marketed as combined bifluorides; however, once these bifluorides are dissolved with water, hydrofluoric acid is formed. Manufacturers recommend caution when using these products. When ammonium bifluoride based cleaners are used to clean stone masonry, the calcium carbonate in the mortar can be converted by the bifluorides into an insoluble material, calcium fluoride. In other words, one deposit is replaced by another. Calcium fluoride can be visible as a grey coloured haze on the masonry surface and on adjacent glass.

Some proprietary cleaners containing milder acids, particularly organic acids such as phosphoric, sulphamic, gluconic, acetic, or citric acid, tend to be potentially less harmful to users and to the substrate. However, even such milder acids may react with minerals in some masonry substrates and cause staining. In one case studied, a mild acid cleaner caused ferrous staining in a limestone façade because the cleaner was applied without pre-wetting the surface, while trials performed on a pre-wet surface did not result in mobilized stains.

Chemicals can leave residues within the stone that can cause problems later on, and once they have been applied their reaction cannot be fully controlled. For example, in Glasgow in the 1990s, there were cases of some sandstone buildings turning green at alarming rates following chemical cleaning, which created ideal conditions for algal growth on the surface of the stone.[18] The development and use of alternative cleaning techniques during the past few years have resulted in significant advances in making conservation methods less intrusive and safer in their use.

With chemical cleaning products, small-scale *in situ* sampling is important as an initial step. Testing of such samples should always be performed to confirm that the chemicals in the cleaner will not cause staining, or other damage. The surface should be pre-wetted with water, trial samples implemented, and the samples allowed to dry after cleaning and rinsing. The sample area should be re-evaluated following a period of at least several weeks to confirm that no staining or other adverse reactions have occurred.

Poultices

Common types of poultice media today include mineral-based materials including diatomaceous earth, attapulgite clay and sepiolite, as well as cellulose-based media including paper pulp and carboxymethylcellulose (CMC, or wallpaper paste). A chemical or solvent is added to the poultice, which is held in close contact with the surface to be cleaned. As the dirt dissolves, the removed soiling is absorbed into the poultice. Poultices offer advantages for building interiors and other applications, where water and microabrasive systems would be costly or difficult to use because of special protection and containment requirements. Poultices may also be effective on ornate and detailed surfaces.

Certain chemicals or solvents can be combined with an absorbent clay for application to deep-seated or persistent stains. For example, poultices containing oxalic acids are effective in removing some types of ferrous staining. Ammonium carbonate (usually in a 10% solution) in a clay or paper poultice has a successful track record of reducing gypsum crusts on

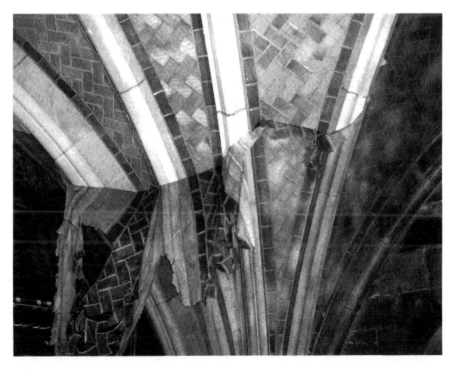

Figure 8.13 Removal of latex film poultice from interior during trial samples of a stone and tile ribbed vault ceiling at the Albany State Capital in New York State, USA. (FTB Restoration, Belgium)

limestone. Another type of poultice is the Mora poultice, which was originally developed in the 1970s for selective cleaning of wall paintings. It contains ethylenediaminetetracetic acid (EDTA) as a chelating agent, and has also been used effectively in the cleaning of gypsum crusts and copper and iron stains from limestones and marbles.

Recently, proprietary rubber latex poultices containing small amounts of EDTA have been developed, based on research and improvements to the Mora packs. The rubber latex poultice requires very little water to loosen and remove dirt from the surface; as such, there is less need for protection and less risk of activating soluble salts within the masonry (Figure 8.13). Over the last five years, the Arte Mundit[R] latex poultice[19] has successfully been utilized to clean interior stonework of the Royal Palace in Brussels, the Cathedral of St. Maurice, Angers, the Monasterio dos Jeronimos in Lisbon, and most notably, St Paul's Cathedral in London.

Containment of cleaning materials

Control of airborne and waterborne cleaners, cleaning debris, and rinse-water is advisable, and may be legally required on some projects due to environmental concerns. Examples of cleaning processes where special collection and disposal are typically required include those involving the removal of lead-containing coatings, the presence of chemicals in cleaning products or cleaning debris that cannot be allowed into the groundwater or sewer water collection system, and dust-generating abrasive methods. Some proprietary chemical cleaning and coating removal systems, usually in the form of pastes or gels, are furnished together with masks that retain the remnants of the cleaner and debris for safe collection and disposal. Certain proprietary micro-abrasive techniques incorporate containment systems to collect and recycle the cleaning medium, as well as to collect and dispose of soiling removed during the cleaning process.

Pressure-wash vacuum containment systems can be used both as water cleaning systems in their own right and as aids in the clean-up and control of run-off from chemical cleaning materials. These systems consist of pressurized water and vacuum clean-up, working within a fully contained system of specially designed hooded hand tools, which not only provide protection to the building from the chemical cleaner overspray that might result from conventional pressure cleaning and rinse cycles, but also provide protection to the operator of the equipment. The pressure-wash vacuum containment systems are applied to the surface to be cleaned. The water pressure, in combination with the vacuum, loosens the soiling which the vacuum then captures. Surface residue is then transferred to a container without any back splash or water run-off.

Biocides

Historically, biocides included copper and fluorides left in place on the masonry surface to inhibit organic growth. Where run-off staining has occurred from copper flashings in stone construction, it is often noted that organic growth does not occur in the stained area. Although presently used less in the UK, the recent approach in the USA is toward a cyclical application of a cleaner containing a biocide to help remove existing growth and inhibit new growth. Biocides may be composed of a solution of detergent, calcium hypochlorite, and a trisodium phosphate-type cleaner, applied to a pre-wetted surface, scrubbed, and thoroughly rinsed with low pressure water. Some proprietary biocides contain quaternary ammonium chlorides.[20]

Biocides vary in their short- and long-term effectiveness, and long-term trials are required to evaluate their effectiveness on a given substrate and to confirm that adverse effects such as staining do not occur. Re-application of the biocide at regular intervals may be necessary to prevent reappearance of biological growth. Biocides are widely used on stone substrates, and although they are not always effective in limiting biological growth, examples of staining or similar problems related to use of these products have not been noted in the authors' experience.

QUALITY CONTROL AND THE EVALUATION OF FAÇADE CLEANING

Trial cleaning should be undertaken and evaluated as part of the cleaning system selection, and again at the beginning of the project with the system actually selected. Cleaning trials that utilize each system under considera-tion are helpful in selecting and confirming the proper system or systems to be used. Trials allow the project team to refine the cleaning procedures, evaluate the effectiveness of the system, and confirm that the proposed protection, collection, and disposal systems are adequate. Trials also allow the building owner and conservation professional to evaluate and approve the level of cleanliness to be achieved. The completed trials should be allowed to remain in place for a minimum of two weeks, and preferably longer, prior to evaluation. In addition to visual review by the project team, it is useful for a conservator or petrographer to examine the cleaned trials and compare them to uncleaned areas of the same stone façade. This process helps to define the effectiveness of the cleaning process, and also to determine whether any damage has occurred. Once the trials are approved, they should be protected during the work and used as a reference for the quality and level of cleanliness required.

Proper project drawings and specifications should document the techniques developed and control measures required. With any cleaning technique, the success of the application is dependent on quality control during application.[21] Trials also allow those performing the work to become familiar with and evaluate the procedures to be used. They also allow refinement of the cleaning process by the architect, conservator, and contractor, and evaluation of the results by the entire project team. Finally, field observation by the conservation professional is an essential part of quality control throughout the work, to monitor the effectiveness and ensure the gentleness of the cleaning process.

CONCLUSION

When the decision is made to clean historic stone structures, whether for aesthetic or performance reasons, the consequent selection of a cleaning system that is gentle but effective must take into account the characteristics of the stone substrate as well as the nature of soiling and staining to be addressed. The composition of the stone is particularly important in determining which cleaning systems will clean effectively without damaging the substrate. The various types of stone commonly used in historic buildings and monuments include sandstone, limestone, marble, and granite. As illustrated by the examples presented in this chapter, the particular physical, mineralogical, and chemical characteristics of the stone are important factors in how the stone reacts to the cleaning processes implemented.

Where inappropriate cleaning methods or materials are used, staining, etching, or other types of damage to the stone surface can result, and can cause long-term problems. Where cleaning is required to remove deleterious surface contaminants such as accumulated pollutants, or even an alteration crust, more aggressive methods may be required than where cleaning is for aesthetic reasons only. In either case, establishing appropriate criteria for the project is an important first step in selecting a process and determining quality control methods. Laboratory testing is useful for evaluating the effectiveness and potential adverse effects of cleaning, and to narrow the selection of cleaning systems to be tested in field trials. The implementation of field trials is critical to the final selection of a cleaning system, and for establishing a standard of quality for the work.

Stone cleaning requires attention to special protection requirements for workers, other persons and animals in the project area, building and site materials, and the environment. Other constraints may be related to the historic character of the building or monument, special concerns that might arise from the project location, and the availability and cost of the proposed cleaning system. Finally, because cleaning of stone substrates is often performed as a cyclical maintenance measure, the effects of a single cleaning programme and future repeated cleanings should be considered, both in specifying the cleaning methods, and in scheduling cleaning over time.

The authors

Kyle C. Normandin, BA, MS Historic Preservation

Kyle C. Normandin is a Senior Associate with Wiss, Janney, Elstner Associates, Inc., in New York City, New York, USA. He is currently a member of ICOMOS/ US and is also a member of American Standards for Testing of Materials Committee E06 on Performance of Buildings. He serves as a board member for the Association for Preservation Technology Northeast Chapter and is a member of the International Scientific Committee on technology for DOCOMOMO International. Kyle C. Normandin and Deborah Slaton are the editors of *Cleaning Techniques in Conservation Practice* (Donhead, 2005).

Deborah Slaton BA, MA, MArch (Structures), FAPT

Deborah Slaton is a Senior Consultant with Wiss, Janney, Elstner Associates, Inc. in Northbrook, Illinois, USA. She is a Fellow of the Association for Preservation Technology International and Vice President of the Historic Preservation Education Foundation. She has published extensively on preservation technology and is the author of a monthly column on material and construction failures for the *Construction Specifier*. She is co-editor of several conference proceedings including the *Preserving the Recent Past* series, and is author of the US National Park Service Preservation Brief on Historic Structure Reports.

References

1   Normandin, K. and Slaton, D., 'Cleaning Atmospheric Pollutants and Contaminants from Natural Stone; Modern and Traditional Methods', *Proceedings of the VDR Conference on Dirt*, October 2002.

2   Fassina, V., 'Environmental Pollution in Relation to Stone Decay', *Durability of Building Materials*, 5, 1988, pp. 317–58.

3   Several references provide an overview of available cleaning techniques from the UK or North American perspective; for example, see Ashurst, N., *Cleaning Historic Buildings, Volume 1, Substrates, soiling and investigations; Volume 2, Cleaning materials and processes*, Donhead, London, 1994. See also Weaver, M. E., *Conserving Buildings: A Manual of Techniques and Materials* Wiley, New York, 1997; Grimmer, A., *Keeping it Clean: Removing Exterior Dirt, Paint, Stains and Graffiti from Historic Masonry Buildings*, National Park Service, U.S. Department of the Interior, Washington, D.C., 1988; Normandin, K. and Slaton, D. (eds.), *Cleaning Techniques in Conservation Practice*, Donhead, Shaftesbury, 2005.

4   Slaton, D., 'Under Pressure', *The Construction Specifier*, December 2000.

5   In comparison, pressures of well over 30,000 psi are considered safe for use in cleaning some metal elements on buildings, and other structures. Water pressures in excess of 30,000 psi have been successfully used to remove existing coatings from sound, high strength concrete substrates without damage to the concrete.

6   An example of a steam cleaning system is the Rotec steam system, distributed by Quintek of Niagara, Ontario, Canada. Another example of a steam cleaning system that utilizes high pressure steam to clean masonry is the DOFF Cleaning System, distributed by Stonehealth Ltd of Dursley, Gloucestershire, England.

7   In the United States, the term 'abrasive' is often used in reference to traditional methods such as high pressure sand blasting, while the term 'microabrasive' is typically used in reference to newer, very low pressure systems using fine particulates. The negative connotation of the term 'abrasive cleaning' in the United States may be in part related to the use of high pressure sand and grit blasting on masonry structures through the 1960s, which resulted in visible damage to the walls of many buildings evaluated years after this cleaning was performed.

8   An example of a wet microabrasive masonry cleaning system is the Rotec Vortex system, distributed by Quintek of Niagara, Ontario, Canada. Another example of a wet microabrasive masonry cleaning system is the JOS/TORC system, distributed by Stonehealth Ltd of Dursley, Gloucestershire, England. All accessory equipment including Standard, Micro and Piccolo nozzles are also made available by this distributor.

9   An example of a dry microabrasive masonry cleaning system is the Façade Gommage system, distributed by Thomann-Hanry, Inc. of Paris, France.

10   Another low pressure microabrasive system, which uses a small amount of water, is the JOS system distributed by Stonehealth of Dursley, Gloucestershire, England.

11   The system described is Sponge-Jet. Recently, Sponge-Jet Europe, based in Blackpool, United Kingdom has developed fine particle media for soft cleaning on a variety of natural stone substrates. This system was recently imported to the United States and is currently being distributed by Sponge-Jet Inc. of Portsmouth, New Hampshire.

12   As an example of the appropriate use of more aggressive sponge cleaning techniques, this system has been used by the authors to remove an alteration crust from a granite substrate. The alteration layer was formed by a previous inappropriate cleaning of the building with strong acid cleaners, and having formed, was trapping moisture against the sound stone substrate beneath. Thus, a more aggressive cleaning method was needed than would have been required had the alteration layer not existed.

13   Further discussion of laser cleaning techniques is provided in publications from LACONA (Lasers in Conservation of Artworks, including *Proceedings of the Fifth International Conference on Lasers in the Conservation of Artworks* (Osnabrueck, Germany, September 2003), Springer, Berlin, 2005. See also Cooper, M., 'Recent Developments in Laser Cleaning', *The Building Conservation Directory 1997*, Cathedral Communications, Tisbury, 1997; *Research Report: Laser Stone Cleaning in Scotland*, Historic Scotland, Edinburgh, 2005; Cooper, M., 'Laser Cleaning of Sculpture, Monuments and Architectural Detail, in Normandin, K. and Slaton, D. (eds.), *Cleaning Techniques in Conservation Practice*, Donhead, Shaftesbury, 2005.

14   Salimbeni, R., Zafiropulos, V. and Radvan, R., 'The European Community Research Concerning Laser Techniques in Conservation: Results and Perspectives', in *Proceeding of Innovative Technologies and Materials for the Protection of Cultural Heritage, (ITECOM) European Conference*, Athens, Greece, 2003.

15   Dwell time is the period for which the cleaning compound is allowed to remain on the surface. Manufacturers' literature typically provides the recommended dwell time for chemical cleaners, which can vary from less than five minutes to more than twenty-four hours.

16   Clean Soap Solution (soap solution), Antique Bronze Ltd, Conservation and Restoration, London, UK, 2005.

17   In the presence of water, these chemicals form hydrofluoric acid.

18   Cooper, M., 'Recent Developments in Laser Cleaning', *The Building Conservation Directory, 1997* Cathedral Communications, Tisbury, 1997. See also Cooper, M., 'Laser Cleaning of Sculpture, Monuments and Architectural Detail, in Normandin, K. and Slaton, D. (eds.), *Cleaning Techniques in Conservation Practice*, Donhead, Shaftesbury, 2005.

19   The Arte Mundit poultice, manufactured by FTB Restoration of Grobbendonk, Belgium, is an example of a system using a chemical cleaner in a latex rubber poultice. Other examples of poultice products combine cleaning

compounds such as sodium bicarbonate, EDTA, and surfactants in a gel or other inert medium.

20   Quaternary ammonium chlorides are compounds found in disinfectants and anti-bacterial products for medical use as well as in building cleaning products.

21   Many proprietary systems require that firms performing the cleaning be certified applicators, and that persons performing the work complete special training courses, prior to using the cleaning systems.

Chapter Nine

Limestone

Nicholas Durnan

INTRODUCTION

Limestone is a spectacularly beautiful stone, both in its natural environment, and when used for architecture and sculpture. It exhibits a range of colours and textures that enhance and adorn countless grand and vernacular buildings. It has been used throughout the centuries for building the coarsest rubble walls to the finest ashlar walling, for bold architectural mouldings to the finest intricacy of screens and monuments, for the immense grotesques on church towers to the delicately modelled features and drapery of the most exquisite figure sculpture (Figure 9.1). Limestone is one of our great natural treasures, and once fashioned into myriad architectural shapes and sculptural forms, it becomes truly a precious stone.

In a limestone area of Britain, one can enter the local church and walk on smooth limestone flagstones, be surrounded by tooled limestone walls and be covered by a painted limestone vault, which is itself protected by a limestone roof. Light streams in through limewashed limestone tracery openings to illuminate polished limestone monuments and finely chiselled limestone corbels, capitals and columns.

This wonderful range of colour, texture, form and scale also presents a wide array of weathering and decay characteristics that challenge the conservation architect and stone conservator at every turn. In this chapter, attention is focussed on the ways in which powdering, crumbling, blistering, cracking, delaminating and eroding limestone surfaces are conserved and repaired.

Figure 9.1 The exquisite beauty of a thirteenth-century head carved in Doulting limestone on the West Front of Wells Cathedral.

CHARACTERISTICS OF LIMESTONE

The great variety of limestones used for architecture and sculpture in Britain range from very dense and hard polishable limestones like Purbeck 'marble' from Dorset to soft chalk limestones such as Beer from Devon. There is an enormous diversity of colour and texture in limestones, from black through to white including brown, orange, buff, yellow, green, grey, pink and cream. There are the coarse, shelly open textures of Ham Hill (Somerset) and Quarr (the Isle of Wight) to the very fine textures of Portland (Dorset) and Beer (Devon), and from highly porous Tufa and Chalk to low porosity polishable limestones like Devonshire 'marble'.

The decay characteristics of each type of limestone may be quite different and dependent on different causes and conditions. A strongly bedded stone like Ham Hill Stone (Somerset) has a tendency to delaminate, and this is exacerbated by the swelling of clay minerals present in this lias limestone. Blue Lias (Dorset, Somerset and at many other locations on the limestone belt) has a high clay content and is susceptible to cuboidal fracturing. Chilmark and Chicksgrove sandy (arenaceous) limestones have some decay characteristics that resemble those of sandstones and can be successfully impregnated with sandstone consolidants. The qualities of mortars used for limestone repair need to reflect the colour, texture and porosity of the stone to be repaired, for reasons of aesthetics, function and durability. The way a given limestone is cleaned also depends on its characteristics – water washing may damage some limestones, abrasive cleaning may be unsuitable for others, and poultice cleaning or laser cleaning may be the correct method for a certain limestone in a particular condition (see the previous chapter for further details on cleaning).

MAIN TYPES OF LIMESTONE DECAY

The weathering and decay patterns of limestone can be broadly divided into surface decay and deep decay. Sulphation of the calcium carbonate of which limestone is composed leads to salt formation, powdering, blistering, exfoliation and cracking (Figure 9.2). These result in surface distortion and surface loss (Figure 9.3). This can all initially occur to a depth of a few millimetres. In time, these processes can lead to deep decay, where the limestone becomes friable to a depth of at least 50 mm. Deep cracking and delamination can result from chemical and physical change of clay or iron minerals, or simply from poorly selected or incorrectly bedded stone. Surface and deep erosion are often the result of limestone surfaces being inadequately protected from rainwater, perhaps due to being situated in exposed areas of a building. Decay can also be caused by hard, cementitious mortars, which act as moisture traps and often lead to the deterioration of adjacent stone (Figure 9.4).

It is important to study the causes and conditions of each particular limestone's weathering behaviour, as this will provide information to tailor the appropriate conservation and repair strategy in each case. The choice of cleaning, consolidation, repair and protection techniques and materials are, to some extent, dependent on the nature of the decay in each particular case, and the general condition of the surface and substrate of the limestone.

Figure 9.2   A fine twelfth-century west doorway carved in Caen limestone from Normandy, at Ruckinge Church, Kent. The stone exhibits signs of sulphation decay, and soot crusts are collecting in sheltered areas.

Figure 9.3   A delicately carved eighteenth-century Chilmark limestone mask head, from the façade of Longford Castle, Wiltshire. Facial features have become distorted due to the formation and exfoliation of gypsum skins.

Figure 9.4 Beer limestone statue of Edward the Confessor, early nineteenth century, Exeter Cathedral West Front. There is deep decay under the hard impervious cement repairs, which are cracking and falling away.

TECHNIQUES FOR LIMESTONE CONSERVATION

Inspection, surface condition recording, geological analysis, mortar analysis, salt analysis, monitoring of rates of decay and the carrying out of trial conservation and repair work are part of the methodology common to all types of stone conservation. But within the areas of cleaning, consolidation, repair and protection, there are techniques that may be particularly appropriate for limestone. Cleaning techniques for limestone include dry brushing, water washing and nebulous sprays, solvents, poultices, abrasives and the laser. For consolidation, repair and protection of limestone, the main methods currently in use in the UK are lime techniques or the 'lime method'. Sometimes incorporated into a lime method strategy for conservation are 'hybrid' techniques involving synthetic resin consolidants and adhesives. For porous limestones, protective lime coatings (sheltercoats) are commonly used, whereas for polishable limestones, synthetic waxes are often favoured for surface protection.

Development of lime techniques

In historic buildings, limestone has historically been used in conjunction with lime in the form of construction mortar, renders and plasters (whether pointing, plain and decorative), and limewash. These materials were used together for the original construction and decoration of a building, and lime was used for the maintenance of limestone whenever re-rendering, re-plastering, re-pointing and re-limewashing were required. Aesthetically, physically and chemically, there are many similarities in the way limestone and lime age and weather, as an inspection of any ancient limestone wall will reveal. These similarities make limestone and lime compatible materials.

This tradition of using limestone and lime together, and of maintaining stone buildings with lime, almost died out during the nineteenth century and first half of the twentieth century. This was largely due to the advent of Roman cement and Portland cement, which became attractive for their qualities of quick setting and high strength. The 1866 specification for Gilbert Scott's restoration of the West Front of Salisbury Cathedral for example instructed: 'all new stone work and building of old stone to be built in Roman cement and pointed in Portland cement in equal proportions of sand and cement, all grouting to be done in Roman cement.'[1]

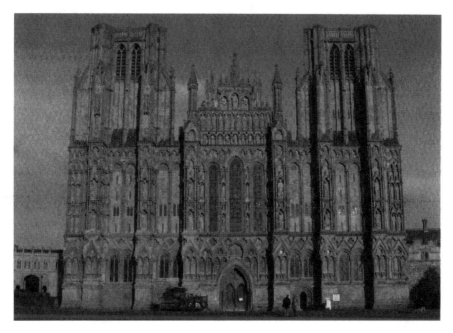

Figure 9.5 A specific methodology for using lime techniques for the conservation and repair of architectural and sculptural Doulting and Dundry limestone was developed during the conservation programme of the West Front of Wells Cathedral (1974–86).

During the 1970s, a growing awareness of the problems caused by hard cement mortars when used with limestone began to develop. The compatibility of lime and limestone both physically and aesthetically, and past traditions of limestone maintenance, were rediscovered. This led to the development of a specific methodology for using lime techniques for the conservation and repair of architectural and sculptural limestone during the conservation programme of the West Front of Wells Cathedral during 1974–86 (Figure 9.5).[2]

The principles of this methodology are straightforward: we wish to conserve ancient limestone surfaces and structures; to do this we look closely at how stone and lime were used historically; we observe where the stone is durable and where it decays; we look at how the lime mortar, plaster or limewash is behaving in relation to the stone. Limestone seems to often survive very well when used in conjunction with lime mortar and vice versa. Lime mortar is usually a softer and more porous material than limestone, and under favourable conditions it will weather at a similar or slightly faster rate than the adjacent stone. In some decay environments lime seems to act in a protective way towards the stone, tending to decay in preference to the stone over time. These compatible and sacrificial properties of lime mortars are harnessed for conservation treatments.

There are also other reasons for using lime techniques for the conservation and repair of limestone:

- Lime can be used for a whole range of specific interrelated repair and conservation requirements – consolidation, pointing, repair, protection, desalination.
- Limestone and lime have similar chemical and physical properties, such as both being primarily calcium carbonate, both being porous and permeable, and therefore behave in similar ways.
- The high level of skill and craftsmanship required in applying lime techniques, especially mortar repairs to statuary and carved work, is a reflection and continuity of the skill and craftsmanship used in the original building.
- The conservator is in full control of the choice of raw materials (the type of lime, aggregates and additives), their formulation for specific applications, and the method of application of treatments.

Cleaning

Cleaning can be defined as the removal of unwanted or harmful material from the stone surface. The purpose of the cleaning may be to reduce rates of decay, see the condition of the stone more clearly, reveal original tooling and polychromy, improve the appearance and appreciation of the building and sculpture, or a combination of all of these. The challenge is always to find techniques that remove the 'dirt' without damaging or altering the stone. In practice, a range of techniques is usually used in a particular sequence. Lasers, chemical poultices, wet and dry abrasive systems, nebulous sprays, solvents, mechanical removal; all have their place, depending on the nature of the 'dirt' and the condition and type of stone. Cleaning trials, followed by a hand lens examination ($\times 10$) of the stone surface to check for any surface damage, are part of an essential preparatory process in finding the appropriate technique.

It needs to be recognized that any cleaning technique can be potentially very damaging to the stone surface. The soft, friable nature of decaying limestone, often combined with the presence of salts, makes it vulnerable to abrasives, which can easily damage the surface. This nature also makes it vulnerable to water, which activates salts and erodes surfaces. Both lead to the possible loss of valuable archaeological information. High pressure water sprays, prolonged washing, grit blasting, and acid based products are all potentially very damaging to limestone, and should be avoided.

Cleaning trials to determine appropriate techniques for the conservation and repair programme of the West Front of Salisbury Cathedral (1994–2000),[3] for example, led to the specification of a sequence of cleaning methods for the Chilmark/Tisbury (a sandy limestone) architectural stone-work (Figure 9.6) as follows: dry brushing to remove algae and lichens; Jos/Torc vortex water/abrasive system to reduce soot crusts (Figure 9.7);

Figure 9.6 The conservation and repair programme for the West Front of Salisbury Cathedral (1994–2000) was preceded by comprehensive trial work to develop specific techniques for treating its architectural and sculptural Chilmark/Tisbury limestone.

Figure 9.7   Salisbury Cathedral, West Front – Jos vortex system
cleaning of thirteenth-century Chilmark/Tisbury limestone architectural
detail during the 1994–2000 repair and conservation programme.

ammonium carbonate poultices to remove stubborn soot crusts; hammer and tungsten chisel to remove old cement repairs and pointing. For the statuary a different sequence was adopted: lime mortar holding repairs followed by dry brushing; application of an ammonium carbonate poultice (Figure 9.8); and finally microabrasive cleaning (Figure 9.9). For the

Figure 9.8 Salisbury Cathedral, West Front – ammonium carbonate poultice cleaning of nineteenth-century Chilmark limestone statuary during the 1994–2000 repair and conservation programme.

Figure 9.9   Salisbury Cathedral, West Front – microabrasive
cleaning of nineteenth-century Chilmark limestone statuary during
the 1994–2000 repair and conservation programme.

interior of the west porch, the Nd:YAG laser was used to clean historically sensitive non-polychromed areas of stonework (Figures 9.10
and 9.11). In recent years, DOFF steam cleaning has been introduced as
a more effective way of removing algae and lichens from copings,
weatherings and string courses.

Figure 9.10   Salisbury Cathedral, West Front, west porch – parts of the thirteenth- and nineteenth-century Chilmark/Tisbury limestone were cleaned using a Nd:YAG laser, avoiding areas of polychromy. The Purbeck and Devonshire 'marbles' on the west front, including those within the west porch, were treated with microcrystalline wax.

At Wells Cathedral, during the 1978–85 West Front campaign,[4] hot lime poultices and timed nebulous sprays were used for cleaning Doulting limestone statuary. Some of the heads of certain mediaeval statues were left uncleaned at this time, due to concern that the delicate soot encrusted surfaces would be damaged by these treatments. During the later 2002 statuary re-treatment work, an Nd:YAG laser was used to safely clean three of these heads (Figures 9.12 and 9.13).[5]

Figure 9.11   Salisbury Cathedral, West Front, west porch – detail of Nd:YAG laser cleaned thirteenth- and nineteenth-century Chilmark/Tisbury limestone mouldings and ornamentation.

For the cleaning of the interior of St Paul's Cathedral (2001–2005), carried out by Nimbus Conservation Ltd and directed by David Odgers,[6] the Arte Mundit® latex system was used, which contains ethylenediamine-tetraacetic acid (EDTA) as the cleaning agent, for the Portland limestone surfaces. The latex poultice medium is sprayed thinly onto the limestone surface, and the nature of the latex allows for a highly controllable cleaning process. Clean-Film is a similar latex cleaning product.

The removal of cement from limestone is a process of separating a hard, dense, brittle material (cement) from an often soft and friable one

Figure 9.12   Wells Cathedral, West Front. Thirteenth-century Dundry limestone head of statue 211, before cleaning in 2002.

Figure 9.13   Wells Cathedral, West Front. Thirteenth-century Dundry limestone head of statue 211, after Nd:YAG laser cleaning in 2002.

(decaying limestone). Techniques range from hammer and tungsten chisel to small cutting discs. Trials are necessary to find the safest technique, as the process of cement removal can be very damaging to the adjacent surviving stone.

Consolidation and repair

Decaying and weathered limestone invariably displays cracks, exfoliation and friable surfaces and substrates, and dealing with such conditions requires a well thought out approach. Emphasis is, of course, placed on

Figure 9.14 Nappers Mite, Dorchester, Dorset, early seventeenth century, before conservation in 2004. Decaying and spalling local limestone ashlar walling, with hard cement repairs and pointing.

preserving the original surface of the stone, as this contains much of the valuable historic and archaeological information. Aesthetic considerations are just as important as the technical and functional performance of any repairs: the colour and texture of mortar repairs and pointing needs to harmonize with the existing patina (Figures 9.14 and 9.15), and their three dimensional form needs to clarify viewers 'reading' of the original construction and design. Ensuring the quality of the materials used for conservation work and taking care in the way they are formulated are thus an essential part of the process.

Figure 9.15   Nappers Mite, Dorchester, Dorset, early seventeenth century, after conservation in 2004. Repointing and mortar repairs to limestone were carried out using putty lime mortars gauged with Metastar 501 (metakaolin) pozzolan.

Application of lime mortar and lime-based treatments for limestone conservation are based on the principle of their being sacrificial, in that they will decay in preference to the conserved stone while being moisture permeable. A range of techniques are used for specific decay conditions:

Cracks and fractures

Where fractures affect structural stability, they require pinning with stainless steel or phosphor bronze rods set in polyester resin, hydraulic lime or lime-casein. Threaded stainless steel rod, grade 316, is commonly used, and is available in a wide range of diameters. When using polyester resin, the hole is drilled, the stonedust removed and the dowel degreased with acetone. The hole is then packed with resin and the dowel slowly inserted, whilst applying additional resin to the sides of the dowel as it goes in. The dowel should be cut so that it terminates at least 6 mm below the stone surface. Excess resin can be cut away from the top of the hole when the resin becomes rubbery (after about 5–10 minutes). When using hydraulic lime or lime-casein as the dowel adhesive, the hole requires flushing out with water several times to both remove dust and ensure that the lime does not harden whilst the dowel is being inserted. Whatever the dowel adhesive, once the dowel has been located correctly, the end of the dowel hole can be capped with a lime-based stone repair mortar. When a cracked or laminated area of stone is unstable or partially loose, it is important to carefully pack or grout the crack or void with lime mortar and allow this to set before carrying out any doweling.

Cracks that pose no structural threat can be grouted or filled with lime grout or fine lime mortar. Cleaning out the crack using dental tools and flushing out with water will improve the depth of the filling. The addition of 1% by volume of casein powder to a grout (before thinning with water) has the double advantage of increasing its flow characteristics and reducing the amount of water required to make the grout suitably fluid. Grouts can be formulated from putty lime and pozzolan (metakaolins are commonly used), or from hydraulic limes.

Where broken or separated sections of limestone require re-adhering, a range of options is available. To maintain the moisture movement between the piece to be re-adhered and the body of the stone, lime putty or hydraulic lime can be used as the adhesive, possibly in conjunction with stainless steel or phosphor bronze dowels set across the fracture line. For structural bonding, a strong fast setting adhesive like polyester resin may be required, but this produces an impervious join. Lime-casein is an effective adhesive, but it also reduces moisture movement. A common technique to avoid this problem is to spot adhere with polyester resin, and once this is cured to fill or grout the remaining crack with lime grout or fine lime mortar. Where there will be a continued shear stress on the re-adhered break, it is normal practice to dowel across the fracture line.

Surface blisters and exfoliating edges

Surface distortion caused by the chemical change of calcium carbonate into calcium sulphate (sulphation) often results in the formation of surface blisters and exfoliating edges. Where these surfaces require conservation, they need to be supported and packed out from behind with lime mortars and sometimes grout. Great care is required with this work, as the distorted surface skins of limestone become much weaker when wet (so a minimum of water should be used).

Friable and powdering stone

Consolidation with limewater, a clear solution of calcium hydroxide, was part of the 'lime method' as developed for the Wells Cathedral West Front repair and conservation programme. There is still much debate about its effectiveness, and its use has become less common of late. The application of dilute lime slurries to strengthen friable limestone surfaces is now a more accepted technique. Lime putty is diluted with water to a milky solution, which is applied by brush in multiple applications. Such lime slurries can be used for surface consolidation (after pigmenting with earth pigments to match the patina of the stone), or as a way of strengthening a friable surface to prepare it to receive a mortar repair.

During the conservation and repair of the West Front of Salisbury Cathedral, eleven of the Chilmark/Tisbury limestone statues had particularly fragile areas of decay on vulnerable areas. These areas, such as fingers and locks of hair were so fragile that lime treatments alone could not save them. After some trial work, ethyl silicate (Wacker OH) was found to be effective on this sandy limestone, and was used on the small decayed areas of each of the eleven statues. The strengthening effect of the ethyl silicate consolidant, which after curing still leaves the stone moisture permeable, allowed lime mortar repairs and sheltercoat to then be applied over the consolidated areas. The moisture permeability of ethyl silicate treated stone increases over time, so a minimum curing time of twenty-eight days after application is necessary to ensure the moisture permeability necessary to allow a good bond with the lime mortar.

A relatively new treatment, Conservare HCT (hydroxylating conversion treatment), can be used as a pre-treatment to improve the consolidation of limestone with ethyl silicate. This method is still at the trial stage in the UK.

Voids and deep decay

The treatment of voids, and missing or deeply decayed areas, requires careful consideration. Whilst it is common practice to fill voids with colour- and texture-matched lime mortars for both conservation and aesthetic reasons, reinstatement of missing detail and form is dependent on the repair and conservation policy decided at the planning stage of the project. A more conservative policy is usually applied to historic sculptures and ornament, where losses are accepted as part of the history of the object and no conjectural repairs are made. In such cases, mortar repairs are used to fill voids or damaged areas just to the point where the existing form is more clearly defined, whilst ensuring that vulnerable areas are adequately protected. For mouldings and repetitive ornament, where remodelling the missing form would not be conjectural, lime mortar repairs are often built up to 'full form'.

Lime mortar repairs need to be placed on a sound substrate, and this can be ensured by either raking away unwanted friable stone or con-solidating the friable stone so it is sound enough to support the repair. Keying the repair to stone can be done by roughening and undercutting the surfaces and edges of the area to be repaired. For large areas of repair, armatures may be required to ensure the continuation of a good bond between mortar and stone. Stainless steel wire and narrow diameter dowels are commonly used, and it is important to set them well back from the mortar surface. This ensures that the armature used does not become visible as the mortar weathers, and reduces the risk of the thermal expansion of the metal disrupting the repair. The dowels are usually fixed into the stone with hydraulic lime, or occasionally polyester resin, depending on the strength required. Ceramic dowels (biscuit fired and unglazed) in the form of 5–7 mm rods or 'T's are also commonly used. These have the advantage of being moisture permeable, so they can be soaked to retain moisture and slow down the drying of the repair, thereby ensuring a good bond to the lime mortar.[7] The typical procedure for applying lime mortar repairs is described in the Appendix.

Surface protection with sheltercoat

Surface protection of limestone with a sheltercoat performs two functions: the practical one of preservation of the original stone surfaces, and the aesthetic one of helping the viewer 'read' the design of the object or monument by integrating the appearance of treated and untreated stonework (Figure 9.16).

Sheltercoat is composed of lime putty, casein, and finely graded stone-dusts and sands. For darker coloured limestones, earth pigments are sometimes added. It is brushed onto and worked into the stone surface. It is designed to match the colour of the stone to be protected, and one coat is the normal application. It is applied to stone surfaces that have been cleaned, and is typically used for vulnerable areas like sculpture, carved work and undercut mouldings. The principle is that it is a sacrificial

Figure 9.16 Salisbury Cathedral, West Front. Nineteenth-century Chilmark limestone statue of St Edmund after cleaning, mortar repair and sheltercoat treatment carried out during the 1994–2000 repair and conservation programme.

coating which will gradually weather away or become sulphated in place of the stone. Because it is sacrificial, it needs to be applied on a regular basis. The typical procedure for application is described in the Appendix.

Limewash

Limewash is an interior or exterior paint composed of lime putty and water. It is compatible with limestone or lime plaster, and has been traditionally used as a paint on these substrates for thousands of years. Applying limewash to historic stonework results in a dramatic change in appearance and should therefore only be considered where there is clear evidence of it being originally applied. Even then, the change in appearance and covering of stone surfaces may be unacceptable for both aesthetic and archaeological reasons. Sheltercoat is preferable for protecting limestone surfaces, as it can be colour and texture matched to the limestone and the character of the original stone surface is retained.

The final colour of limewash is sensitive to the dampness of the substrate. The longer limewash takes to dry (cure), the closer it is to its wet colour; the quicker it dries, the paler it becomes. For a successful result, it should be allowed to dry out slowly and evenly over a period of one to two days.

Conservation and repair of polishable limestones

The conservation and repair of hard polishable limestones like Purbeck 'marble' and Devonshire 'marble' are special cases. Purbeck 'marble' was prized in medieval times for its rich dark colours when polished, and columns made of this stone are found at many medieval churches and cathedrals. Prior to the conservation and repair of the West Front of Salisbury Cathedral (1994–2000), conservator Mike Burleigh carried out trials on a cluster of Purbeck shafts in the cloister. As a result, a lime/casein repair mix was developed that set hard enough to take a polish, adhered well to the stone surface, and could be coloured to emulate the distinctive markings of the stone. These lime-casein mortars were subsequently used to repair both Purbeck and Devonshire marbles across the entire West Front. Burleigh also tested a range of wax surface protective treatments. Renaissance (microcrystalline) wax was found to be the most suitable in terms of penetration, clarity and colour enrichment. This, too, was used for treating the Purbeck and Devonshire marble across the West Front, in the cloister and elsewhere.[8]

SELECTION OF LIME FOR CONSERVATION AND REPAIR

There is much debate within the conservation and traditional building professions as to which limes and additives are appropriate for the range of application situations that arise in conserving and repairing historic limestone. Ellis, from his experience of analysing a wide range of historic mortars, describes the materials that they contain, and gives recommendations for producing a durable putty lime mortar.[9]

Many conservators have a preference for putty lime and pozzolanic putty lime mortars, plasters and renders over hydraulic limes in terms of workability, the fact that batches can be premixed and can be stored until required, and to ensure the mortars remain sacrificial to the stone. Both high calcium limes and chalk limes are now easily available, with chalk limes offering the advantages of better workability and less shrinkage. The strength of lime putty mortars can be increased by the addition (gauging) of small amounts of reactive materials known as pozzolans. The varieties most used in the UK are the metakaolin Metastar 501 (calcined china clay), certain reactive brick dusts and Trass (a volcanic ash). The addition of 5–10% pozzolan to lime putty is the typical range. The practice of gauging putty lime with hydraulic lime is contentious, and the complex issues surrounding the gauging of putty lime with pozzolans and the gauging of putty lime with hydraulic lime are clearly described in an article by Ellis.[10]

The higher strength of modern hydraulic limes makes them useful for more exposed situations on historic buildings, but with this increased strength comes the disadvantage of being less workable, and a reduction of moisture permeability. The less hydraulic grades, especially NHL2, are better suited for work on historic limestone.

When it comes to replacing or matching an existing mortar, an experienced conservator can, in many situations, from close examination, produce a suitable replacement mortar. On larger projects, or where requirements demand it, mortar analysis can provide information about the binder and aggregates. Such analysis is not necessarily to ensure an exact replication of the existing mortar, but more to ensure that one has as much information as possible to aid decision-making on the most appropriate replacement material. It may be that the existing mortar is too soft, too earthy, or too hard for its purpose and requires adjustment. Alternatively, the mortar may be performing well and it is desirable to produce a close replica. Ellis describes what can be achieved from mortar analysis and outlines the current analysis techniques.[11]

In any event, whether one is replicating or replacing historic mortars, or designing conservation repair mortars, the carrying out of trials to ensure the correct colour and texture is good practice.

INSPECTION, MAINTENANCE AND RE-TREATMENT

The principle behind lime techniques is that they protect the stone through their sacrificial properties. Thus it is essential that any major conservation and repair project should include provision for future inspection and maintenance, so as to observe the ongoing behaviour of the treated stone. Five-yearly cycles of inspection are typical. For high-level work, the inspection can be carried out from a hydraulic platform (spider or cherry picker), or by a rope-access trained conservator. Drawn,

Figure 9.17   Exeter Cathedral, Image Screen. Fifteenth-century Beer limestone statues (numbered C19 and 20). Since the main conservation and repair programme in 1978–85, the Image Screen has been regularly inspected. As part of the continuing maintenance programme, further re-treatment in the form of putty lime mortar repairs to some of the statues, and re-application of sheltercoat treatment, has been carried out in 1992 and 1999. The Image Screen is protected from nesting birds by a stone coloured 50 mm mesh polyethylene netting system.

photographic and video records of the inspection can be reviewed, and a strategy for further repair work implemented if necessary. This process has been undertaken for example at Wells, Exeter (Figure 9.17) and Salisbury West Fronts since their respective conservation programmes were completed. Revisiting previously treated work is a very useful exercise for two reasons: the areas most at risk of future decay can be clearly identified, and

Figure 9.18   Wells Cathedral, West Front. Statue 151 in 2002, before re-treatment. Extensive mortar repairs had been carried out in 1983 to the left and right arm, chest, and lower drapery. These were mostly still sound, except for some on the lower parts of the statue drapery.

the behaviour and effectiveness of the lime treatments can be assessed (and if necessary formulations can be adjusted for re-treatment work). An inspection and evaluation of the effectiveness of lime treatments at various sites has highlighted areas of success and those where further research is necessary.[12]

For example, re-treatment work at Wells Cathedral West Front in 2002 was found to be necessary following regular inspections of conservation

Figure 9.19   Wells Cathedral, West Front. Statue 151 before re-treatment in 2002, showing detail of mortar repair breakdown – note the exfoliating skin of mortar, and powdery surface where the skin has fallen away. The base layers of mortar were sound.

and repair work from the 1974–86 programme.[13] The inspection process revealed that surfaces of some of the 1974–86 mortar repairs were breaking down. This was happening in a sacrificial way as originally intended, as the adjacent Doulting limestone remained sound. The failing repairs were removed, and replaced with a mortar designed to be a little more durable while still preserving the sacrificial function (Figures 9.18, 9.19 and 9.20). At the same time the opportunity was taken to re-treat this area of statues

Figure 9.20 Wells Cathedral, West Front. Statue 151 after re-treatment, showing detail of lower drapery of the statue. The friable upper layers of the 1983 mortar repairs were removed, and replaced with new mortar repairs in 2002 over the sound 1983 base layers.

with sheltercoat where after 16–18 years, the first application had partially weathered away.

A recent and ongoing study of rates of stone decay, at St Catherine's Chapel, Abbotsbury, Dorset by English Heritage, is using laser imaging techniques to map the rate of surface loss at selected locations over annual cycles. The resulting 'colour maps' provide easily accessible information about the locations and depths of stone loss over a given area. From such illustrative information about patterns of decay, a policy for conservation treatment, re-treatment or further monitoring can be decided. Such techniques as these could be extended over the whole or partial elevation of a building, allowing the conservation architect and conservator to pinpoint the fastest decaying areas of stonework.

The author

Nicholas Durnan DiplCons

Nicholas Durnan has over 30 years experience working on the conservation and repair of stonework on cathedrals, churches and historic buildings. After a masonry apprenticeship at Canterbury Cathedral and a diploma in carving at the City and Guilds of London Art School he trained as a sculpture conservator at Wells Cathedral. For most of his career he has worked as a sculpture conservator and conservation consultant. He has been involved in both these roles for the major repair and conservation programmes of the West Fronts of Wells, Exeter and Salisbury Cathedrals.

References

1 Scott, Sir G. G., 'Specifications of Works to West Front of Nave', un-published specification for the Dean and Chapter, Salisbury Cathedral Archives, 10 August 1866.
2 Drury, M. and Durnan, N., 'Conservation and Repair, 1994–2000', in Ayers, T. (ed.) *Salisbury Cathedral – The West Front: A History and Study in Conservation*, Philimore, Chichester 2000, pp. 139–168.
3 Ibid.
4 Sampson, J., *Wells Cathedral West Front: Construction, Sculpture and Conservation*, Sutton, Stroud, 1998, pp. 1–9.
5 Durnan, N., 'Wells Cathedral: West Front 2002, Report on the Re-treatment of statues (abridged version with note on polychromy and laser cleaning)', *Conservation News*, No. 35, March 2004.
6 Stancliffe, M., De Witte I. and De Witte E., 'St Paul's Cathedral: Poultice Cleaning of the Interior', in Normandin, K. and Slaton, D., *Cleaning Techniques in Conservation Practice*, Donhead, Shaftesbury, 2005, pp. 87–104.
7 Nim T's ceramic dowels available from Nimbus Conservation Ltd, Eastgate, Christchurch Street East, Frome, Somerset BA11 1QD.

8 Drury and Durnan, *op. cit.*
9 Ellis, P., 'The Importance of Complex Aggregates in Historic Renders and Repair Mixes', *SPAB News*, Vol. 21, No. 2, 2000, pp. 31–3.
10 Ellis, P., 'Gauging Lime Mortars', *The Building Conservation Directory 2001*, Cathedral Communications, Tisbury, pp. 165–7.
11 Ellis, P., 'The Analysis of Mortar: The Past 20 Years', *Historic Churches*, 2002.
12 Woolfitt, C., 'Lime method evaluation: A survey of sites where lime-based conservation techniques have been employed to treat decaying limestone', *English Heritage Research Transactions: Stone*, Vol. 2, James and James, London, 2002, pp. 29–43
13 Durnan, *op. cit.*

Further reading

Ashurst, J., Mortars, 'Plasters and Renders', *Conservation EASA*, Second Edition, December 2002.
Ashurst, J., 'The cleaning and treatment of limestone by the lime method', in Ashurst and Dimes, *Conservation of Building and Decorative Stone*, Vol. 2, Butterworth-Heinemann, London, pp. 169–176, 1990.
Ashurst, J. and Ashurst, N., *Practical Building Conservation Volume 1: Stone Masonry*, Gower Technical Press, Aldershot, 1988.
Ashurst, J. and Ashurst, N., *Practical Building Conservation Volume 3: Plasters, Mortars and Renders*, Gower Technical Press, Aldershot, 1988.
Durnan. N., 'Wells Cathedral: West Front 2002, Report on the Re-treatment of statues', *Journal of the Building Limes Forum*, Vol. 10, 2003.
Fidler, J., 'Lime Treatments, An overview of lime watering and sheltercoating of friable historic limestone masonry', in *English Heritage Research Transactions, Vol. 2, Stone*, James and James, London, 2002, pp. 19–28.
Holmes, S. and Wingate M., *Building with Lime, A Practical Introduction*, revised edition, ITDG Publishing, London, 2003.

Materials and suppliers

Singleton Birch Chalk Lime and Casein Powder
Rose of Jericho, Horchester Farm, Holywell, Nr Evershot, Dorset DT2 0LL

Singleton Birch NHL2 hydraulic lime and Metastar 501 (metakaolin)
Limebase Products Ltd, Walronds Park, Isle Brewers, Taunton TA3 6QP

Nim T's ceramic dowels
Nimbus Conservation Ltd, Eastgate, Christchurch Street East, Frome, Somerset BA11 1QD

Renaissance Wax
Picreator Enterprises Ltd, 44 Park View Gardens, Hendon, London NW4 2PN

Arte Mundit cleaning system
FTB Restoration, Bouwelven 19, B-2280 Grobbendonk, Belgium

Jos/Torc and DOFF cleaning systems, and Clean-Film system
Stonehealth Ltd, Bowers Court, Broadwell, Dursley, Gloucestershire, GL11 4JE

Phoenix Conservation Nd:YAG laser
Lynton Lasers Ltd, Lynton House, Manor Lane, Holmes Chapel, Cheshire CW4 8AF

Wacker OH stone consolidant
Triton Chemical Manufacturing Company Ltd, Unit 5 Lyndean Industrial Estate, Abbey Wood, London SE2 9SG

Conservare HCT (hydroxylating conversion treatment)
Tensid UK plc, Aquila House, Wheatash Road, Addlestone, Surrey KT15 2ES

Notes

Laser cleaning at Wells Cathedral West Front 2002 was carried out by:
Nic Boyes, Nicolas Boyes Stone Conservation, 46 Balcarres Street, Edinburgh EH10 5JQ

Mortar analysis at Salisbury Cathedral was carried out by:
Peter Ellis, Horchester Farm, Holywell, Nr Evershot, Dorchester, Dorset DT2 0LL

Close range 3D laser scanning at St Catherine's Chapel, Abbotsbury was carried out by:
The Scan Team, 5 Ravenscroft, Harpenden, Hertfordshire AL5 1ST

Chapter Ten

Sandstone

Colin Muir

INTRODUCTION

Sandstone is amongst the most widespread of geological building materials, with a long history of use. Its layered formation has enabled it to be easily quarried, split and built with, from as far back as the Neolithic period. Such use has resulted in some of the earliest surviving stone-built structures, such as those at Skara Brae and Maeshowe in Orkney. Whilst sandstone has sometimes been regarded as a less desirable building stone than the more easily worked limestone, its attractive range of colours and textures has ensured its extensive use around the world. Historic sites such as the Red Fort in Delhi, the city of Petra in Jordan and Karnak Temple in Luxor all attest to the diverse uses of the material.

The quartzite material of which sandstone is composed is the granular debris of ancient igneous rock, namely granite. This ancient rock has been eroded, broken down and sorted, by water and wind action, into depositions of similarly sized grains. Once chemically cemented together, the resultant sandstone is a very different material to its parent rock. In terms of strength, appearance and characteristics it is an altogether new material. When sandstone decays it weathers back to its constituent aggregate of loose granular silica, ready to be deposited all over again. This process results in an ongoing cycle of decay, deposition and stone formation.

Sandstone has been a popular building stone largely due to its relative softness and ease of carving. However, the quartzite grains it contains take a heavy toll on cutting equipment, quickly blunting chisels and saws. Ironically, wetted sandstone is often used to sharpen such dulled edges. Some sandstones can be inconsistent in their characteristics due to their sedimentary formation: inclusions such as stones, clays, and fossils can interrupt fine carving, occasionally weakening the material as well.

SANDSTONE CHARACTERISTICS

Sandstones have been deposited throughout the globe, and derive from a number of different geological periods; indeed their formation is ongoing. Sandstones consist mainly of medium-sized quartz grains (although small proportions of micas, feldspars and other minerals may be present), cemented together by one of a number of mineral binders. The type of binder plays a vital role in determining durability and decay of sandstones. Indeed, sandstone is only as strong as its binder, since the individual silica crystals are so structurally strong as to be effectively indivisible. The various types of sandstone are named after their predominant binder material as follows.

Sandstone type	Binder material
Ferruginous	Iron oxides
Calcareous	Calcite
Argillaceous	Clay
Silicaceous	Silica
Dolomitic	Dolomite (Gypsum)
Micaceous	Mica

SANDSTONE DECAY AND TREATMENT

The weathering and decay of sandstones by environmental agents is affected, to a large extent, by the stone's internal structure and the mineralogy of its binder. The most common manifestations of sandstone decay are described below, roughly in order of increasing severity, with notes regarding their causes and possible treatments.

Pollution crusts

These crusts build up on sheltered areas of sandstone, such as beneath overhanging carving and canopies. They are usually black in colour, and appear as lumpy accretions on top of the stone (Figure 10.1). The surface of such crusts is hard and brittle, and if removed often reveals friable, disaggregating stone beneath.

Figure 10.1   A pollution crust formed on the underside of a carving.

Cause

These build-ups are pollution products, combining calcareous elements from the stone or soluble wash-off from the mortar, with atmospheric sulphur and carbon deposits.[1] They are usually found in urban environments, and the surrounding stone will normally show a level of carbon soiling as well.

Treatment

The removal of pollution crusts may cause some damage to the friable stone that has been created underneath. Whilst they may be removed using air abrasive systems it is usually preferable and less damaging to remove them by hand. They are best removed using a combination of wood and steel tools to lift and separate the accretions, taking care to retain as much of the stone as possible. In some cases it may be necessary to use a small (3 mm) tungsten-tipped chisel to chip away at a mass until it separates. Spraying small amounts of water on the surface can also aid in separation of the materials. Laser cleaning has proven successful in removing such deposits, but tests would be required to ensure that the type of sandstone being cleaned did not react (bleach or lighten) to this method.

Disaggregation

Disaggregation, friability or 'sanding' is evident where the surface of a stone appears soft and poorly bound, and where aggregate is being shed from the substrate (Figure 10.2). It can either affect just the upper grains of stone, or indicate much deeper binder failure (to a depth of a centimetre or more). In extreme cases, sandstones can completely disintegrate through this process.

Cause

This problem occurs where the structural integrity of the stone binder has been compromised. This can occur when binder minerals have been dissolved by water or chemical reaction. Alternatively the cause may be the mechanical stress exerted by internal salt expansion (known as crypto-fluorescence), or one of the various fluctuation cycles, such as freeze/thaw or wetting/drying.

Treatment

Some form of deep consolidation is required to halt this type of deterioration. Where salts are present either as the cause, or in addition,

Figure 10.2   Sandstone exhibiting disaggregation loss.

desalination will be required prior to the application of a consolidant. This is a particularly difficult decay form to treat as it affects the whole stone, surface and substrate. Consolidation is an inexact science at present though the best results on sandstones so far have been achieved with silane-based treatments.

Preferential erosion

Preferential erosion is visible as the accelerated decay of one part of a stone, leaving surrounding stone relatively intact.

Cause

This process is the visible manifestation of the difference between adjacent hard and soft materials. It can often be seen in the striated natural weathering of sedimentary stones, as softer areas yield faster to exposure. It can also occur through the inappropriate use of materials. The most common occurrence is where a hard cement mortar is left standing proud, after the softer surrounding sandstone has weathered back (Figure 10.3).

Figure 10.3   Preferential erosion of sandstone related to hard, cement pointing.

Treatment

Prevention is better than cure in this case, and the use of hard cement mortars for pointing or repairs to sandstone should be avoided. Where damage has occurred, the offending repair or pointing material should be carefully removed, using small chisels, and replaced with a softer lime-based mortar.

Alveolar erosion

Alveolar erosion is often associated with maritime locations, and is typified by the formation of smooth, hemispherical depressions in the surface of a stone. These depressions can become so numerous that they join together, forming a honeycomb-like appearance (Figure 10.4).

Cause

This process is believed to occur through the formation of salt-induced disaggregation pockets, which then weather preferentially into cavities (or alveoles). This form of decay is usually associated with areas experiencing wind turbulence, which causes both accelerated drying and

Figure 10.4   Alveolar erosion of sandstone showing distinctive weathering pattern.

salt crystallization, as well as with physical wind erosion. As a depression forms, it is gradually enlarged to the point where it creates a micro-environment within it. Within this environment, air-pressure, drying rates, disaggregation and abrasive micro-eddying will differ from unaffected areas, further enhancing the erosion of the depressions.[2]

Treatment

This phenomenon affects wide areas at a time, and it is difficult to know how to halt it without further research into its development. The 'sculptural' effects of this erosion can be minimized by the filling of alveolar depressions with colour-matched repair mortar. This also improves the ability of the surface to shed wind-flow, rather than trapping it in the hollows.

Efflorescence

Efflorescence is the visible crystallization of soluble salts on the surface of a stone. This most commonly appears as a loose, powdery white deposit (Figure 10.5). Salts may also crystallize internally, in which case the result is known as 'cryptoflorescence', as they are hidden from view. This latter

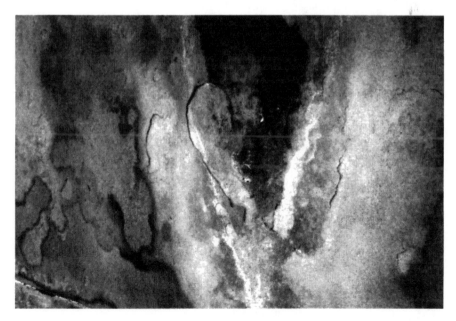

Figure 10.5   Efflorescence formation in sandstone, and associated damage.

form is particularly damaging to the structural integrity of stone, as there is initially no visual indication of its occurrence; it is only when it starts to cause blistering, substrate separation or disaggregation that its presence becomes evident.

Cause

Salt deposition can result from a number of sources. Soluble salts can be absorbed from groundwater, rain and marine environments. Ordinary Portland cement is also responsible for significant salt contamination of associated masonry. More direct sources can relate to salt-storage areas, splash-back from salted winter roads, and salt-laden chemical sprays such as fertilizers and insecticides.

Treatment

Where salt deposition is present, damage is likely to be occurring. Desalination is necessary to remove as much of the saline contaminant as possible. However, removal of salts from stonework will only be effective in the long term if the source of contamination is identified, and either eliminated or isolated. Where objects are portable, such as grave slabs or small sculptures, it is possible to carry out immersion desalination over a period of months. Such objects can then be returned to their original locations once the source of the salts has been addressed; alternatively they can be isolated from contaminated areas, such as wall cores, by plastic or lead membranes beneath or around them. Whilst immersion-desalination is an effective way of removing the vast majority of salts from a stone, it is not practical for architectural elevations. For desalination on such a large scale, a series of poultice applications is made to the surface to harmlessly draw salts into the poultice material. Poultices used for architectural elevations can use clays, such as sepiolite, or acid-free paper pulp as their medium. In architectural locations, efforts must be made prior to poulticing to assess the source and route of any salt-laden moisture, and to then effectively treat the condition. Often, simple measures, such as fixing defective roofing and guttering, or providing adequate drainage around the base of walls, will staunch the ingress of descending or ascending moisture.

Blistering

Blistering causes rounded extrusions to form on the surface of sandstone. These protuberances are hollow and frequently break, revealing the friable substrate beneath (Figure 10.6).

Cause

This decay form is also associated with contour scaling and hollowness. Blisters may indicate locations of salts concentrations rather than contour scaling where salts are more evenly distributed.

Treatment

Blister sites are best left intact, to retain as much of the stone for as long as possible. They are often associated with efflorescence and should be dry-brush cleaned of salt deposits and desalinated where necessary. When a blister has broken open, the stone should be taken back to a supportable edge (not necessarily flush with the surface), and the interior edges should be injected with a solution of 5% acrylic resin in 50/50 acetone and industrial methylated spirit (IMS). The edges of the blister sites should

Figure 10.6   Blistering leading to surface loss in sandstone.

then be edge-pointed, to support them and keep out water. The interior parts of the blister should be brush cleaned, and can then be surface filled with repair mortar.

Contour scaling

Contour scaling is a decay pattern associated primarily with sandstone. It appears similar to delamination, but the separation follows the surface contours of the stone rather than the bedding planes (Figure 10.7). Scaling layers vary in thickness, from a couple of millimetres to as much as two centimetres.

Cause

Contour scaling has been thought to relate to internal horizons within the stone that are the limit of moisture penetration and salt transportation. It is now believed that the formation of gypsum (from mortar or atmospheric sources) within the outer layer of the stone may cause changes in the mechanical behaviour of the material, resulting in stress fatigue, and its eventual separation from the substrate.[3]

Figure 10.7   Contour scaling of sandstone surface perpendicular to the bedding plane.

Treatment

Contour scaling is often only noticed once parts of the stone surface have been lost, though it may have been detectable prior to this as hollowness. Once areas have been lost, the usual treatment is to clear the friable edges of debris using a soft dry brush. If salts are visible, then desalination-poulticing may be necessary prior to further conservation treatment. Loose edges that show substrate separation are injected with a solution of 5% acrylic resin in 50/50 acetone and IMS. This will bind and stabilize the edges and surroundings. Edges should then be edge-pointed using a lime or acrylic-based repair mortar. The intention is to fill and seal loose, undermined edges, to support them and to keep out the negative effects of the weather, primarily rain.

Hollowness

Hollowness is often not discernible visually, but is revealed by a hollow sound when a surface is tapped. This indicates the separation of the surface from the substrate, usually parallel to the face. Cracks can also sometimes indicate such a situation, where the thin surface layer has been differentially stressed (Figure 10.8).

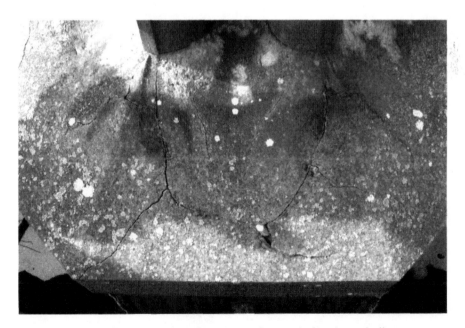

Figure 10.8   Shallow micro-cracking in sandstone, indicating a hollow detached surface.

Cause

Depending on the orientation of the stone, this may point to either delamination or the early stages of contour scaling. The interface between surface and substrate may be a clean division, such as in delamination, or the internal stone may be friable (if the action of salts or loss of binder has broken down its structure).

Treatment

Areas of hollowness can be filled and stabilized by opening a small aperture at the top of the void. Into this is alternately fed fine dry sand (<600 microns, >160 microns), and a solution of 5% acrylic resin in 50/50 acetone and IMS. This layering system will ensure filling and saturation of the void, and when filled the aperture can be capped with acrylic repair mortar. Alternatively, a fine, lime-based gravity grout can be fed into the pre-wetted void in the same way. Care should be taken in the case of liquid grouts that the pressure of the liquid does not cause the exterior surface to deflect, or indeed to separate entirely.

Delamination

Delamination, also known as exfoliation, is observed as the separation of a stone along its bedding planes. The layers may be very thin and affect the stone only near the surface (Figure 10.9), or divisions can split throughout the stone in layers a number of centimetres thick.

Cause

Delamination is primarily caused by the division of stone along weakened bedding planes. The layers that become compromised may differ from adjacent ones by being more permeable, or containing poorly bonded or more soluble elements, such as micas, fossil carbon debris, or clays. These physical inconsistencies can cause water ingress to affect some layers of stone more than others. Water ingress can then result in associated problems of salt contamination, wetting/drying stress or frost expansion.

Treatment

Where the edges of bedding planes are accessible (such as on gravestones), injection of acrylic resin can prove an effective and reversible means of

Figure 10.9 Delamination of sandstone along the bedding planes.

adhering adjacent surfaces deep within the stone. Where the edges cannot be accessed, small holes drilled through the face can give access to the separating layers within and facilitate injection. When this technique is used, the series of holes should be injected and then filled from the bottom upwards to ensure overall coverage. Acrylic resin has a limited bridging capability, but the addition of a fine sand to it can enable gap filling, and will support the layers of stone on either side.

Cracking

Cracking can occur in any direction of a stone face (Figure 10.10). It can be divided into two basic categories. Micro-cracking is seen as the development of a fairly shallow network of fine fissures. Macro-cracking, on the other hand, is exemplified by singular deep divisions in the stone.

Cause

Micro-cracking may be formed by fluctuation cycles, particularly wetting/drying, which can cause fine stress fractures to form. These are particularly seen in raised areas that dry out quickly, such as cusps and carved details. Such cracking may also form on surfaces that are detached from their substrate, and can therefore be a good indicator of hollowness

Figure 10.10   Cracks forming in sandstone, independently of bedding plane direction.

(Figure 10.8). Macro-cracks may originate from natural flaws in the stone, quarrying trauma, rust-jacking, or from a shift in weight-loading. Water quickly exploits such cracks, and frost expansion can then cause further splitting to occur, sometimes on a massive scale.

Treatment

Micro-cracking may cover areas of disaggregating stone, and it is prudent to try to stabilize this substrate prior to filling the surface cracks. This may be carried out by injecting the area with a reversible solution of 2.5–5% acrylic resin in 50/50 acetone and IMS. Once the cracks and interior have been treated, the cracks can be filled using a colour-matched repair mortar based on lime or acrylic resin.

Larger macro-cracks can point to serious structural issues that affect not just a specific masonry element, but also the structure as a whole. The cause of these defects may be settlement, subsidence, seismic activity, or changes to the loading of the masonry, often through 'unrelated' building works. The use of crack-monitoring plates is recommended, to establish if movement is still occurring. If this is the case, it may be necessary to involve a structural engineer to oversee and advise.

Even when large cracks are stable, they can be difficult to bond to any depth, and the emphasis should be on sealing the crack-site with a repair mortar, to ensure water cannot continue to gain access. Dropping further material into a crack should be avoided, as this can wedge the crack open and hasten its widening.

CLEANING

Few stone types highlight the controversial issues surrounding stone cleaning as much as sandstone does. Its granular, porous characteristics, and often-variegated colour makes for an attractive building medium. However, these same qualities also lead it to readily absorb salts, water, paint, inks and atmospheric pollutants, and to chemically react inconsistently over its surface. Its porous surface retains moisture, providing an ideal environment for biological colonization. Initially, this is usually algal in nature, but can then attract moss or lichen growth, depending on how wet or dry the surface generally is, and what kind of weather it is exposed to.

Sandstones accumulate soiling in the locations that retain moisture the longest. This is not true of limestones, where rain-washed areas appear the cleanest (due to the solubility of limestone to acidic precipitation). Soiling patterns on sandstones, however, are related to the complexity of the surface.[4] This is true on a macro level, where complex mouldings, carvings or tooling act as water traps, inhibiting drainage and drying. On the micro level, the granular, highly porous nature of sandstone means it has a much larger surface area than its apparent X, Y, Z dimensions would suggest. As a result, this complex surface is capable of retaining moisture for extended periods. The black soiling found on sandstone in urban areas is from the adhesion of atmospheric carbon deposits (industrial and domestic soot, car fumes, and the like) onto wet surfaces. When these carbon particulates dry, they form insoluble concretions on the stone surface. Ongoing soiling adheres further soot deposits to those already in place. This accumulation of matter lines the pores, and thus reduces both surface area and its ability to trap water. When such surfaces are cleaned, they once again provide a hugely complex terrain that retains water, traps soot particles, and provides a vast and sheltered environment for biological colonization. This accounts for the rapid re-soiling and biological growth noted on some sandstone buildings after they have been cleaned.

Over time, the original colour of the stone can change as chemical interaction with the natural environment causes iron-oxide rich areas to darken, or binder elements on the surface to be lost, causing greying.[5] Some changes in colour are considered acceptable and 'natural',[6] or even desirable, and are described in terms of a patina acquired through age. But changes caused by salt efflorescence, localized water-staining, unwanted paint, pollution accretion and biological greening are generally thought to be objectionable. In some cases, this is due to the harmful side effects of these visual symptoms, such as internal damp, or salt related decay. Often, though, the desire to remove an unattractive surface appearance is the reason for cleaning. Such negatively altered surfaces can be seen as undermining the aesthetic appreciation and value of a structure, or its details.

The ethics and aesthetics of what may be considered 'cosmetic' cleaning, which imparts no conservation advantage to the material, are complex and vary internationally.[7] One of the reasons why the subject generates active debate is the variety of cleaning techniques available, and in some cases the abuse of these methods by commercial contractors in the past. The inappropriate use of chemical cleaning agents or mechanical abrasive systems has caused considerable damage in many historic cities globally. Another issue to consider, prior to cleaning, is whether the stone will be adversely affected by the chemicals, or the loss of surface, and how quickly the soiling will reappear (thereby necessitating further cleaning). It has been shown that sandstone surfaces cleaned of algae can often be re-colonized very rapidly, frequently in less than six months. This process can accelerate where the surface has been roughened by acidic or abrasive stone cleaning systems that increase the surface area.[8]

Cleaning techniques pertinent to sandstone can be generalized as steam, chemical, abrasive and laser. Steam cleaning utilizes the enhanced solvency of super-heated water, the sudden heat-expansion of pollution layers to separate them from the stone surface and the force of the steam-pressure to wash away detritus. Chemical systems may be biocidal (for the removal of biological growth), acidic (for the removal of pollution products) or solvent-based (for the removal of paint or graffiti). Abrasive systems vary in detail, and usually involve the projection of an abrasive against the stone surface using pressurized air, or air and water. Abrasives can vary both in the size of the particles and the hardness of the material used. Aluminium oxide is amongst the hardest abrasives used, while organic sources, such as ground walnut shells and peach stones, are often used for softer abrasives. Some low-pressure abrasive systems create a flow-vortex to deliver the abrasive at an acute angle to minimize frontal impact and enhance the abrasive's lateral 'chisel' action. Laser cleaning is becoming more common in conservation labs, though it is still best suited to sculptures and small architectural details rather than the cleaning of entire façades. Whilst laser cleaning is a non-contact system, it is erroneous to think it cannot cause damage to the stone substrate. It requires sensitive operation of the equipment to ensure that only soiling is vapourized, and that no underlying stone is affected. This is particularly true where the stone is decayed or friable. Laser cleaning is most effective on dark soiling of a light coloured stone surface. It should be noted, however, that laser cleaning can 'bleach' or grey some sandstones, as the laser can affect minerals in the stone's binder.

Certain types of cleaning are more effective and appropriate on specific forms of soiling. There follows an overview of commonly occurring types of soiling, their causes, and what type of cleaning might be best suited for each. It should be noted that this is not an exhaustive or definitive list, and as always, varied cleaning trials should be undertaken prior to deciding on a methodology. These tests should be carried out on an unobtrusive area, and start with the least harmful/invasive technique, and advance until an appropriate level of cleaning is achieved. It should also be realized that a pristine level of cleaning is neither likely, nor appropriate on historic stone surfaces.[9]

Paint

Cause

This may be the result of a previous surface finish, or a maliciously applied marking, such as graffiti. How well it is adhered will be dependent on its age and the type of paint used (e.g. oil, acrylic, emulsion, vinyl, cellulose and so on).

Removal

Care should be exercised when attempting to remove paints, since all paints applied prior to the 1960s should be regarded as possibly containing lead.[10,11] Various proprietary paint removers are available, including solvent poultices, and these should be tested in progressive order of strength, from weakest to strongest. Heat guns and dry-abrasion systems should be avoided, due to the hazards of toxic fumes and dust. Health and safety guidelines and regulations must be strictly observed, to protect the operatives, public and the environment. Special care should be taken to wash off or neutralize surfaces as per the manufacturer's instructions. Always obtain data sheets for the preparations that are to be used and study them.

Salts

Cause

Salt staining can result from contaminated groundwater, adjacent concrete/cement mortars, or by reaction of the stone with previous chemical cleaning materials, acidic rainfall, or bird and animal excretions. Direct salt deposition can occur from salted roads, seawater, or via a maritime atmosphere.

Removal

The visible signs of salts are often easily removed by water; however water will also draw more salts to the surface. Salt efflorescence should therefore be removed by dry brushing, and the salts collected and safely disposed of to ensure contamination is not spread. As discussed previously, any treatment of salts will only be successful where the source is identified and dealt with. Once the source has been addressed, poulticing is an effective means of reducing any internal salt content and its visual effects.

Iron and cuprous staining

Cause

Iron staining can occur from oxidizing ferrous fittings, such as hinges and gutter supports, or from hidden internal fixings, such as cramps and dowels. It can also result from dripping or wash-off from ferrous structures above or nearby, such as corrugated roofing or steel beams. Cuprous staining results from copper-salts washed off from oxidizing copper, brass or bronze features, such as copper roofing and brass nameplates, or bronze sculptural elements.

Removal

Effective removal of metallic corrosion products from sandstone usually requires the use of chemical poultices, since the staining can often be absorbed deep into the pore structure. The 'Mora' poultice mix,[12] which contains a chelating agent, ethylenediaminetetraacetic acid (EDTA), is effective, though treating large-scale staining may prove more problematic.

Carbon deposits

Cause

Carbon deposits result in a blackened surface and are associated with industrial pollution (either historic or contemporary), car emissions and domestic coal burning. They may be localized in a fireplace or a building that has burnt down, or be widespread, especially in an urban environment.

Removal

These dark deposits can be removed from sandstone using a variety of methods, including laser cleaning (though this is only suitable for small areas of soiling). More normally, a low pressure water and abrasive system, such as Jos, is used. Whilst this is effective in removing the soiling, it will naturally also remove small amounts of stone. It has been suggested that the removal of surfaces that display carbon soiling and associated mineral absorption may result in accelerated weathering.[13]

Bio-films, lichens, mosses, algae

Cause

Biological growths will colonize areas that can supply adequate moisture, light and nutrition and lie within a suitable range of pH and temperature.[14] Their growth is particularly accelerated where animal or bird droppings accumulate, such as beneath roosting areas, which provide nutrient-rich environments.

Removal

Initial removal of biological growth is best achieved by using wooden tools, such as scrapers and bristle brushes; first dry, and then using wet-brushing and rinsing with water sprays. High pressure water-sprays and hoses should be avoided to minimize the likelihood of damage to hidden areas of decay, and to limit the amount of water driven into the stone. An environmentally 'friendly' biocide may then be used to delay organic re-colonization.

CONSOLIDATION

Consolidants are usually applied as liquids to ensure deep penetration. These then solidify within the pore structure of the stone to attempt to recreate the characteristics of sound stone. Ideally, this process would result in a material that had similar strength, permeability, colour and thermal properties to the original sound stone. Stone consolidants have often tried to mimic the host material's chemistry, so different types have been developed for different stone types. Whilst various resins have been used to attempt to bind and consolidate friable sandstone, most have proven either short lived in their effect or lacking in the penetration required to effect significant change. Vinyls, polyesters, epoxies and polyurethanes have all been tested for use as sandstone consolidants, and all found to be unsuitable for various reasons. In comparison to these, some acrylic resins, such as ethyl methacrylate, are more suitable, being very colour-, heat- and UV-stable, and they are widely used in conservation as adhesives and binders. However, they display poor penetration, and as a result, their benefit outdoors tends to be short lived. Silane-based systems have so far proven to be the most successful means of consolidating sandstone, and these are continuing to be developed and refined. Silane consolidants penetrate deeply into the stone, where they form a silica gel. As the gel dries out, it creates a permeable silica network within the stone's pore system, knitting the stone together. Since silica (SiO_2) is the principal constituent of sandstones, many of these products are now marketed solely as sandstone consolidants. Those most prevalent for use with sandstones are the ones containing tetra-ethoxy silane (ethyl silicate).

Despite early trials with Brethane, an alkoxysilane, the British conservation establishment has tended to be very wary and conservative in its use of silanes, largely because of their irreversible nature, unknown aging characteristics and the possibility of their darkening the stone. In Europe and the United States, however, their use is frequent and widespread. Continental Europe and the Eastern Seaboard of the US undergo vast numbers of freezing/thawing cycles each winter, and far greater extremes of heat and cold annually than are experienced in the UK. This leads to accelerated rates of stone decay, and the need to combat this is therefore seen as all the more urgent. The acceptance of silane use in these locations may therefore correlate with the more extreme environmental conditions experienced.

Whilst silanes may not be ideal, they are the most effective forms of consolidant presently available for sandstone. Over time, the silica formed by silanes can suffer from micro-fracturing, lessening the stone's overall strength and cohesiveness. To combat this, some forms of silane are now available with added elasticizers, to ensure that the silica deposited is flexible and does not fracture on drying.

POINTING AND BEDDING MORTARS

Traditionally, lime mortars would have been used for bedding and pointing of sandstone buildings. These varied in their mixtures, both historically and geographically. The source of the lime, how thoroughly it was processed, and the aggregates and additives used, all varied hugely. Raw materials most often came from very close to the site, and the older and ruder a construction, the more likely the materials were gathered and processed locally. In maritime locations, seashells and beach sand were regularly used as aggregates. Whilst these were readily available, they were also salt laden, and often transferred salts to the associated stone work.

Seashells, especially oyster shells, were also used as packing in random rubble construction, as were slates and thin stones. In certain localities, 'galleting' was used to minimize the exposed areas of broad joints between undressed stones. This involved the insertion of small stones into the wet mortar, and lengthened the life of the pointing by decreasing its surface area, and thus its rate of erosion. A decorative form of this, known as 'cherry pointing' is particularly evident in the northeast of Scotland, where granite was the predominant building material.

When replacing historic mortars, it is usually preferable to use a material as close to the original as possible. To this end, it is often worth taking samples of original mortar to test and analyze. The intention of this analysis is to help 'reverse-engineer' the mortar from its constituent parts. However, whilst it is useful to know what the original mortar consisted of, laboratory tests can tell us little about how it was mixed, stored, applied and tended. It is therefore essential that the contractors used are familiar and confident in the use of lime mortars.

In some cases, matching the original mortar may not be possible or appropriate. Historic mortars incorporating salt-laden components, beach sand for instance, should not be replicated, for obvious reasons.

The choice of lime binder, whether non-hydraulic lime-putty or hydraulic lime, will depend on the hardness and rapidity of set required, and the level of weather exposure expected. Lime putty will usually be the preferred option if the original mortar was non-hydraulic. However, calcium carbonate in lime-putty mortars may react with acid rain to form calcium sulphate, which has on occasion been associated with the decay of neighbouring sandstone. Whilst it is possible for these processes to occur, experience shows them to be rare, provided the mortar is tended properly to ensure thorough carbonation. Sandstone decay is more likely to result from cement gauging or salt-laden aggregate. Natural hydraulic limes have a lower free lime content, so there is less risk of calcium sulphate contamination of the masonry blocks when they are used on sandstone. Hydraulic limes have proven useful on sandstone structures, particularly in Scotland. Their initially rapid set makes them more suitable for use in cold, wet and maritime locations than non-hydraulic mortars

PLASTIC REPAIR

A number of materials have been used for the plastic repair of sandstone in the past, including coloured cement or epoxy-based mortar systems. These have now been largely discredited, due to issues with salts, impermeability and over-hardness. Two very different forms of plastic repair are now in use for repairing sandstone. One is a traditional lime-mortar based repair the other is an acrylic resin-based one.

Lime mortar repairs

Lime mortar, whilst not homogenous to sandstone, can achieve good, long-lasting repairs. The effectiveness of the process is dependent on a number of factors. The aggregate needs to be well graded and colour matched, and the resulting mortar thoroughly mixed. The stone surface requires wetting and preparation, including dovetailing of any edges of the repair site, keying of the surface and the fitting of armature supports where required. The mortar then needs to be applied and tended with an understanding of the material, ensuring that it is not overworked. It requires skilled application, and is time consuming to apply and tend. Colour matching of lime mortar repairs to some sandstones can be particularly difficult, especially the dark red sandstones. The whitening effect of the lime tends to bleach pigments, and can result in patches of repair becoming obviously visible over time.

Resin mortar repairs

Resin mortars are often thought of as interior mortars, though they have been used successfully in outdoor locations. In the past, resin mortars consisted of a mixture of sand and an organic resin, usually shellac, though this tended to darken with age. The modern equivalent is a UV-stable mix of acrylic resin and colour-matched sand. Both these mixes have the advantage of being reversible with the application of a solvent, usually acetone. Resin-based mortars can achieve very good visual matches to the stone, they adhere well, are slightly flexible, and are permeable to an extent. The disadvantages of these mortars are that they have less longevity in exposed locations, and are unsuitable for replacing large masses. Resin mortars can only be relied on to last between two and five years externally, though they may survive much longer in some locations. As a result of such short service-lives, resin mortars are rarely used commercially, and tend to only be practical for those public heritage bodies that can afford to carry out regular and ongoing conservation to their properties.

In conclusion, if the repair site is easily accessible, indoors or very sheltered, an acrylic resin mortar may be ideal. However since such conditions are not the norm, most exterior repairs to sandstone are best effected with lime mortars. Whilst this material requires skill and labour intensive preparation and application, a sound repair can last indefinitely.

The author

Colin Muir BA(Hons), MSc, ACR, FSA Scot.

Colin Muir graduated from Grays School of Art, Aberdeen in 1988 with a BA(Hons) in Sculpture. He obtained an MSc in Architectural Stone Conservation from Bournemouth University, and went on to work for Cliveden Conservation. For the last ten years he has worked throughout Scotland as a Stone Conservator for Historic Scotland. His current role involves the provision of specialist advice and the conservation treatment of sculptural and decorative stonework.

Acknowledgements

Thank you to Jean Marie Muir for her assistance and proofreading. All illustrations are copyright of the author.

References

1   Masonry Conservation Research Group (MCRG), *Stone Cleaning in Scotland, Research Report 1*, Historic Scotland/RGU/ Scottish Enterprise, Edinburgh, 1992, pp. 15–18.

2   Amoroso, G. and Fasina, V., *Stone Decay and Conservation*, Elsevier, Amsterdam, 1983, pp. 33–34.

3   Ashurst J. and Dimes F. (eds.), *Conservation of Building and Decorative Stone Volume 1*, Butterworth-Heinemann, London, 1990, pp. 158–159.

4   Amoroso and Fasina, *op. cit.*, p. 138.

5   MCRG, *op. cit.*, pp. 18–19.

6   Maxwell, I., 'Stone Cleaning, for Better or Worse? An Overview', Webster, R. G. M. (ed.), *Stone Cleaning and the Nature, Soiling and Decay Mechanisms of Stone*, Proceedings of the International Conference held in Edinburgh, UK (14–16 April 1992), Donhead, London, 1992, p. 33.

7   Andrew, C., 'Towards an Aesthetic theory of Building Soiling', Webster, R. G. M. (ed.), *Stone Cleaning and the Nature, Soiling and Decay Mechanisms of Stone* Proceedings of the International Conference held in Edinburgh, UK (14–16 April 1992), Donhead, London, 1992, pp. 63–81.

8   MCRG, *Biological Growths on Sandstone Buildings*, Technical Advice Note (TAN) 10, Technical, Conservation, Research and Education Group (TCRE), Historic Scotland, Edinburgh, 1997, pp. 19–20.

9   Ashurst, N. *Cleaning Historic Buildings*, Volume 1, Donhead, London, 1994, pp. 14–16.

10 www.defra.gov.uk/environment/chemicals/lead/advice3.htm (accessed 12 May 2006).

11 www.health.state.ri.us/lead/environmental/removepaint.php (accessed 12 May 2006).

12 Ashurst, J. and Ashurst, N., *Practical Building Conservation Volume 1: Stone Masonry*, Gower Technical Press, Aldershot, 1988, pp. 74–75.

13 Bluck, B., 'The Composition and Weathering of Sandstone with Relation to Cleaning', Weaver, R. G. M. (ed.), *Stone Cleaning and the Nature, Soiling and Decay Mechanisms of Stone*, Proceedings of the International Conference held in Edinburgh, UK (14–16 April 1992), Donhead, London, 1992, p. 127.

14 Ashurst, N. *Cleaning Historic Buildings*, Volume 1, Donhead, London, 1994, pp. 74–75.

Further reading

Amoroso, G. and Fasina, V., *Stone Decay and Conservation*, Elsevier, Amsterdam, 1983.

Ashurst, J. and Ashurst, N., *Practical Building Conservation,* Volumes 1 and 2, Gower Technical Press, Aldershot, 1988.

Ashurst, N., *Cleaning Historic Buildings, Volumes I and 2,* Donhead, London, 1994.

Caple, C., *Conservation Skills,* Routledge, London, 2003.

Dallas, R., *Measured Survey and Building Recording,* Historic Scotland, Edinburgh, 2003.

GB Geotechnics Ltd, *Non-Destructive Investigation of Standing Structures,* Historic Scotland, Edinburgh, 2001.

Howe, J. A. *The Geology of Building Stones* (reprint of the 1910 edition), Donhead, Shaftesbury, 2001.

Hyslop, E., *The Performance of Replacement Sandstone in the New Town of Edinburgh,* Historic Scotland, Edinburgh, 2004.

Hughes, J. and Valek, J. *Mortars in Historic Buildings,* Historic Scotland, Edinburgh, 2000.

Leary, E., *The Building Sandstones of the British Isles,* B.R.E., Garston, 1986.

Schaffer, R. J, *The Weathering of Natural Building Stones* (reprint of the 1949 edition), Donhead, Shaftesbury, 2004.

Young, Ball, Laine and Urquhart, *Maintenance and Repair of Cleaned Stone Buildings,* TAN25, Historic Scotland, Edinburgh, 2003.

Chapter Eleven

Marble

Jonathan Kemp

INTRODUCTION

Geology

The word 'marble' derives from the Greek 'marmaros', meaning 'shining stone'. There is often confusion about its definition as applied to decorative stones: both the stone industry[1] and Faustino Corsi, an early nineteenth-century geologist and collector (cf. the Corsi Collection of Marbles at the University of Oxford[2]), consider marble to designate all stones composed of calcium carbonate that can take a polish.

In geology, the term has a more specific meaning: marble is a crystalline, compact stone, formed by metamorphosis of limestones that consist primarily of calcite ($CaCO_3$), dolomite ($CaMg\,(CO_3)_2$), or a combination of both minerals. The high temperatures and pressures generated during metamorphosis result in the destruction of any fossils and textures in the original stone and the recrystallization of the calcite and dolomite. It leaves a saccharoidal crystalline structure in the marble that may be relatively isotropic (exhibiting similar properties in all crystallographic directions), or anisotropic (where properties vary when measured in different directions). Stone that has undergone these kinds of metamorphic processes will have their origins in the deepest and oldest layers of the earth's crust, and most marbles are Palaeozoic or pre-Cambrian.

Marble itself might be subject to further metamorphic episodes and geologic upheavals, sometimes being smashed to pieces and then re-cemented to form a brecciated marble, in which distinguishable marble fragments are cemented by silica, calcite or iron oxides in a fine-grained matrix.

The purest form of marble is statuary marble, such as the marbles from Carrara, Italy, which are white. They exhibit relatively strong isotropism, and are composed of pure calcite,[3] resulting from metamorphosis of a very pure limestone. Because calcite has a low index of refraction, light seems to penetrate several millimetres into a pure statuary marble before being scattered out, resulting in a highly prized translucency.

The characteristic array of colours and veining in many marbles are due to the abundance of various mineral impurities; for example, iron oxides and hydroxides (mainly haematite) produce pink, red, orange and brown; diopside results in blue; limonite forms yellow veining; green veins can be from the presence of iron silicates such as chlorite; and black can be the result of traces of graphite derived from organic matter.

Varieties of marble

Some historic marbles, named after the locations of their quarries, include: from Greece, Pentelic (from which the Elgin Marbles from the Parthenon were carved), Thasssos, Carystian, and Parian (all with quarries still active); from Italy, the active quarries of Carrara (used by Michelangelo for *David* and by Canova for *The Three Graces*), and Rosso Verona; Turkey produces, among others, the ancient and highly prized Procconesus marble; and Numidian marble from Tunisia has recently been used for the new portico at The National Gallery in London. Although some of these marbles are still available today, they may differ in quality and appearance from their historic counterparts.[4]

Use of marble

From the canon of extant examples, it appears that the Greeks used marble primarily as building blocks, and for fine sculpture. For example, the Temple of Apollo at Delphi was rebuilt in Parian marble in about 510 BC, and at the Parthenon in Athens Pentelic marble was used for the extensive sculptural pediment friezes (parts of which are the Elgin Marbles in the British Museum).

It was the Romans who first fully exploited marble architecturally, using it both as building blocks and for decorative stonework. Marble slabs were used on a large scale, as, for example, on the Colosseum (AD 69–80), a building of four storeys that exemplified the first-century AD's technical achievements of cladding, concrete and the arch. Emperor Augustus boasted that he found Rome in clay and left it in marble,[5] and many of these buildings survive today. Techniques of marble construction were exported throughout the Mediterranean countries of the Roman Empire.

In Britain, the Romans used indigenous stone for construction and imported marble was only used for sculpture, either by being imported as a finished artefact or in block form to be worked by carvers in the British Isles. Finds from the Temple of Mithras in Londinium (London) include figures carved from Carrara marble, probably made in Italy, and others of marble from Proconnesus in Turkey. For Roman sculptors, marble was a cultural symbol of tradition and refinement,[6] but this tradition was discontinued in Britain after the Romans left in approximately AD 410.

From the late medieval period until the Reformation, alabaster was the medium of choice for religious sculpture in the British Isles, being easier to work and readily available from sources in Nottinghamshire. Important alabaster workshops in Nottingham, York, Burton-on-Trent and London managed to survived after the sixteenth century by focussing on the carving of tombs for the wealthy. Marble was used sporadically for memorials in Britain throughout the medieval period, and with the gradual rediscovery of Classicism in the sixteenth century, combined with a new passion for garden design, the seventeenth century saw a spate of commissions for marble monuments. Marble was used expressively, especially from the 1750s onwards, in both internal and external monu-ments and for architectural embellishments. The most notable solid marble structure is Marble Arch in London, made of white Carrara marble in 1828, to a design by John Nash based on the triumphal arch of Constantine in Rome (Figure 11.1). The first known example of marble used in a façade in the British Isles was in the 1890 building at 101–104 Piccadilly, London, now the Japanese Embassy, with blocks of White Saltern marble from Norway in its façade (Figure 11.2).[7] True calcite marbles have rarely been used for building in the UK; as solid masonry they are too expensive (and there are many good indigenous limestones as alternatives), and as cladding they lose their polish (whereas granite, which is cheaper, retains its finish). Where marble has been used externally, apart from in monuments, is in the detailing of shop fronts. Examples can be seen in Princes Street, Edinburgh, and Tottenham Court Road, St James's Street and Jermyn Street in London (Figures 11.3 and 11.4).

Figure 11.1 Marble Arch, London, *c*.1828.

Figure 11.2 101–104 Piccadilly, London, *c*.1890.

Figure 11.3   Shop front, St James's Street, London, *c.*1946. Italian
Arebescato marble.

Figure 11.4   Shop front, Jermyn Street, London, *c.*1969. Unidentified
green marble.

MARBLE DECAY MECHANISMS

Marble exhibits a narrower range of variability in its mineral composition, textural distinction, degrees of hardness and pore/capillary ratios than many other stones. Whilst it is susceptible to similar modes of decay as other calcareous stones, its relative homogeneity can lead to more significant alterations to its crystalline structure, particularly in strongly anisotropic marbles.

An important decay mechanism affecting marble is thermally induced microcracking. When heated, calcite crystals do not expand equally in all directions. This can cause stress, particularly along grain boundaries, resulting in microcracking. Furthermore, different component minerals exhibit different thermal expansion coefficients: darker minerals will absorb heat more readily and cool more quickly than lighter ones, causing micro-stresses and fracturing along mineral grain boundaries. In addition, grain size, shape and texture influence the degree of disintegration, and any presence of water in the pores further enhances such thermal stressing.

Thermal microcracking increases the porosity of marble. Whilst most marbles, when newly quarried, have very low porosity compared with most limestones and sandstones, an increase in porosity over time due to thermal microcracking enhances water penetration. This increases the susceptibility of marble to deterioration by wetting and drying, by freeze thaw action, and by the crystallization of soluble salts.[8] Increased porosity also increases the effective surface area on which chemical weathering can attack. These physical processes generally weaken the substrate, and eventually lead to granular (or saccharoidal) disintegration.

In a wet or humid climate, the rate of decay is intensified (in drier regions marble can remain resistant to disintegration for far longer) as rain, a naturally weak carbonic acid, reacts with the calcium carbonate to form water soluble calcium bicarbonate that is washed away, resulting in pitting and etching of the marble surface. For this reason, marble installations in wet climates will always lose any polished finish; it also helps to explain why there have been few examples of extensive use of marble externally in the British Isles. This decay process is accelerated in polluted environments, where sulphur dioxide and nitrogen oxide in the atmosphere combine with water to form sulphuric and nitric acids (Figures 11.5–11.7).

If marble is in an exposed position and regularly washed by rain, then the reaction products will be washed away and the surface will recede; if,

Figure 11.5 Detail of etching to marble walling, 101–104 Piccadilly, London.

Figure 11.6 Detail of etched marble surface, Marble Arch, London.

Figure 11.7 Detail of surface erosion and pitting, architectural panel, Whitechapel, London.

however, the stone is sheltered, then any reaction products will accumulate and form gypsum crusts on the surface, often incorporating atmospheric particulates including carbon, which gives the crusts their characteristic blackness (Figure 11.8).[9]

Calcium oxalate is the reaction product of oxalic acid with calcium carbonate, and is widely found as a yellowish skin or patina on marble monuments. It has often been described as a protective epidermis, often known as 'scialbatura', as exemplified on the Parthenon.[10] These skins, specific to marble, are thought to be derived from the incomplete combustion of fossil fuels, biological agents such as lichens (which produce oxalic acid), or, as is often the case with marble monuments in the UK, the transformation of previous oil or wax conservation treatments (Figure 11.9).

Marbles may also be subject to oxidization of accessory minerals. For example, a marble containing pyrite (FeS_2) may suffer from rust spots, with the sulphur being converted to sulphuric acid in the presence of water, which will dissolve calcite and produce pitting.

Cladding with natural stone is not a recent phenomenon, but for the last sixty years, thin sheet cladding with marble has raised questions over its

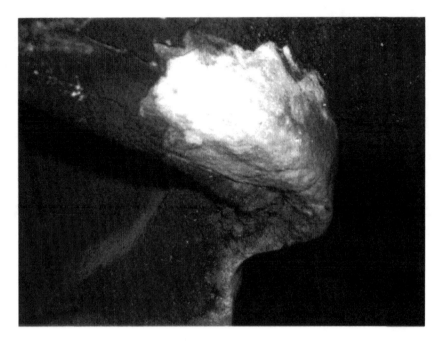

Figure 11.8 Detail of black crust on a figure, Westminster Abbey, London.

Figure 11.9 Detail from Queen Anne Monument, St Paul's, London, *c*.1886, with calcium oxalate patina traces.

durability, due to examples of extreme warping, associated porosity/ volume increases, brittleness, and loss of strength leading to collapse. Expensive re-cladding schemes have been undertaken at the Finlandia Concert Hall, Helsinki, the Amoco Tower, Chicago, and there is an ongoing problem at the University Library building in Göttingen, Germany. In the UK, marble examples on a smaller scale exist, for example some inscriptional panels at Westminster Abbey, and the interior panelling of Aberfeldy Chapel, Scotland. Suggested causes of warping include poor dimensional specification, inappropriate fixing regimes, lithology and inappropriate marble selection, thermal expansion, freeze-thaw cycling, the anisotropic behaviour of calcite, and moisture uptake and hygric expansion.[11]

CONSERVATION OF MARBLE

Cleaning

Mechanical cleaning

Micro-air abrasive systems, in conjunction with abrasive powders of different hardnesses and shapes (for example, soft bicarbonate of soda; rounded grog, harder aluminium oxide, rounded calcite and so on), can be used with circumspection on decorative marble (they have been used to remove black crusts/gypsum and calcite deposits), but with the injunction in mind that abrasive particles fired at velocity cannot differentiate between dirt accretions and marble substrate. Pressures should be kept low (<20 psi/2 bars), and a small nozzle size (1.5 mm) is recommended for optimum results (i.e. efficient removal with minimum damage to substrate).

Water cleaning

Where soiling is water-soluble, steam cleaning and nebulized sprays, followed by soft brushing can be used, with the provision of suitable water run-off/suppression apparatus. Non-ionic detergents are sometimes used, as are de-ionized water poultices for some stain removals and the softening of crusts. Steam cleaning with a conservation grade pencil cleaner is a very effective method for removing many biological accretions, but caution is urged as prolonged steam-jet contact time can induce thermal micro-cracking to the marble, whatever its condition.

In the case of desalination, poulticing with de-ionized water can be disadvantageous if elements are still attached to the parent structure, as the process may mobilize soluble salts from deeper within the structure, and fail to tackle the source of contamination. Poulticing using clay-based materials, paper pulps and cellulose fibres have been used, and the resulting reduction in salt levels monitored by salt conductivity testing. In the case of efflorescent salts, their removal with vacuum cleaners or brushing away (provided the detritus is collected and removed from site to prevent their redistribution by rainfall) is sufficient treatment, although they should also be taken as potentially indicative of subfluorescent salt deposits.

Chemical cleaning

Chemical cleaning techniques on marble should be used with caution. Chemical complexing or sequestering agents, such as EDTA and ammonium citrate, have been used in poultices for rust reduction, salt removal, and iron and copper stain removal from marble. However it should be remembered that poultices containing chelating agents cannot distinguish between the stain and the substrate itself, and so can affect both if used without caution.

Poulticing to remove sulphation from marble with ammonium carbonate should be executed with care. Percentage test poultices made with de-ionized water and cellulose paper pulp in discrete test areas (typically 5–20% ammonium carbonate in de-ionized water) should be carried out by a qualified conservator before any large works are embarked on. The ammonium carbonate reacts with the calcium sulphate to form calcium carbonate and soluble ammonium sulphate, which must then be rinsed off thoroughly with water. Pre-wetting helps prevent the entry of the solution into the substrate. Again, caution must be exercised, because although ammonium compounds leave no salts themselves, they can oxidize other minerals such as pyrites, which will result in the deposition of harmful sulphates.

Generally, alkaline cleaners should be avoided when considering the cleaning of marble. Their use can introduce chemical complexes to the surface that might condition future reactions through their continued interaction with the environment.

Laser cleaning

In recent years. laser cleaning systems have been developed for use in external environments, and although cleaning rates for large surface areas are often uneconomic, they are commonly used for the cleaning of architectural details, and have the advantage of being able to retain patinas and any extant scialbatura. There have been problems in cleaning some substrates using infrared wavelengths, which can cause marble to discolour, and also in removing some darker pigmented lichen/fungi containing melanins and carotenes, which can be burned into the crystal matrix by the laser, resulting in black staining. Caution must be exercised where polychromy is suspected, as lasers can discolour some pigments such as vermillion. Recent developments with lasers include the testing of the combination of ultraviolet light with the standard Q-switched Nd:YAG laser, which avoids marble substrate discolouration.[12]

Biocides and biochemicals

Biocides can be used to eliminate and prevent future bioinfestations, but they are the subject of strong debate, and furthermore the choice of the correct biocide is complex. They can be useful to facilitate the removal of the biological growth and to hinder recolonization. However, large doses of caution and testing should be applied, as biocides treatments can discolour marbles (and other light stones) and aid in certain pigment releases from bio-infestations. For example, products containing quaternary ammonium salts can produce staining in the marble if used on some black cyano-bacteria layers, and biocides in general, including borate-based biocides (such as Wykabor 10), might produce a temporary discolouration.

Biochemical compounds of microbacteria and enzymes have been used in tests for the elimination of insoluble calcium oxalate patinas from monuments, because some bacteria use the oxalate salts as their sole source of carbon and energy. Biomineralization has been investigated, using specific biological molecules in order to re-precipitate new calcite crystals to improve the stone's superficial mechanical strength, and also to find non-pathogenic organisms that will destroy salt crusts.[13] The treatment of sulphation by gypsum inversion has been implemented, using recarbonation pastes of ion exchangers that replace the sulphate with carbonate ions.[14]

Consolidation

Pre-consolidation and surface consolidation

Treatment may be required to secure flakes of stone or pigment, or to stabilize a surface before dismantling an object or removing it from site, or before another conservation technique, such as cleaning, is carried out. Pre-consolidation is often carried out in conjunction with temporary facing-up of vulnerable surfaces with acid-free tissue paper. Common pre-consolidants used on marble are acrylic co-polymers (such as Paraloid B72) in concentrations of 5–10% in solvent, although colour changes can sometimes occur. Polyvinyl acetate (PVA), if used in a viscous solution, can have poor penetration and be brittle; but if it is used in a sufficiently low concentration to achieve good penetration it is too weak to have significant consolidating effect. Polyvinylalcohols (PVAls such as Mowlith DM477, formerly DMC2) and acrylic dispersions (Primal B60A for instance) are often used for temporary facing-up operations, as the former is reversible in water and the latter in acetone. However, if left for too long in bright and hot conditions, PVAl can crosslink and become more insoluble and therefore more difficult to remove.

The acrylic co-polymer Paraloid B72 has also been used extensively on marble as a surface consolidant, especially in Italy. A long-term study in Rome raised concerns that incomplete impregnation could form distinct interfaces between treated and untreated areas, thereby creating new zones of stress. There is also empirical evidence of darkening of marble through its use.[15]

Deep consolidation

It is the silane family that is most frequently used on stone for deep consolidation, with two compounds being dominant: methyltrimethoxysilane, MTMOS, and tetraethoxysilane (TEOS) on its own, or mixed with other alkyl-alkoxy silanes (commercial products include Dow Corning Z6070 and Wacker Silres BS OH 100). Originally developed for sandstones, they have been used surprisingly successfully on marble. Many investigations have centred on the poor adhesion between calcite and the silicon polymer in silanes when used on limestones. However, for marbles the most common form of decay is granular disintegration; and as marble is largely made of calcite grains in direct contact with no cementing agent, its porosity is low (even in the case of decayed marble). Furthermore, as the shape of the intergranular spaces is anistropic, the alkoxysilane solutions enter these spaces, gel, and then shrink, and, although they do not adhere to the grains, they can nearly fill the entire space, preventing the grains from being removed mechanically.[16]

Many experiments have been carried out with acrylic polymer/ alkoxysilane mixes, including Racanello E55050, a mix of Paraloid B72 and MTMOS, and what is known as the 'Bologna cocktail' (Paraloid B72 together with Dri-Film 104), a partially pre-polymerized alkoxysilane and solvent. Sometimes they have achieved a near regal status in their application to limestone and marble sculptures in museums and externally in, for example, Bologna, Italy. This stemmed from the idea that Paraloid B72 adds the adhesive and gap bridging properties that an alkoxysilane lacks. However this composite gel is now considered to be weaker than neat MTMOS gel, and the acrylic polymer is thought to inhibit the hydrolysis of the silane ester due to its hydrophobic properties.[17]

Perfluoropolyethers were investigated in the 1980s and 1990s for their suitability for use on marble, but found to be unstable and lacking cohesion, with a mobility that inhibits performance over time. However, they do seem to have better results in low porosity stones (in the 1990s they were experimented with by the National Trust for England's Statuary Workshop). They are now used as the basis for some anti-graffitti treatments and some water repellents – their addition to acrylic and acrylate/ methacrylate co-polymers is also being investigated.[18]

The use of the inorganic consolidant calcium hydroxide $Ca(OH)_2$ (limewater) has been attempted on some marble surfaces, e.g. the Library of Hadrian at Athens in 1992, but with no published results. Because of marble's low porosity, and the poor solubility of calcium hydroxide in water combined with the lack of CO_2 at depth, limewater seems an unlikely candidate for the consolidation of marble. However experiments to improve stability and solubility have been conducted with the dispersion of $Ca(OH)_2$ in propan-1-ol. Furthermore, research is being carried out on marble items from the Ince Blundell Collection, Liverpool, by the Polymer and Surface Chemistry Group, Loughborough University, England. They propose to develop an approach to consolidation based on 'charge stabilized colloidal calcite and the nucleation and growth of calcite crystals directly onto the internal surfaces of weathered calcite from Calcium Hydroxide solutions in the presence of carbon dioxide'.[19]

Another proposal for the consolidation of marble has been to use ammonium oxalate on gypsum free surfaces to produce a calcium oxalate protective layer (because of the relative insolubility of the oxalates weddellite and whewellite).[20]

Structural repairs

Replacement of ferrous fixings is a common conservation operation when dealing with marble structures, particularly in the case of wall monuments. Generally, new fixings should be grade 316 anti-corrosion stainless steel that re-use, as far as possible, old fixing holes. Other fixing materials that might be considered are carbon fibre (e.g. on isolated items of elongated shape, such as fingers) and slate, where, in a like-for-like regime, old slate fixings are to be replaced.

Stainless steel and carbon fibre fixings can be adhered to their mount points with polyester resin, epoxy resin or methacrylate resin. Coating fixing holes with an acrylic co-polymer such as Paraloid B72 will aid later reversibility (although the structural requirements of the fixing should be evaluated, as the exothermic curing of a polyester resin will reach a minimum of 115°C, which can compromise the acrylic co-polymer). Slate dowels can be fixed with a lime-based mortar.

Pointing and surface fills

Pointing

Pointing should be carried out with softer sacrificial lime mortars, which are more permeable and flexible than the marble. Hard mortars impart mechanical stresses to marble through the inhibition of its effective thermal expansion, and so stress cracking and bowing may result. Mixes of 3:1 aggregate to lime putty, with or without the addition of softer pozzolans depending on the degree of exposure expected, are recommended. The use of hydraulic lime gauging to impart increased strength to non-hydraulic lime putty has been a common, though questionable, practice, with some doubts over longevity and is discouraged by some authorities. However, the use of natural hydraulic limes such as NHL 2 and NHL 3.5 may be appropriate in exposed or aggressive situations.

Surface fills

Surface repairs can be carried out with suitable lime mixes, with the addition of earth pigments for colour and tone matches. Such mortars are a good match for opaque, weathered marble, and they are durable in an external environment. However, for fine cracks and fissures, lime mortars are often too coarse. Instead there has been a tendency to use acrylic co-polymers (e.g. Paraloid B72), in percentages between 15–25% (the lower concentration sometimes used for initial penetration, followed by the more viscous solution), mixed with acetone (though IMS, ethanol or white spirit can be used where slower evaporation rates are required), combined with various fillers, such as onyx or glass microballoons, and colour matched earth pigments. This technique can be useful for small fills as it provides a good match for unweathered marble, but it is not suitable generally for external use because there are durability issues to consider.

Epoxy fills are not recommended for external use because of their general irreversibility and deterioration under ultraviolet light. They can be used in structural fixings, where they remain hidden from the surface, and occasionally they might find use in below-surface adhesive gap filling. The coating of all substrate joints with an acrylic co-polymer (e.g. Paraloid B72) is recommended to prevent resin creep and to aid reversibility, and the epoxy material should remain below surface level to enable capping by a mortar or acrylic co-polymer fill.

Preventative conservation

Hydrophobic coatings

Hydrophobic coatings have been applied to stone for centuries to reduce water ingress – limewashes with admixes (e.g. tallow), waxes, linseed oil mixes (producing the typical orange-yellow oxalate staining in marble described above), as well as more recent adventures in alkoxysilane, silicone, fluorinated acrylic, and fluoropolymer based water repellents. Marble, because of its low porosity and relative compactness, is rarely treated hydrophobically, except where it is consolidated, in which case hydrophobicity is a design component of the consolidant (e.g. Wacker SILRES® BS OH 100, which also might prevent some bio-infestations).

The use of microcrystalline wax coatings externally as a hydrophobic treatment is inadvisable, because they reduce the permeability of marble further still and inhibit the movement of moisture that might contain soluble salts which would become trapped. Furthermore, microcrystalline waxes are generally unstable in ultraviolet light.

New decay phenomena can begin soon after the completion of any conservation programme, and monitoring and maintenance regimes should therefore be considered. Many potential macro strategies can be executed that positively influence the conditions in which the item is situated, including environmental planning, traffic management and community adoption schemes.

The author

Jonathan Kemp BA(Hons), PGDip, MSc, CGLI

Since graduating in 1989 from the PGDip Stone Conservation course at Weymouth College, Jonathan Kemp has worked extensively on a range of movable and immovable cultural objects dating from between around 2000 BC to the twentieth century, made of stone, plaster, fresco, ceramic, artificial stone and metals. He has worked as a senior conservator and consultant to both public and private collections and has worked internationally on projects in Spain and Ukraine. He has trained students and graduates of various nationalities and from various institutions and has taught stone conservation to under/post graduate students at The City & Guilds London Art School. He has recently been appointed to the V&A Museum, London.

Acknowledgements

My thanks go to Graciela Ainsworth (private conservator, Edinburgh) and Vanessa Simeoni (Head Conservator, Westminster Abbey, London) for invaluable discussions.

References

1   www.qmj.co.uk/nss/stoneexplained/marble.htm (accessed 2 May 2006).

2   For some examples of classical descriptions of antique marbles see: Corsi, F., *Delle Pietre Antiche*, Toscanelli, Rome, 1845; Porter, M. W., *What Rome was built of,* Henry Frowde, London & Oxford, 1907; Hull, E., *A Treatise on the Building and Ornamental Stones of Great Britain and Foreign Countries,* Macmillan & Co., London, 1872; Merrill, G. P. *Stones for Building and Decoration*, 3rd. edition, John Wiley & Sons, New York, 1903; www.oum.ox.ac.uk (accessed 2 May 2006).

3   The common mineral pure calcite is a crystalline form of calcium carbonate, $CaCO_3$, formed hexagonally and colourless or white when pure, but of almost any colour because of the presence of a range of impurities. It can be transparent, translucent, or opaque as well as vitreous or dull; many crystals, especially the colourless ones, are vitreous, whereas granular masses, especially those that are fine-grained, tend to be dull. Three perfect cleavages give calcite its six-sided polyhedrons, with diamond shaped faces; the angles defining the faces are 78 and 102 degrees – this means that when light passes through, it is split into two rays that travel at different speeds, and in different directions – a phenomenon known as birefringence. Calcite exhibits double refraction that can be observed with the naked eye, and William Nicol in 1828 found that by cutting the crystals in the appropriate direction, one could make an optical device which eliminated one of the rays and permitted the other to emerge as plane polarized light. This allowed the creation of a technology that was used in microscopes and applied to the study of minerals. Concomitantly, crystallography also developed from the study of the cleavage and crystal forms of calcite.

4   For more information, see the UK stone trade standard reference book, *Natural Stone Directory*, QMJ Publishing Ltd, a directory of suppliers of all stones in the UK, including marbles with colour plates and descriptions. More readily accessible is 'The Stone Network', an on-line resource site for the stone industry and allied professions at http://stone-network.com (accessed 2 May 2006), with a marble image portal at http://stone-network.com/marble.html (accessed 2 May 2006). Frederick Bradley's *Fine Marble in Architecture*, (Studio Marmo W.W. Norton & Company, New York, 2001) is a lavish guide outlining the technical characteristics of marble, and giving information about its production, historical use, and suppliers, and includes photographic samples of sixty varieties, including a gallery of their use in buildings. The Corsi Collection and the Natural History Museum's Building and Decorative Stones Collection are also invaluable resources to visit, details online at www.oum.ox.ac.uk/collect/minpet.htm (accessed 16 June 2006), and www.nhm.ac.uk/research-curation/collections/departmental-collections/mineralogy-collections/rocks/building-decorative-stones.html (accessed 2 May 2006).

5   www.geopolymer.org/science_archaeology/roman_cement_concrete/high_durable_buildings.html (accessed 2 May 2006).

6   Vitruvius, *The Ten Books of Architecture*, translated by Morgan, M. H., Dover Publications, New York, 1960, Book X Chapter 2 Sections 15 p. 15 'I will digress a bit and explain how these stone-quarries were discovered. Pixodorus was a shepherd who lived in that vicinity. When the people of Ephesus were planning to build the Temple of Diana in marble, and debating whether to get the marble from Paros, Proconnesus, Heraclea, or Thassos, Pixodorus drove out his sheep and was feeding his flock in that very spot. Then two rams ran at each other, and, each passing the other, one of them, after his charge, struck his horns against a rock, from which a fragment of extremely white colour was dislodged. So it is said that Pixodorus left his sheep in the mountains and ran down to Ephesus carrying the fragment, since that very thing was the question of the moment. Therefore they immediately decreed honours to him and changed his name, so that instead of Pixodorus he should be called Evangelus. And to this day the chief magistrate goes out to that very spot every month and offers sacrifice to him, and if he does not, he is punished.'

7   Robinson, E., *London: Illustrated Geological Walks* Vols. 1 and 2, Scottish Academic Press, Edinburgh, 1985, Vol.2, p. 89.

8   See discussions in: Zesig, A., Weiss, T. and Siegemund, S., *Thermal Expansion and its Control on the Durability of Marble*, Geological Society Special Publications 205, London, 2002, pp. 57–72; Weiss, T. *et al*, 'Weathering of stones caused by thermal expansion, hygric properties and freeze-thaw cycles', in *Proceedings from the 10th International Congress on the Deterioration and Conservation of Stone*, Stockholm, 2004, Vol. 1, pp. 83–90; Hansen, K. K. and Vardinghus-Nielsen, K., 'The influence of microstructure on properties of marble', in *Proceedings from the 10th International Congress on the Deterioration and Conservation of Stone*, Stockholm, 2004, Vol. 1, pp. 139–146.

9   Moroni, B. and Poli, G., 'The Weathering of Marble and Calcereous breccia in the Lateral Facade of Foligno Cathedral: Influence of Lithology and Role of Exposure', in *Proceedings from the 8th International Congress on the Deterioration and Conservation of Stone*, Berlin, 1996. Vol. 1, pp. 121–134.

10 www.thebritishmuseum.ac.uk/gr/kouzelicompositionpaper.pdf (accessed 2 May 2006).

11 See: *Testing and Assessment of Marble and Limestone. State of the art report Task 1.2* TEAM – A European research project within EU's 5th Framework Program – Competitive and Sustainable Growth (GROWTH) (2000–2005) interim report 2001 (a literature survey of 190 papers on the causes and mechanisms of marble warping); Koch, A., 'Browning of marble panels: on-site damage analysis from the University Library Building at Göttingen, Germany', in *Proceedings from the 10th International Congress on the Deterioration and Conservation of Stone*, Stockholm, 2004, Vol. 1, pp. 171–178.

12 For a basic summary of laser cleaning see Cooper, M., www.ihbc.org.uk/context_archive/72/laser/cleaning.html (article 2001) (accessed 2 May 2006); for development cited see: Frantzikiaki, K., *et al*, 'The cleaning of the Parthenon West Frieze: an innovative laser methodology', in *Proceedings from the 10th International Congress on the Deterioration and Conservation of Stone*, Stockholm, 2004, Vol. 2, pp. 801–807; also Cooper, M., 'Laser Cleaning of Sculpture, Monuments and Architectural Detail, in Normandin, K. and Slaton, D. (eds.), *Cleaning Techniques in Conservation Practice*, Donhead, Shaftesbury, 2005.

13 See for example: Lal, Gauri K. and Chowdrey, A. N., 'Experimental studies on conversion of gypsum to calcite by microbes', in *Proceedings from the 6th International Congress on the Deterioration and Conservation of Stone*, Torun, 1988, Vol. II, pp. 545–550; Ranalli, G., *et al*, 'The use of microorganisms for the removal of nitrate and organic substances on artistic stoneworks', in *Proceedings from the 8th International Congress on the Deterioration and Conservation of Stone*, Berlin, 1996, Vol. III, pp. 1421–1427; and www.biobrush.org (accessed 2 May 2006).

14 For example, see Protz, A., 'The cleaning of the Hirschfeld tomb by recarbonation of gypsum crust', in *Proceedings from the 8th International Congress on the Deterioration + Conservation of Stone* Berlin, 1996, Vol. III, pp. 1387–1393.

15 Roby, T. C., '*In situ* assessment of surface consolidation and protective treatment of marble monuments in Rome in the 1980s, with particular reference to two treatments with paraloid B72', in *Proceedings from the 8th International Congress on the Deterioration and Conservation of Stone* Berlin, 1996, Vol. II, pp. 1015–1029.

16 Wheeler, G., *Alkoxysilanes and the Consolidation of Stone*, The Getty Conservation Institute, Los Angeles, 2005, pp. 45–46.

17 Wheeler, G., Wolkow, E., Gafney, H., 'Microstructures of B72 acrylic resin/MTMOS composite', in Vandiver, P. (ed.), *Materials in Art and Archaeology 3*, Materials Research Society Proceedings 267, Pittsburgh, 1992, pp. 963–967; and researches carried out at San Marco Basilica in Venice evaluating

the recent past use of the Bologna Cocktail (in 1982–86 and 1996–98) – among other observations was that the methylsilicone was partially still soluble, reducing its consolidant effects – see Vigato, P., 'Science and Technology for Cultural Heritage at Institute of Inorganic and Surface Chemistry', in *Mediterranean Magazine,* March 2004, www.dai3cnr.net/pdf/ magazine_1_04.pdf (accessed 2 May 2006). See also: Haake, S. and Simon, S., 'The Bologna Cocktail – evaluation of consolidation treatments on monuments in France and Italy after 20 years of natural aging', in *Proceedings from the 10th International Congress on the Deterioration and Conservation of Stone,* Stockholm, 2004, Vol. 1, pp. 423–430.

18   Chiantore, O., Poli, T. and Aglietto, M., 'Effect of fluorinated groups on photo-oxidative stability of polymeric protectives applied to calcereous stone', in *Proceedings from the 9th International Congress on the Deterioration and Conservation of Stone,* Venice, 2000, pp. 215–223.

19   Larson, J. H, Madden, C. E. and Sutherland, I., 'Ince Blundell: the preservation of an important collection of classical sculpture', *Journal of Cultural Heritage,* Vol. 1, 2000, pp. 79–87.

20   Matteini, M., Moles, A. and Giovannoni, S., 'Calcium oxalate as a protective mineral system for wall paintings: methodology and analyses', in Zezza, F. (ed.), *Proceedings from the First International Symposium on Conservation of Monuments in the Mediterranean Basin,* Grafo, Brescia, Italy, 1989, pp. 155–62. See also two student projects: Todd, K., *Calcium oxalate as a protector of marble',* California State Science Fair, 2004, Project SO514 www.usc.edu/CSSF/History/2004/Projects/S0514.pdf (accessed 2 May 2006); Cezar, T., 'Calcium oxalate: a surface treatment for limestone' in *Journal of Conservation and Museum Studies,* 1998, No. 4. http://palimpsest.stanford.edu/jcms/issue4/cezar.html (accessed 2 May 2006).

Further reading

Bradley, F., *Fine Marble in Architecture,* Studio Marmo W.W. Norton & Company, New York, 2001. www.archinform.net/index.htm – international database of architecture.

Dubarry de Lassal, J., *Identifying Marble,* H. Vial Editions, Dourdnan, France, 2000.

Guilding, R., *Marble Mania: sculpture galleries in England 1640–1840,* Sir John Soane's Museum, London, 2001.

Chapter Twelve

Polychrome Stone

Christopher Weeks

INTRODUCTION

The conservation of polychrome stone on the outside of buildings and inside churches is a comparatively recent and specialized discipline within conservation. What is unusual about the problems associated with polychrome stone? Are there a set of common practices in this area among conservators, and are there any deficiencics?

This chapter focuses upon medieval, decoratively painted exterior stonework, particularly post eleventh-century northern European church façades, and interior stonework including sculpture in churches and cathedrals, such as reredos, rood screens and choir screens, monuments and chantries.[1] British funerary monuments of the fourteenth to seventeenth centuries are also of particular interest. Examples outside northern Europe and Britain cannot be explored here.

MONUMENTAL POLYCHROMY IN MEDIEVAL AND
RENAISSANCE CULTURE

The debate surrounding historic polychromy on monumental and architectural sculpture in stone is resurgent today. It is now widely known that most pre-modern western architecture and sculpture in stone would once have been decorated with paint.[2] This is true from the earliest civilizations through the Classical and medieval periods, the Middle Ages, the Renaissance, the Age of Enlightenment, and even the industrial age (albeit as an antiquarian interest allied to the growth of scientific archaeology). It is true despite the existence of traditions counter to the norm, such as neoclassicism in Romanesque sculpture in Italy,[3] or the late

Gothic art exemplified by the work of Tilman Riemenschneider.[4] As Sauerländer suggests in a recent essay, it is indeed 'curious' that the debate about the nature and role of polychromy in sculpture is so markedly absent from the vast bibliography on Romanesque and Gothic sculpture that appeared between 1920 and 1970.[5] The struggle to interpret the scant survivals is clearly seen in recent reviews.[6] In Europe there is, perhaps, too little stone polychromy remaining for detailed stylistic comparison. To add to the confusion, the complexity of the cultural significance and interpretation of colour is now being exposed by historians.[7]

The discoveries associated with contemporary conservation documentation have even begun to shake our assumptions regarding those periods of history during which it was previously thought that paint played no role in Western sculpture. Fifteenth-century Renaissance church monuments in Florence, for example, retain many traces of polychromy, albeit of an eclectic nature fitting to the period.[8] During conservation assessment of eighteenth-century wall monuments in the cloisters at Westminster Abbey, grey washes were found to have been applied, apparently to enhance chiaroscuro effects.[9]

POLYCHROMY TECHNIQUES AND STYLE

Those in search of original treatises relating to polychrome sculpture techniques from the classical or medieval periods will find the great majority of sources silent on the subject, or at best ambiguous.[10] Instead we are forced to rely on plentiful physical, quantitative data, such as petrology, pigments, media, and techniques, published and unpublished, collected by conservators, historians and scientists, particularly during the last twenty-five years. Several writers have attempted to rationalize and interpret this data across various geographical areas.[11]

Because degraded, dirty and discontinuous paint layers are extremely hard to interpret visually, the importance to the conservator of familiarity with the materials and techniques of historic polychromy cannot be overstated. Figure 12.1 shows how complex the simplest of remains may be. Thankfully, the techniques of wall painting, panel painting and painting on sculpture in the Middle Ages are closely related, and, in northern Europe at least, according to Howard, independent of substrate.[12] With regard to porous supports, such as wood, stone and plaster, this may be true, but less porous stones were prepared and painted differently. Techniques of alabaster painting in England during the later Middle Ages

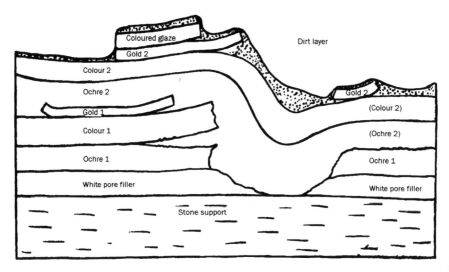

Figure 12.1   Diagram of typical cross section through simple polychromy remains on limestone or sandstone.

sometimes took clear account of the translucency of the stone;[13] and south of the Alps, where the use of white marble for sculpture was common throughout the medieval period, the intrinsic beauty of the stone, and perhaps its antiquarian interest, militated for a more partial polychromy.[14]

Practicalities impinge forcefully upon style and technique. The porosity of the stone dictated the nature of its preparation. The very open, porous limestones and sandstones of northern and central-western Europe were commonly prepared with a white ground layer containing white lead, sometimes referred to as pore-filler (*bouche-pores*). Preparation of this kind is not a prerequisite for painting on marble or alabaster. Such preparatory layers are associated with full polychromy, where the 'picture layers' cover the entire sculpture. Picture layers were applied over the pore-filler and, often, over supplementary coloured preparatory layers. These would have been mixed from the cheaper pigments, such as ochres, and sometimes admixtures with red or white lead. There is every indication that the subtlety of hue these colours gave the picture layers was fully appreciated by the artists; for instance red preparation for flesh tones, or red or black beneath azurite (blue).[15] Twelfth-century texts such as Suger's *De Administratione* or the *Eight Marian Homilies* of Amadeus of Lausanne evoke this sensibility.[16]

What did medieval polychrome sculpture look like in context? Church monuments are relatively small, and the descriptions of paint survivals in the conservation literature are very evocative of the original whole. Some idea of the level of sophistication in colour and texture is given by the fifteenth-century polychromed limestone effigies of William Fitzalan and Joan Nevill, in the Fitzalan Chapel, Arundel (Figure 12.2). But with regard to objects on an architectural scale, the literature is often short on qualitative assessment. There have been, nevertheless, attempts to marry minute archaeological and analytical observation with qualitative evocations of past paint schemes.[17] For the twelfth and thirteenth centuries, the well preserved ensembles at Senlis, Lausanne and Vezzolano (the rood screen on the interior of the church) are very evocative. The stylized faces are highly coloured and refined. The draperies are extremely complex: garments lined in contrasting colours, especially green and red; imitation embroidery, painted or in applied relief over coloured or gilded grounds; gilded or otherwise decorated hems; colour and modelling built in successive, often translucent, layers. The play of colour contrast often extended to the background stonework, with successive registers of sculpture set against each other. Mouldings were emphasized with contrasting colours or metal leaf. The well preserved stonework in the sanctuary of Westminster Abbey (fourteenth century) gives us an idea of just how elaborate the decoration of sculpture could be. With every surface painted, and in some instances large portions of the entire façade, the overall impression would have been fairly overwhelming.[18] Changes in costume fashion or architectural decoration are reflected, even in restoration schemes, such as that dating from the late fifteenth century at Amiens' *Portail de la Mère Dieu*.[19]

Inside churches, paint schemes could be more or less complex. Fictive ashlar work is common throughout the medieval period. Fragments of painted stone from the interior of the Benedictine Priory in Coventry give some indication of how elaborate interior polychromy could be.[20] A study of the interior of Chartres Cathedral relates the polychrome interiors to the original stained glass.[21]

The elaborate polychromy of medieval architectural sculpture was at least equalled by that of English church monuments. Increasingly elaborate tombs and chantry chapels were constructed by the wealthy between the fourteenth and seventeenth centuries. Some still retain very elaborate polychromy, although these tend to be the earlier examples.[22] During the sixteenth and seventeenth centuries, under the influence of Italian artistic fashion, the use of decorative stones in construction became ubiquitous, and with it the style of painting changed. Indigenous stones such as alabaster, slate or Purbeck limestone were valued for their intrinsic beauty. Alabaster was commonly used in large quantities. It is interesting that the

Figure 12.2   The fifteenth-century polychromed limestone effigy of Joan Nevill, in the Fitzalan Chapel, Arundel. Illustrated above are the draperies over the feet with applied wax brocades. (courtesy of The Norfolk Estate)

effigy, the other human figures and the heraldic devices were generally fully polychrome, whereas the aedicule, the architectural structure, was painted in a more continental style: mouldings, fillets and sometimes inscriptions were picked-out with oil gilding; foliage and flowers, perhaps, naturalistically painted on a white preparatory layer. The parochial nature and apparent ubiquity of Tudor funerary monuments in England has resulted in a startling disregard for their conservation, particularly in relation to their polychromy, which is very poorly understood and documented. While the horrors of over-painting may be receding, the quality of conservation work in this area requires closer scrutiny.

Recently, a full catalogue of pigments identified to date on medieval façades in France has been published.[23] This and other sources indicate that the pigments encountered on polychrome stone, outdoors and in, are as varied as those in any other art form. During the pre-industrial period, these included the blues lapis-lazuli or natural ultramarine, azurite, artificial copper blues,[24] and, during the later Middle Ages, smalt[25] and indigo[26]; the reds vermilion, red ochre, red lead, red lake; the whites white lead, lime or chalk and bone white; the greens malachite, green earth, verdigris, and copper resinate; and blacks. Yellow, commonly yellow ochre, was rarely used decoratively, although orpiment and lead tin yellow have been found on the West Fronts of Salisbury and Exeter Cathedrals respectively. Pigments with poor covering power were sometimes mixed with white lead (e.g. azurite). Oil and water gilding were both used extensively, often as a ground for other paint layers.[27] Tin and silver leaf, applied over a thick mordant, rarely survive; the organic glazes with which their use would often have been associated (in the case of silver to obviate its immediate corrosion) have not been found on exterior sculpture.[28] Even lead leaf was used.[29] Glazes such as red lake are very delicate and rarely encountered, though their widespread use, to subtle effect, can be inferred from other media and from those fragments that do survive.[30] Green copper resinate glazes used over verdigris and white lead are very common.

The media with which pigment was bound in the Middle Ages was very varied, often even on the same object. Although animal proteins predominated, wax, resins and oils, alone or in admixture, appear early in the record, oil having been identified on twelfth-century sculptures at Bourges, for example.[31] It is often extremely difficult positively to identify ancient binding media, as the polymers may be degraded or largely depleted through leaching, or through digestion by micro organisms. This depletion is not often uniform, and poses great problems for the conservator, as we shall see.

DISTRIBUTION OF POLYCHROMED FAÇADES IN EUROPE

The best surviving examples of medieval exterior polychromy on stone are to be found in France (for example, Senlis, Amiens),[32] Switzerland (Lausanne, Bern),[33] Italy (Baptistery at Parma, Portal of St Andrew at Vercelli),[34] and Spain (Toro).[35] Almost nothing comparable survives in Britain. Whilst the humid climate of the British Isles has played a role in the dearth of surviving medieval polychromy, there are other factors to consider.

In France, for example, grand churches from the late twelfth-century onward were designed with deeply recessed western portals, the gigantic central porch of Amiens Cathedral being a case in point, which is extensively decorated with limestone sculpture in three-quarter relief on every surface and at every level. There is no doubt that the design of such porches has contributed to a considerable degree to the protection and survival of their polychromy. By stark contrast, the West Front of Salisbury Cathedral, precisely contemporary to that of Amiens, is a fine example of a flat, 'curtain' façade, upon which the sculptures are cruelly exposed to the weather.

Similarly, the vicissitudes of history have been relatively unkind to buildings in Britain, where religious upheaval saw a great proportion of our ecclesiastical sculpture defaced, vandalized, or simply destroyed. Calvinistic currents in religious politics in sixteenth-century Switzerland led to the painted portal of Lausanne being whitewashed, and incidentally, preserved more or less intact. Italy, having escaped Protestant purges, also enjoys a kinder climate and more resilient natural stone. In Germany, eastern Europe, and the Iberian peninsula, the renewal of elaborate paint schemes has remained a lively tradition until very recently. In this manner for example, the original polychromy of the west portal of the cathedral of Toro, for example, had been preserved beneath layers of overpaint until its restoration, completed in 1994.

Nineteenth-century restoration plays an ambiguous role in the preservation of early paint schemes. In Britain, perhaps more than anywhere else in Europe, the ancient vestiges of paint on architectural edifices were not respected, a fact amongst others that led directly to the 'anti-scrape' campaigns of Ruskin and Morris. Viollet le Duc, ubiquitous French architect of *Monuments Historiques* appears, when charged with its preservation, to have taken a singularly conservative approach to ancient paint.[36]

THE CONTEMPORARY STATE OF PRESERVATION OF PAINTED STONE

How, then, does historic polychromy on stone appear today? Except in unusual cases, it is not easy to spot. This is due to the chemical degradation (colour change) of pigments and binding media, as well as to the physical degradation of the paint layer and its underlying support. An example of thirteenth-century polychromy in an outdoor location, and in typical condition, is shown in Figure 12.3.

The discolouration of certain pigments over time and in specific conditions is well documented. Thus, for example, red lead (minium, Pb_3O_4) can sulphate or oxidize and turn brown-black. Vermilion (HgS) can also darken under certain conditions (this may or may not be the result of crystallographic change to its brown form, meta cinnabar). Azurite (basic copper carbonate, $2CuCO_3.Cu[OH]_2$), a beautiful, deep sky blue, can fade to a weak green in the presence of chloride ions (formation of copper chloride), or by transition to its green form, malachite. White lead (basic lead carbonate, $2PbCO_3.Pb(OH)_2$,) can oxidize to form platternite (lead dioxide, PbO_2) (Figure 12.4). Green resinate glazes, widely used and notably hardy at Amiens, for example, darken with age (polymer degradation). The dynamics of these changes are not well understood;

Figure 12.3   Detail of limestone arcade mouldings, Salisbury Cathedral, West Porch.

Figure 12.4 Monument to Richard Cornwallis, St Peter's Church, Cretingham, Suffolk (limestone, *c*.1600). Above: a fine example of late English provincial polychromy. Below: discolouration and detachment of lead white.

their variety and complexity cannot be dwelt upon here, and are covered well in the literature. In addition new examples are continually coming to light.[37] It should always be assumed that the causes of any discolouration encountered may be complex.

Unfortunately, red lead, vermilion and above all white lead were used extensively in medieval stone polychromy. White lead in particular is almost always present, forming a compact, well bound layer against the stone, as well as in admixtures for flesh tones and other colours, or as an extender for pigments with poor covering power. The relative fragility of picture layers means that often the pore-filler is today exposed by their loss. Where the lead white is discoloured, it assumes a dull grey or a brown cast.[38] In extreme cases, white lead can feed the formation of a compact sulphation crust that incorporates fly-ash. The susceptibility of white lead to darkening, allied to that of red lead and vermilion, make flesh tones very vulnerable to discolouration. Such degradation products are commonly thought of as dirt layers to be removed; attempts to do so are fraught with difficulty (see below).

Paint will also normally be discoloured by particulate accretion. Surface roughness, electrostatic charge between particles, and the chemical composition of paint and particulate, all contribute to this accretion.[39] While fluctuations in relative humidity might draw pollutants into the surface, creating a very superficial discoloured layer, it is a matter of common experience that this kind of soiling is relatively poorly bound to most painted surfaces, provided these have not previously been treated with preservative oils, waxes or other substances. Unfortunately, the polychrome parts of church architecture and sculpture have also attracted more than their fair share of maintenance in the past. Alkali silicates, commonly used in pure form or as ingredients in patent preparations during the nineteenth century for the consolidation of historic stonework, for example, have had a marked effect on lead white.[40]

Lacunae (gaps) are common in historic polychromy (see Figure 12.2). Direct exposure to the full force of the elements would normally all but eradicate paint, but in more sheltered locations, where substantive quantities of paint remain, the causes of lacunae may be complex. Differential shrinkage or embrittlement, particularly where associated with thick, multi-layered over-paint, can result in flaking and cupping. Weak bonds between strata are common. A notable case of this is the central trumeau sculpture of the Virgin in the 'Portail de la Mère Dieu' at Amiens Cathedral, which supports, in places, up to twenty-six discrete paint layers.[41] Some of these layers are commonly less well bound than others. Ochre layers, in particular, are very susceptible to swelling during centuries of fluctuations in ambient relative humidity (ochre pigments are complex in composition and contain hydrophilic clay minerals). Since ochre layers were often used as secondary preparation in the medieval period, and subsequently in preparatory layers for over-paint, ochre pigments often precipitate substantial losses from the entire stratigraphy, or large portions of it.

Sometimes, motifs applied to the picture layer (gilded, painted or in wax-resin or gesso relief) are lost. What remains may be as little as a shadow of differential soiling in the surviving paint layer, which can be very difficult to spot. Such remains are common, for example, on early Renaissance marble sculpture, on which gold leaf was often applied to motifs painted in plain oil size, particularly on draperies.[42] Cleaning can easily eradicate these ghost images. The utility of infrared (IR) imaging as an aid to identifying and visualizing such remains cannot be understated.

The term 'partially polychrome' is commonly applied to sculptures or ensembles of sculpture that preserve islands of polychromy (what some refer to as 'picture layers'), but which otherwise present bare stone or the remains of preparatory layers. The appearance of these is often very dark, due to the accretion of pollution layers, especially to exposed carbonates (lead white pore-filler, calcium carbonate stone).

Decay of the underlying stone is, of course, a considerable problem. The subject cannot be covered comprehensively in this chapter, but issues specific to the treatment of decayed, painted stone are dealt with below.

PRACTICAL ISSUES OF CONSERVATION

From the relative wealth of articles relating to the conservation of polychrome stone, two driving currents of practice are apparent. One emerges in the work of the *Institut Royal du Patrimoine Artistique* in Brussels, where, in the 1960s and 1970s, a centre of international repute in the conservation of painted sculpture was being established. Paul Philippot produced seminal work on the philosophical understanding of patinas and lacunae in painted artworks, while Agnes Ballestrem collated and published a bibliography for conservators of polychrome sculpture.[43] In more recent times, under the influence of the current acting director, Miriam Serck-Dewaide, the Institute has increasingly lent its expertise to the problem of the conservation of outdoor polychrome stone. This current is characterized by a marked emphasis on pre-cise preliminary documentation and analysis, and careful, close working methods, exemplified elsewhere by the thirty-year restoration of the Painted Portal at Lausanne.

The second current is driven from the private sector, particularly in France, and has emerged in response to the growing political will to see monumental stone conserved, or more particularly, cleaned. This current is represented by, for example, the conservation of the West Fronts of Amiens Cathedral and Notre-Dame in Paris.

It will immediately be apparent that the relatively slow pace and high academic aspirations of museum conservation are incompatible with the treatment of an object the size of Amiens Cathedral's West Front. This begs the question whether the work to clean and conserve such enormous, precious objects should be undertaken at all, a debate that has emerged with force recently.[44] I hope that I can demonstrate, through analysis of the problems posed by real examples, that it is indeed possible to achieve the requisite high standards of conservation treatment on such a scale.

TREATMENT

It is hard to find a published, reasoned, general discussion of the treatment of polychrome stone. Lazzarini and Laurenzi Tabasso's *Il Restauro della Pietra* is an intensely practical, technical guide, but it contains very little specific discussion of the treatment of polychrome stones, except with regard to their cleaning.[45] In English, Ashurst and Dimes' *Conservation of Building and Decorative Stone* has fulfilled a similar function; it contains an essay on the cleaning of painted stone.[46]

It is certainly difficult to express in writing the myriad subtleties and petty decisions involved in daily conservation work. As a result, the literature is very short on detailed information. This is a pity, because discussion of decision-making in conservation, especially in relation to complicated objects, is precisely what a lot of conservators are looking for. Another result of this difficulty is that accounts remain predominantly concerned with the treatment of objects in isolation from their wider environment, in ways that might suggest no progress in stone conservation had been made over the last twenty-five years.

The presence of paint lends the surface of three-dimensional works of art a particular importance. This was clearly elucidated by Philippot. With regard to the cases in question, because of the fragility of the remains and their rarity, the conservator is forced to consider the evaluation and preservation of every particle of surface. In building conservation, such a consideration is not normally applied. Economies of scale are required to achieve large projects in shorter timescales (<10 years). During the last thirty years, English cathedral façades, for example, have been cleaned with water (timed mist sprays) abrasives (wet and drying grit-blasting, micro air abrasion) and chemical poultices (notably ones based on ammonium carbonate). None of these techniques including, I would contend, micro air abrasion, even practised in highly controlled ways, can achieve the finesse required for the treatment of polychrome or part-polychrome sculpture.[47]

Consequently, the problem of what to do with cleaned stone (consolidation, re-fixing etc.) has been similarly compromised. Treatments based on the British 'lime method', for example, include consolidation with limewater (involving repeated saturation with water) and 'sheltercoating', which properly involves vigorous rubbing. Neither is physically or chemically compatible with the preservation of surface detail and polychromy.

In 1986, Lazzarini and Laurenzi-Tabasso wrote: 'the only examples of cleaning on a vast scale of polychrome sculpture that have been achieved to date (the cathedral of Ferrara, the cathedral of Chartres) are, from the point of view of conservation, considered satisfactory.'[48] Today the examples are too numerous to mention. In an unusual and very interesting recent essay, Véronique Vergès-Belmin of the *Laboratoire de Recherche des Monuments Historiques* presents the results of a survey, the aim of which was to identify which conservation treatments are commonly being used in the conservation of 'partially polychrome portals' in France.[49] The article attempts to rationalize the relationship between the choices of conservation treatment, incompatibilities between certain surfaces and certain treatments, and the role of economics and political expediency in the choices made. As Vergès-Belmin points out, there is a startling lack of homogeneity in those choices.

Documentation and analysis

The objects I have been discussing are often so large, complex and degraded, that they present a truly daunting prospect. They pose some of the greatest technical, ethical and aesthetic challenges a conservator might face. The role of preliminary observation, documentation and analysis is therefore vitally important. Multi-disciplinary co-operation is essential. Rather than enumerate the set of all possible preliminaries, I should like to distinguish clearly between that which conservators need to know, and that which, for the purposes of treatment, they do not.

Preliminary surveys often begin with the taking of paint samples and the commission of analyses of these. This stage would better be preceded by an extensive period of looking: looking with the naked eye, with the binocular microscope, in raking light, under ultra-violet and infra-red illumination. It is conservators, with their peculiar expertise and practically trained eyes, who should be engaged in this exercise and in documenting what they have seen. Gathering as much data as possible should be the aim, and the methods of documentation are immaterial, provided they offer a sufficiently rich record.[50] Two dimensional representations of three dimensional works of art are limiting, but they can be supplemented by macro and micro photography, video, UV and IR images, sketches and text. Conservators need to differentiate pigmentation from patination, 'dirt' from discolouration, and to establish the nature of the interface between them. They need to identify and characterize the remains of past preservation treatments. They must also characterize the state of conservation of the stone and wider supporting fabric. Simultaneously, documentary sources relating to the restoration history of the object should be trawled and collated. They need to establish and record the distribution of the remains and their stratigraphy,[51] but they do not need exhaustively to characterize every fragment of paint at this stage.

Only after this extensive, potentially expensive, exercise is complete should samples of paint be taken. The removal of samples is a serious matter and should be avoided whenever possible. There is no point in taking a paint sample with a view to confirming the obvious. The analysis of paint cross sections can help decipher complex stratigraphies, and can identify pigments and media within these. It can pinpoint discontinuities or weaknesses in the layer structure. It may sometimes be used to investigate the relationship of the upper layers of paint or stone with past treatments, such as waxes or patent nineteenth-century chemicals. Degraded or depleted organic media can sometimes be very hard to identify; the use of highly discriminating instrumental techniques such as HPLC (high performance liquid chromatography), by scientists experienced in the analysis of artworks, may be necessary.

It is absolutely essential that the conservator involved in the survey and documentation process be charged with any conservation work that may arise. The size of the overall contract must not be allowed to dissuade the bodies responsible from ensuring that this is the case.

Environmental survey

Before any action is taken to remedy any gross manifestations of decay, it is essential to establish the rate of that decay. It is remarkable how little consideration this factor commonly receives. There are clearly some objects that exhibit rapid and obvious decay, but they are exceptions. Close monitoring over an extended period of, say, five years would seem to be a minimum requirement; good photography in raking light can help. An assessment of the environmental conditions surrounding the object would also ideally form part of this. Unfortunately, although point measurements of temperature, relative humidity and incident radiation are easily achieved, characterization of the intensely complex, dynamic situation as a whole is still unattainable.

Cleaning

Cleaning is an important part of the treatment of polychrome stone. Particularly in outdoor locations, cleaning can be required even before a proper assessment of further conservation requirements can be made: mineral crusts, heterogeneous dust layers and the nests, feathers and droppings of pigeons that have accumulated over several centuries may obscure large portions of the stone. The deleterious effects, physical, catalytic and biological, of these deposits on stone, let alone ancient paint, are very poorly understood. These various accretions are unlikely to be distributed uniformly; mineral crusts may form evenly toward the less sheltered parts of an ensemble otherwise protected from direct precipitation, and not at all in parts remote from the exterior, where minimal airflow has failed to transport atmospheric particulates. Dust and pigeon mess tend only to build-up upon horizontal or angled surfaces. Indoors, the soiling may be less acute (aside from the problem of bat excreta), but the extremity of the environment is still considerable, and soils on the surface can be encouraged to penetrate just as readily with fluctuations in relative humidity here as outside.[52] The likelihood of the interior polychrome stone having been subjected to repeated treatment with waxes, oils and resins during its lifetime is also far higher.

For the gross removal of heavy, superficial accretions of dust and droppings from partially polychrome stone, micro air abrasion has been used very effectively, but necessarily with great circumspection to avoid the dislodgement of islands of polychromy. Soft brushes and vacuum cleaners are equally hazardous. Further to these preliminaries, which are essential for any subsequent laser cleaning, soiling layers that obscure or discolour medieval paint, except those associated with the pigment transformations, particularly of lead pigments as mentioned above, will usually be the result of more recent coatings and treatments such as waxes, oils and silicates.

Unfortunately, the darkened preparatory layers of lead pigment commonly exposed on partially polychrome stone cannot be 'cleaned', unless we are to accept the stripping of the first microns of the affected paint layer as 'cleaning'. Micro air abrasion has been used for this to regrettable effect on the central and north portals of Amiens cathedral (conserved 1997–2000).[53] Such surfaces represent a classic instance of the limits of this cleaning technique, which is unable effectively to cope with hard, brittle soils overlying much softer original material. Poultices of de-ionized water can sometimes soften these surfaces, after which they may be more amenable to treatment, but at present, there is no wholly satisfactory answer to the aesthetic problem posed by the existence of such discoloured layers.

Micro air abrasion may still be useful for the removal of black mineral crust from bare stone, but it is impossible to see any advantage over the use of Nd:YAG laser for this.[54] Choice of abrasive is irrelevant (corundum, glass micro spheres, stone dusts, vegetable powders etc. in different grades), since the operative parameter is the kinetic energy of the air abrasive stream. Laser cleaning, by contrast, is highly spatially discriminating and avoids damage to surrounding sensitive surfaces associated with micro air abrasion, as well as the indiscriminate deposition of abrasive waste. The conservator can at all times see what they are doing, and can also work under magnification.[55]

With regard to the removal of degraded waxes or other coatings, or overpaint from medieval polychromy, it is impossible to generalize regarding the desirability or technique for this. Nd:YAG laser can sometimes prove effective for removing discrete films from unpainted stone. If solvents are used to remove coatings or overpaint, proper care should be taken to ensure chemical compatibility with any underlying polychromy.[56] Ammonium carbonate and EDTA, in particular, endanger certain pigments and surfaces.[57] The use of preparatory formulations based on latex risks physical damage. Gels (poultices) that retain or confine the active ingredients, and barrier membranes such as Gore-Tex, should be used wherever possible.[58] Removal of overpaint by scalpel under magnification is still reliable but it is very slow, may be uneconomic on vast surfaces, and is difficult where there are weak layers or very degraded substrates.

Several cleaning and consolidation strategies will be required on each object. The deleterious effects of laser radiation, particularly Nd:YAG laser, on a small range of the pigments commonly encountered on polychrome sculptures, is well documented.[59] The causes of damage are various but, as yet, poorly understood. The latest available research confirms that its effects on some pigments such as white lead are dependent upon the operator surpassing a threshold level of laser energy.[60] With practice, a skilled and qualified conservator, working with low laser energy (fluence), a well regulated laser beam, and a very low laser pulse rate, can achieve spectacular results.[61] Nevertheless, until further research is done, IR and visible lasers should be used with extreme care. It would be a terrible pity if, as a result of this necessary circumspection, lasers were not more widely used for cleaning exposed stone and preparatory layers on partially polychrome stone in favour of micro air abrasion or chemical poultices that are relatively destructive.

Consolidation of the substrate and paint layers

The consolidation of stone is dealt with elsewhere in this volume. Suffice it to say that the decision to apply an imperfect treatment is even harder to make in the case of a polychrome object of singular importance. Today, the total consolidation (with epoxy resin grouts and acrylic silane) of the sculptures of the *Portail Royal* at Chartres seems, at best, unfortunate, as does that of the sculptures of the *Bergportaal* in Maastricht (with tetraethoxysilane) in 1992.

The problem of how best to secure fragile remains of paint outside, or in otherwise aggressive environments, is a difficult one. This is principally because of the nature of the layers and their decay. Medieval stone polychromy typically exhibits some layers from which the original binder has been partially leached, digested or compromised by the hydration of minerals. This results either in exposed, powdery ochre layers, or well bound paint overlying such layers. Often, there is no physical bridge between these. The best (most benign in the long term) consolidants for stone at our disposal, such as tetraethoxysilane, are not designed to bridge gaps, and lend but little strength to loose powder. Long chain polymers, such as natural proteins (sturgeon glue for instance), and acrylics, such as Paraloid B72, are better suited to this. However, their deployment at useful concentrations inevitably entails the formation of a skin of paint and stone of reduced porosity. Good results can be achieved with sturgeon glue at relatively low concentrations, typically 2–3% hydrated solid by weight in solution, compared to between 5–10% for Paraloid B72 (though conservators may prefer to use acrylics because of the range of suitable solvents, not to mention their pedigree in conservation). Solutions are typically applied by brush or pipette.[62] Flakes of pigment can be pressed gently into position with a heated spatula while the consolidant is still tacky, or after a flake of consolidant cut from a dried film has been inserted behind the paint. At Vezzolano (façade) and the Portail de la Mère Dieu of Amiens cathedral, Primal AC33 acrylic dispersion was used for re-fixing polychromy at a concentration of 5% in water, applied by brush or pipette.[63] In the central portal (*Portail du Beau Dieu*) of Amiens, Paraloid B72 in solution was used for this, followed by more general consolidation with tetraethoxysilane.[64] The application of silanes to architectural sculpture is usually by spraying. This technique results in uneven depth of penetration. It also entails prolonged physical stress to weak paint layers as they are repeatedly soaked over a period of up to twelve hours.

Medieval polychrome stone in humid environments confronts the conservator with physical, chemical and biological systems, the complexity of which is poorly understood. Chemical consolidation and the application of water repellents or anti-graffiti treatments that add to this complexity should remain a last resort.

Retouching

The scale of the objects in question, and of the losses they generally have suffered, coupled with the difficulty of isolating and characterizing a given colour scheme, renders retouching particularly problematic. In addition, the surfaces in question are, by definition, distressed and decayed. In order to 're-paint' polychrome sculpture, unacceptable damage to the extant remains would result. It is not possible to 're-paint' polychrome sculpture. It may sometimes be necessary to camouflage previous restorations or break surfaces. Film-forming retouching media (e.g. acrylics) are unsuitable for outdoor use in general because of their adverse effect on surface permeability. Retouching executed in these media tends to stand out in damp weather. Watercolour, or dry mineral pigments fixed subsequently with acrylic solution, may be preferable (provided permanent pigments are used). Parishes sometimes ask for inscriptions or heraldic devices on church monuments to be retouched; there are preferable alternatives to this, such as cleaning or the installation of interpretative material nearby.

Environmental management

Active management of the environment is very hard in outdoor locations. The Painted Portal at Lausanne is today enclosed behind glass, an
installation facilitated by the dimensions and design of the porch. The
environment is monitored and controlled by machinery below floor-level.
In this manner, it is hoped that the rate of deposition of soils, for example,
can be dramatically reduced, and nesting birds have been permanently
excluded. Such measures are very unusual; yet, if we are to take seriously
the long-term survival of these rare and enigmatic survivals of our past, we
inevitably must move away from conservation interventions that address
the effects of decay rather than the causes.

CONCLUSION: FUTURE TRENDS

In this chapter, the reader will have remarked upon those areas in relation
to which little is known. We need a better understanding of how pigments
and media darken or fade, for example, or the role of stone growing flora
in the decay cycle, or the effect of pollutant accretions on objects. We need
better environmental mapping (and control), and perhaps using computer
modelling to interpret remotely captured data.

Developments in spectral imaging and computer image processing are
already having a marked effect on the analytical power available to
conservators, and hence the quality of the documentation they can
produce.[65] Better analytical instruments are also becoming available, such
as Raman spectroscopy, that are non-destructive, portable, and very
discriminating.[66] The elimination of destructive sampling is an eventual
goal. Allied to this will be better laser tools that perhaps incorporate
high photon-energy analytical beams and computer analysis capable, for
example, of laser induced florescence spectroscopy (LIFS). Even standard laser cleaning protocols and methods can be further explored and
developed.[67]

Faster computers will facilitate better laser scanning and other forms of
digital three-dimensional capture. Such images can be used to assess decay
rates and movement, and to create virtual reconstructions of objects in
previous states.[68]

The size and complexity of many of the objects discussed in this chapter
is a singular impediment to their conservation. The costs involved are very
high, as are the contract values. Setting competitive teams to work on the

same object (currently common in France) cannot be the way forward. It is to be hoped that the collective political will to see them properly conserved will be strengthened.

The author

Christopher Weeks ACR

Christopher Weeks has practised as a conservator in France, Italy, Eire and the UK, largely on architectural sculpture. His particular interest is the conservation of painted stone, and he now runs an independent conservation practice in Hertfordshire.

References

1   The eleventh century marked an important turning point for European sculpture, a point after which the decoration of church façades became increasingly important. See Duby, G., 'Preface', in *Sculpture: From Antiquity to the Present Day*, Taschen, Cologne, 2002, p. 247.

2   Melucco-Vaccaro, A., 'La polichromia nell'architettura e nella plastica antica: stato della questione', in *Ricerche di Storia dell'Arte*, 24, Nuova Italia Scientifica, Rome, 1984. Also Jones, A. and MacGregor, G., *Colouring the Past: The significance of colour in archaeological research*, Berg, New York, 2002.

3   Rossi-Manaresi, R., 'Observations à propos de la polychromie de la sculpture monumentale romane et gothique', in Verret, D. and Steyaert, D. (eds.), *La Couleur et la Pierre: Polychromie des Portails Gothique*, Éditions Picard, Paris, 2002, pp. 57–64.

4   See Guillot de Suduiraut, S., 'Glow and Afterglow of Gothic (1400–1530)', in Duby, G. and Daval, J.-L. (eds.), *Sculpture: From Antiquity To The Present Day*, Taschen, Cologne, 2002, pp. 517–518; Knipping, D., 'Le Portail Ouest de l'église du Saint-Esprit à Landshut', in Verret, D. and Steyaert, D. (eds.), *La Couleur et la Pierre: Polychromie des Portails Gothique*, Éditions Picard, Paris, 2002, p. 51.

5   Sauerländer, W., 'Quand les statues étaient blanches. Discussion au sujet de la polychromie', in Verret, D. and Steyaert, D. (eds.), *La Couleur et la Pierre: Polychromie des Portails Gothique*, Éditions Picard, Paris, 2002, pp. 27–34. More generally this essay is an excellent introduction to historic attitudes to polychrome stone.

6   See, for example, the excellent Williamson, P., *Gothic Sculpture 1140–1300*, Yale University Press/ Pelican History of Art, New Haven and London, 1995, pp. 6–7, 58–59. As recently as 2004 the published proceedings from a conference organised to celebrate and interpret the most splendid and famous extant example of Gothic polychromy, the Painted Portal of Lausanne Cathedral, omitted any colour illustrations or explicit discussion of the painted decoration; Kurmann, P. and Rohde, M. (eds.), *Die Kathedrale von Lausanne und ihr Marienportal im Kontext der europäischen Gotik*, Post

prints of the Freiburg Colloquium, 1998, Scrinium Friburgense Neue Serie – Band 13, Berlin/New York, 2004.

7 Pastoureau, M., *Blue: The History of a Colour,* Princeton University Press (trans. Cruse, M. I.) 2001; Gage, J., *Colour and Meaning: Art, Science and Symbolism,* Thames and Hudson, London, 2000; Gage, J., 'Colour and Culture', in Lamb, T. and Bourriau, J., *Colour: Art & Science,* Cambridge University Press, Cambridge, 1995, pp. 175–193.

8 Danti, C., Giusti, A., Lanfranchi, M. R. and Weeks, C., 'Scultura e affresco: novità dal restauro del monumento Marsuppini', in *OPD Restauro* 10, 1998, pp. 36–56; Weeks, C., 'Sculpture and colour: recent discoveries in the monument to Carlo Marsuppini, Santa Croce, Florence', in *Burlington Magazine,* December 1999, pp. 732–738.

9 Vanessa Simeoni, personal communication.

10 It is interesting to speculate upon the reasons for this. The *Montpellier Manuscript,* also known as *Liber diversarium arcium,* possibly dating from the late fourteenth or early fifteenth century, appears to refer to polychrome sculpture. See Clarke, M., *The Art of All Colours: Medieval Recipe Books for Painters and Illuminators,* Archetype Publications, London, 2001, pp. 22, 91.

11 Brodrick, A., Painting techniques of early medieval sculpture, in *Romanesque: Stone Sculpture from Medieval England,* Henry Moore Institute, Leeds, 1993, pp. 18–27; Rossi-Manaresi, R., *op. cit.,* 2002 [Ref. 3]; Rossi Manaresi, R., 'Considerazioni tecniche sulla scultura monumentale policromata, romanica e gotica', in *Materiali lapidei,* supplement to *Bollettino d'Arte,* 41, Ministero Beni Culturali e Ambientali, 1987, pp. 173–186; Pallot-Frossard, I., 'Polychromies des portails sculptés médiévaux en France: contributions et limites des analyses scientifiques', in Verret, D. and Steyaert, D. (eds.), *La Couleur et la Pierre: Polychromie des Portails Gothique,* Éditions Picard, Paris, 2002, pp. 73–90.

12 Howard, H., *The Pigments of English Medieval Wall Painting,* Archetype Publications, London, 2003, pp. 206–207.

13 Brodrick, A., 'Medieval painterly techniques on monuments', in *Proceedings of the Joint Forum for Conservation Issues, 7/11/2000,* Council for the Care of Churches, 2001, p. 16. For illustrations see Boldrick, S., Park, D. and Williamson, P., *Wonder: Painted Sculpture from Medieval England,* Henry Moore Institute, Leeds, 2002.

14 Rossi-Manaresi, R., *op. cit.,* 2002 [Ref. 3].

15 Howard, H., *op. cit.,* 2003 [Ref. 12], p. 207; Brodrick, A., *op. cit.,* 1993, p. 20 [Ref. 11].

16 Bavaud, G. (trans.) *Amédée de Lausanne: Huits Homélies Mariales,* Éditions du Cerf, Paris, 1960, p. 79. For Suger see Frisch, T.G., *Gothic Art 1140 –c.1450 Sources and Documents,* Medieval Academy of America, 1987, pp. 4–13.

17 See for example Sinclair, E., 'La polychromie des façades de cathédrales en Angleterre, témoinage fragmentaire d'un monde presque disparu', in Verret, D. and Steyaert, D. (eds.), *La Couleur et la Pierre: Polychromie des Portails Gothique,* Éditions Picard, Paris, 2002, pp. 129–138; and Steyaert, D., 'Notre Dame de Senlis: étude de la polychromie du portail du Couronnement

de la Vierge', in Verret, D. and Steyaert, D. (eds.), *La Couleur et la Pierre: Polychromie des Portails Gothique*, Éditions Picard, Paris, 2002, pp. 105–114.

18   Small traces of medieval paint (colour wash?) remain high on the façades of Salisbury and Amiens cathedrals. For an excellent evocation of medieval painted sculpture see Park, D., in Boldrick, S., *op. cit.*, 2002 [Ref. 13].

19   In this scheme the draperies are painted in imitation of fashionable Flemish silk brocades and the roll moulding with 'barber's pole' figures. See Weeks, C., 'The 'Portail de la Mère Dieu' of Amiens Cathedral: its Polychromy and Conservation', in *Studies in Conservation* 43, 1998, pp. 101–108.

20   The fragments are on show in the Priory Visitor Centre, Coventry.

21   For Chartres see Michler, J., 'La cathédrale Notre-Dame de Chartres: reconstitution de la poychromie originale de l'intérieur', in *Bulletin Monumental*, vol. 147, no. 2, 1989, pp. 117–131. More generally, see *Architecture et décors peints, Actes du colloque d'Amiens 1989*, Ministère de la Culture, Éditions Picard, 1990. For French and German examples, see Nussbaum, M., (trans. Kleager, S.), *German Gothic Church Architecture*, Yale University Press, New Haven & London, 2000, p. 61, especially notes 179 and 180.

22   Brodrick, A., Darrah, J., 'The fifteenth-century polychromed limestone effigies of William Fitzalan, 9th Earl of Arundel, and his wife, Joan Nevill, in the Fitzalan Chapel, Arundel', in *Church Monuments*, 1, 1986, pp. 65–94; Brodrick, A., *op. cit.*, 1993 [Ref. 11]; Brodrick, A., *op. cit.*, 2001 [Ref. 13]; Howard, H., *op. cit.*, 2003 [Ref. 12].

23   Pallot-Frossard, I., *op. cit.*, 2002, pp. 73–90 [Ref. 11].

24   Sinclair, E., *op. cit.*, p. 132 [Ref. 17]. For Exeter, see also Hulbert, A., 'Medieval paintings and polychromy', in *Exeter Cathedral: a Celebration*, Dean and Chapter of Exeter, 1991, pp. 91–98.

25   For example at Fribourg in the fifteenth or sixteenth century. See Arn, W., Nussli S., Savelli and E., *Cathédrale St Nicholas de Fribourg, portail ouest. Investigations des polychromies, 1992–1994, intermediate report*, unpublished.

26   Steyaert, D., Réflections á propos de la polychromie des portails gothiques, *Annales d'Histoire de l'Art et d'Archeologie, Tirage á Part, XIX*, Université Libre de Bruxelles, 1997, pp. 78–79.

27   Piel, C., 'La restauration de la Vierge Dorée, a la cathédrale d'Amiens: une longue histoire', in *Monumental* 10–11, 1995, p. 154–161.

28   Sinclair, E., *op. cit.*, p. 133 [Ref. 17].

29   Lead leaf plate armour was found by Brodrick and Eastham on the effigy of Sir Richard Herbert in Abergavenny Priory, Wales. See Brodrick, A., *op. cit.*, 2001 [Ref. 13], p. 18.

30   For example at Amiens and Angers cathedral West Fronts. See Pallot-Frossard, I., *op. cit.*, 2002, p. 87 [Ref. 11].

31   Rossi-Manaresi, R.and Tucci, A., 'The polychromy of the portals of the Gothic Cathedral of Bourges', in *ICOM 7th Triennial Meeting, Copenhagen, 10–14 September 1984: preprints*, ICOM, Paris, 1984, section 84.5, pp. 1–4.

32   For Senlis see Steyaert, D. and Demailly, S., 'Notre-Dame de Senlis: etude de la polychromie du portail du Couronnement de la Vierge', in Verret, D.

and Steyaert, D. (eds.), *La Couleur et la Pierre: Polychromie des Portails Gothique*, Éditions Picard, Paris, 2002, pp. 105–114. For Amiens see Weeks, C., *op. cit.*, 1998 [Ref. 19] and Zambon, L., Grunewald, D. and Hugon, P., 'La polychromie du portail central de la cathédrale d'Amiens: conservation, restauration et investigations scientifiques', in Verret, D. and Steyaert, D. (eds.), *La Couleur et la Pierre: Polychromie des Portails Gothique*, Éditions Picard, Paris, 2002, pp. 233–248.

33   For Lausanne see Furlan, V. and Pancella, R., 'Portail Peint de la Cathedrale de Lausanne, analyses pour une restauration', in *Chantiers* 12, 1981, 13–20; Hermanès, T., 'La riscoperta del colore nel moumento: il caso delle cattedrali di Ginevra e Losanna', in *Il colore nel medioevo: arte, simbolo, tecnica, atti delle giornate di studi*, Lucca, 5–6 maggio 1995, Istituto storico lucchese, Lucca, 1996, pp. 41–65. For Bern see Schweizer, J., 'Les sculptures de la cathédrale de Berne', in Verret, D. and Steyaert, D. (eds.), *La Couleur et la Pierre: Polychromie des Portails Gothique*, Éditions Picard, Paris, 2002, pp. 175–182.

34   For Parma see Zanardi, B., 'La polycromie des reliefs de Benedetto Antelami et les deux phases décoratives du Baptistère de Parme', in Verret, D. and Steyaert, D. (eds.), *La Couleur et la Pierre: Polychromie des Portails Gothique*, Éditions Picard, Paris, 2002, pp. 115–118. For Vercelli see Rava, A., 'Le jubé de Vezzolano et les reliefs antélamiques du portail de Saint André à Vercelli', in Verret, D. and Steyaert, D. (eds.), *La Couleur et la Pierre: Polychromie des Portails Gothique*, Éditions Picard, Paris, 2002, pp. 163–174.

35   Katz, M. R., 'The mediaeval polychromy of the majestic west portal of Toro, Spain: insight into workshop activities of late medieval painters and polychromers', in Roy, A. and Smith, P. (eds.), *Painting Techniques: History, Materials and Studio Techniques*, Contributions to the Dublin Congress, 7–11 September 1998, IIC, London, 1998, pp. 27–34.

36   Weeks, C., *op. cit.*, 1998 [Ref. 19].

37   Such as vivianite, a deep-blue iron phosphate; see Howard, H., *op. cit.*, 2003, p. 38 [Ref. 12].

38   Chiari, G., Colombo, F., Fiora, L., Compagnoni, R., Rava, A., Perino, G. and Barni, E., 'Santa Maria di Vezzolano: restoration of the façade', in *Conservation of Stone and Other Materials*, Vol. 2, RILEM, Paris, 1993, pp. 468–478.

39   A lucid discussion of these dynamics is included in Wolbers, R., *Cleaning Painted Surfaces: Aqueous Methods*, Archetype, 2000, pp. 1–7.

40   Weeks, C., *op. cit.*, 1998 [Ref. 19].

41   Hugon, P., *Report No. 851D, Amiens 80-Somme (Picardie) Cathédrale, portail sud de la façade occidentale, étude de la polychromie*, Laboratoire de Recherche des Monuments Historiques, Paris, 1992.

42   See Plate 33, in Weeks, C., *op. cit.*, 1999, p. 737 [Ref. 8].

43   Philippot, P., 'Problèmes esthétiques et archéologiques de conservation des sculptures polychromes', in *Preprints of the contributions to the New York conference on conservation of stone and wooden objects*, I.I.C., New York, 1970, pp. 59–62. Ballestrem, A., 'Sculpture Polychrome – Bibliographie', in *Studies in Conservation* 15, 1970, pp. 253–271.

44 For an example of such polemic see, Serck-Dewaide, M., 'Méthodes d'examen, recherches et traitements de polychromies du Moyen-Age à l'Institut Royal du Patimoine Artistique', in Verret, D. and Steyaert, D. (eds.), *La Couleur et la Pierre: Polychromie des Portails Gothique*, Éditions Picard, Paris, 2002, pp. 91–101. See also Serck-Dewaide, M., 'De l'étude et du sauvetage de la polychromie des sculptures en pierre', in *Proceedings of the Vth international congress on deterioration and conservation of stone, Lausanne, 25–27 September1985*, Presses Polytechniques Romandes, Lausanne, 1985, pp. 1115–1119.

45 Lazzarini, L. and Laurenzi Tabasso, M., *Il Restauro della Pietra*, CEDAM, Padua, 1986, pp. 146–152.

46 Finn, C., 'The cleaning of painted stone', Ashurst, A. and Dimes, F. G. (eds.), *Conservation of Building and Decorative Stone, Volume 2*, Butterworth-Heinemann, London, 1998, pp. 214–218. The essay is written with relatively recent architectural paint in mind, includes outdated prescriptions entirely unsuitable to objects of value, and no footnotes.

47 Vergès-Belmin, V., Pichot, C. and Orial, G., 'Élimination de croûtes noires sur marbre et craie: à quel niveau arrêter le nettoyage?', in *Conservation of Stone and Other Materials*, Vol. 2, RILEM, Paris, 1993, pp. 534–541.

48 Lazzarini, L. and Laurenzi Tabasso, M., *op. cit.*, 1986, p. 149, (translation: Weeks) [Ref. 45].

49 Vergès-Belmin, V., 'Restauration de la pierre dans les portails aujourd'hui partiellement polychromés', in Verret, D. and Steyaert, D. (eds.), *La Couleur et la Pierre: Polychromie des Portails Gothique*, Éditions Picard, Paris, 2002, pp. 151–162. The term 'partially polychrome' is intended to suggest the state of conservation of the portals in question rather than their original design, and to distinguish them from those rare ensembles that preserve extensive or near-complete schemes.

50 See, for example, Groux, D. and Weeks, C., *Cathédral d'Amiens, portail sud, investigations sur la polychromie*, 2 Vols., unpublished report submitted to *Monuments Historiques*, France, 1994.

51 For an interesting contribution to this challenge, see Barros Garcia, J. M., 'The use of the Harris Matrix to document the layers removed during the cleaning of painted surfaces', in *Studies in Conservation* 49, 4, 2004, pp. 245–258.

52 Paine, S., *Bats in churches: guidelines for the identification, assessment and management of bat-related damage to church contents (furnishings, fittings and works of art)*, English Heritage/English Nature, published online at www.english-heritage.org.uk/ (accessed 16 June 2006).

53 Many excellent plates are published in Egger, A. and Fraudreau, M., *Amiens: la Cathédrale Peinte*, Perrin, Paris, 2000.

54 Bougrain-Dubourg, R. and Serck-Dewaide, M., 'L'application du micro-sablage au traitement des sculptures polychromes', in *Bulletin de l'IRPA*, 18, 1980–81, pp. 119–130. Scalpel and 'Mora' poultice were used for the painted portions in this case study.

55   It is important to use safety spectacles that transmit at least 70% visible light. Dark, dual wavelength (1064nm/532nm) spectacles are unacceptable.

56   See Vergès-Belmin, V., *op. cit.*, 2002, for a very useful table of common incompatibilities [Ref. 49].

57   Azurite can fade if exposed to very basic solutions; EDTA (ethylene diamine tetra acetic acid) is an aggressive metal ion grabber.

58   Wolbers, R., *op. cit.*, 2000 [Ref. 39].

59   Weeks, C., *op. cit.*, 1998 [Ref. 19]; Pouli, P. and Emmony, D.C., 'The effect of NdYAG laser radiation on medieval pigments', in *Journal of Cultural Heritage* 1, 2000, pp. 181–188.

60   Schnell, A., Goretzki, L. and Kaps, C., 'IR-laser effects on pigments and paint layers', in Dickmann, K., Fotakis, C. and Asmus, J. F. (eds.), *Lasers in the Conservation of Artworks V, Proceedings, Osnabrück, Germany, September 15–18, 2003*, Springer Verlag, Berlin, 2005, pp. 291–296. Used in alternating combination with water poultices, it has been possible to remove light mineral crusts from white lead. See Weeks, C., *op. cit.*, 1998 [Ref. 19].

61   Chiari, G., *et al.*, *op. cit.*, 1993 [Ref. 38]; Weeks, C., *op. cit.*, 1998 [Ref. 19].

62   Horie, C. V., *Materials for Conservation*, Architectural Press, Oxford, 1998, pp. 103–112.

63   For terminology see Cooper, M., *Laser Cleaning in Conservation*, Butterworth-Heinemann, Oxford, 1998.

64   Zambon, L., *et al.*, *op. cit.*, 2002 [Ref. 32]. The silane in question was *Wacker OH*; the method of application is not stated.

65   For example the *Artist* multi spectral video system from Art Innovation BV, Zutphenstraat 25, 7575 EJ Oldenzaal, The Netherlands.

66   Clarke, M., 'Anglo-Saxon manuscript pigments', in *Studies in Conservation* 49, 4, 2004, pp. 231–244.

67   The high photon energy of UV lasers has encouraged experimentation with their use for varnish and overpaint removal from paintings; however, because of the computer process control necessary to limit their effect on underlying layers, and because of the very dark glasses that are required to protect the eyes of the user, it is not possible to foresee a time when lasers of this type could be used on scaffolding to treat polychrome sculpture.

68   Ruiz de Arcaute Martinez, E., 'Reconstitution des polychromies par ordinateur. Possibilités et limites', in Verret, D. and Steyaert, D. (eds.), *La Couleur et la Pierre: Polychromie des Portails Gothique*, Éditions Picard, Paris, 2002, pp. 259–267; Geary, A., 'Three dimensional virtual restoration applied to polychrome sculpture', in *The Conservator* 28, 2004, pp. 20–34.

Chapter Thirteen

Church Monuments

David Carrington

INTRODUCTION

Church monuments come in many forms. This chapter focuses specifically on those found inside and constructed entirely or largely of stone. The Hedda Stone of circa AD 800 in Peterborough Cathedral and pre-conquest 'hogbacks' are forerunners of the medieval effigial monument of which an early example is the Tournai marble slab commemorating Bishop Nigellus (d.1169) in Ely Cathedral. Throughout the Middle Ages this tradition flourished, encompassing large canopied tombs and chantry chapels. The Reformation brought an influx of foreign sculptors and changes in fashion, with wall monuments becoming increasingly common. Monuments, primarily of marble, continued to be popular throughout the eighteenth and nineteenth centuries, really only becoming less popular after the First World War. War memorials are perhaps the most common twentieth-century monument.[1]

Note that floor ledger slabs and brasses are not specifically covered here, although much of what follows will also be relevant to them. Polychromy is also an important aspect of many monuments. This is beyond the scope of this chapter (although reference is made to issues arising when dealing with painted and gilt surfaces), but is considered in greater detail in Chapter 12 by Christopher Weeks.

MATERIALS COMMONLY USED

Freestones

Freestone is a general term describing stone that can be carved in three dimensions, and is usually applied to sedimentary stones. Prior to the fifteenth century (by which time alabaster was generally the material of choice), the vast majority of monuments were carved from relatively local freestone. In North Yorkshire, for example, of the 124 surviving pre-Reformation monuments there are two of Purbeck 'marble', three of wood and ten of alabaster – the remainder are of relatively local stone, in particular the fine-grained magnesian limestone quarried at Hazelwood and Tadcaster, but there are also many examples of monuments made from local sandstone.[2] One freestone that merits particular mention is clunch. Clunch is a soft, fine-grained Cretaceous limestone quarried in Cambridgeshire and Bedfordshire[3] that was very popular for monuments throughout the East Midlands, northern Home Counties and East Anglia up until the late seventeenth century.

Alabaster

Alabaster is a form of gypsum (hydrated calcium sulphate) that has been quarried in many parts of Britain including Glamorgan and Yorkshire, but most notably in Staffordshire and Derbyshire, where a thriving alabaster carving industry was established from the fourteenth century until the eighteenth century, by which time supplies began to dwindle. It is still obtainable periodically today from Fauld in Staffordshire. Alabaster is very easy to carve, and when polished has a wonderful translucent finish that also takes polychromy and metal leaf well – all ideal qualities for medieval statuary.[4]

Polishable limestones

There are several limestones that can be polished to look like marble and are often referred to as 'marbles'. Touch is a grey Carboniferous limestone that can be polished to an almost black shiny finish, quarried primarily at Ashford-in-the-Water in Derbyshire.[5] Other black 'marbles' that have been used in monuments include Belgian black (such as Tournai) and Kilkenny 'marble' (particularly from the eighteenth century onwards). Raunce is a mottled-red polishable limestone obtained from the Low Countries. Ashburton 'marble, quarried in Devon until relatively recently, is a polishable Devonian limestone that varies in colour from dark-grey to black with white, yellow and red patches and veins. Another 'marble' is Cockleshell, which enjoyed a relatively brief period of popularity in the Midlands during the seventeenth century.[6] Touch and

Figure 13.1 Cockleshell marble insets to the alabaster monument to Sir Henry Pierrepont (d.1615) at Holme Pierrepont, Nottinghamshire. The inscription panel is of black Carboniferous limestone ('Touch').

Raunce in particular were very commonly used in conjunction with alabaster during the sixteenth and seventeenth centuries.

Purbeck marble is by far the most famous of the polishable limestones. It is a fossiliferous limestone of the late Jurassic period with a polished colour varying from russet-red to greenish-brown and blue-grey. It began to be used extensively for decorative coffin lids and effigies and architectural parts of monuments from the twelfth century onwards. It was also popular for ledger slabs in which brasses were set. By the mid-fourteenth century, Purbeck effigies were out of fashion. However, by the mid-fifteenth century, tomb chests and canopied tombs (generally London-made) composed of this material had become very popular – invariably incorporating brasses. This fashion continued until the mid-sixteenth century, after which the use of Purbeck marble for monuments virtually ceased. It is not infrequently used in conjunction with alabaster, for example in the sarcophagus of the Kelwey monument of circa 1580 at Exton, Rutland, and was also used for column shafts.[7]

Three other similar 'marbles' are also worthy of mention. Alwalton 'marble', quarried near Peterborough, is often mistaken for Purbeck, and was used, for example, for a series of ecclesiastical effigies in Peterborough

Figure 13.2   The Purbeck marble sarcophagus being reinstated to the Kelwey monument at Exton, Rutland. Note the arrangement of the slings for lifting.

Cathedral. Frosterley 'marble', quarried in County Durham, is a Carboniferous limestone with numerous large pale grey or white fossils against a dark background, occasionally used in monuments. Finally there are a number of Wealden 'marbles' – also known as 'Paludina marbles', after the large distinctive fossils that they contain – including Bethersden, Petworth and Sussex 'marbles'. These were certainly used locally as a substitute for Purbeck marble in monuments but, like Alwalton, they can be difficult to distinguish from the Purbeck variety in a weathered state.

True marbles

Marble, in the true sense of the word, is metamorphic stone consisting largely of calcite (crystalline calcium carbonate). There are some localized sources of true marble in Scotland and Eire, but these do not appear to have been exploited for use in monuments to any significant degree. Much more important are imported marbles, especially Italian – the most famous of all being from Carrara in Tuscany. Italian marble began to be used in earnest for monuments in the early seventeenth century, and within 100 years it had almost totally supplanted alabaster. As well as pure white statuary marble, there are also varieties of grey-veined white marble from Carrara. The most common yellow marble is from Sienna, and the best known red

Figure 13.3 Detail of the monument to Samuel Tufnell (d.1758) at Pleshey, Essex, showing Sienna marble cladding (partly detached) used in conjunction with white statuary Carrara marble. The monument is by Henry Cheere.

from Verona. Brecciated (or Breccia) marbles were also used extensively. These comprise secondary formations of marble in monuments, in which fragments of stone are incorporated into a marble matrix.[8]

Fixings

It is important to remember that the fixings of a monument, although not generally visible, are an important part of its structure. In a typical tomb chest, these might be simple wrought iron dog cramps set between side panels and tying them back to a stone and mortar core, but more complex or unusual fixings might also be found. An example is the limestone tomb chest beneath the two oak effigies, believed to be of Sir Ralph and Cecilia Reynes of circa 1333 at Clifton Reynes, Buckinghamshire, rebuilt as part of a conservation programme in 1987. It was found not only to have ferrous cramps fixing adjacent side panels to one another, but also to have three oak ties running from side to side, dovetailed into the top of the panels.[9] Wall monuments, by their very nature, require numerous and often more complex fixings. Usually they are supported on key elements that are set well back into the wall (and sometimes additionally held with large ferrous fixings) acting as corbels, perhaps with a shelf or entablature also rebated in the wall, but some may rely purely on iron supports. It is not unusual to find carefully made wrought iron ties on late sixteenth- or early seventeenth-century alabaster monuments, running horizontally through an entablature and linking to dowels set vertically through a column shaft and capital. Although it is often the corrosion of this ironwork that necessitates an intervention to start with, it must be remembered that these carefully made fixings are just as much part of the monument as the alabaster or marble.

Medieval and later masons were clearly aware of the potential problems of using ironwork in monument structures, and other fixing methods were sometimes employed. For example, the canopy of the monument to Sir Richard Willoughby (d.1471) and his wife at Wollaton, Nottinghamshire, was fixed using 'secret key' joints between lintel stones, with molten lead poured into the joint lines. By the mid-nineteenth century, copper alloy pins were increasingly used to fix minor elements together, and it is not uncommon to find wooden dowels in less vital structural contexts on monuments of any period.

The use of natural resins should also be mentioned. Marble veneer, for example, is often found to be fixed to a limestone backing-panel using rosin.

Figure 13.4 Iron pins (set in lead) through the alabaster capitals of the Kelwey monument at Exton, and the end of a fish-tailed iron strap running right across the top of the entablature. Cracks can be seen in the capitals, arising due to corrosion and expansion of the iron.

Bedding and pointing

In early (medieval) monuments, lime mortar was almost invariably used to bed and point stone elements. By the later sixteenth century, plaster of Paris was increasingly common, being the material of choice for alabaster and marble monuments. Portland cement is occasionally encountered in (generally) early to mid-twentieth-century restoration work, and PVA and silica sand mortars are found in some monuments conserved in the 1970s to 1990s.

THE HISTORIC BUILDING ENVIRONMENT

By their very nature, church monuments belong in churches. Churches are not museums, and typically are of a traditional form of construction, employing porous building materials and incorporating no damp-proof courses. The average parish church has a pattern of periodic use, causing fluctuations in the internal temperature and relative humidity. It is this context that makes the field of monument conservation very different from sculpture conservation in the museum environment, or in parks and gardens or in private houses. It is therefore vital that a conservator looking at a monument considers not just the monument, but also the building environment in which it is set, and an understanding of that context is one of the most important aspects of monument conservation.

A BRIEF HISTORY OF MONUMENT RESTORATION AND CONSERVATION

Monument restoration and conservation has a history as long as that of the monuments themselves. This can be said with some confidence, because evidence is regularly found of repairs that have been made on site to monuments which were damaged in transit to their original placement. It is easy to imagine the frustration of the masons who unpacked the separate elements of the monument to Richard Earle (d.1697) as it arrived from its long journey by cart up the Great North Road from Thomas Green's workshop in Camberwell to the remote parish church at Stragglethorpe in Lincolnshire, only to find that the inscription panel had broken in two. The masons improvised a repair using a flat slab of stone obtained locally, fixed to the back of the two halves of the marble panel using plaster of Paris and iron cramps.[10] This is typical of the approach to repair and maintenance until the nineteenth century, it being done by the same craftsmen who carve and fix monuments using the same range of techniques.[11] One such example is Edward Richardson, a sculptor who was responsible for drastic restoration work, including much speculative re-carving and piecing-in, to many monuments from 1842 onwards, including most notably the Temple church effigies and the alabaster tombs at Elford in Staffordshire.[12] Even at the time, there was much criticism of the extent to which often speculative restoration of this nature was carried out. By comparison, Sir George Gilbert Scott oversaw a relatively 'conservative' programme of consolidation, cleaning and repair to the Royal tombs at Westminster Abbey in the 1850s and 60s. This included the attempted consolidation of deteriorating Purbeck marble using shellac diluted in alcohol, injected using a 'gardener's syringe', as well as cleaning the bronzes using 'acids of oxides' (probably oxalic acid or hydrogen peroxide).[13]

There was much contemporary criticism of Scott's proposals by The Society of Antiquaries and the Royal Archaeological Institute, reflecting the public interest in restoration and concerns that too much might be done. In 1876, the Society for the Protection of Ancient Buildings (SPAB) was formed, and it helped campaign for the preservation of historic fabric rather than unnecessary 'restoration' (that is, replacement) of buildings. This approach is equally reflected in the treatment of monuments, with for example Fred Crossley (author of many books on church architecture and art) working, in association with A. R. Powys of SPAB and the antiquary Sir William St John Hope, on the monuments at Paulerspury church (Northamptonshire) between 1915 and 1920. The work they carried out there, as documented in the SPAB archives, could truly be called conservation in the modern sense.

The treatment in the 1930s of the alabaster tombs at Swine Church in the East Riding of Yorkshire is another comparatively rare example of such work being well documented. In this case it was published, with photographs, both in the Yorkshire Archaeological Journal and a Council for the Care of Churches (CCC) report.[14] It is remarkable not only for the level of recording achieved, but also as an attempt at isolating the monuments from damp, although the means is not entirely clear. This seems to have been a new concept, and one that was increasingly adopted as the century progressed. Although the work at Swine was carried out by local craftsmen under the direction of the church's architect, it became increasingly common for there to be a museum involvement with the treatment of monuments, particularly after the Second World War as the concept of conservation became more widely established.[15] The 1970s were a particularly formative time for monument conservation. The use of damp-proof membranes was becoming more widespread, and they were used in the rebuilding of three alabaster monuments at Breedon-on-the-Hill, Leicestershire in 1974 – in this case with a cement and concrete block core, lime mortar as a bedding medium, and Polyfilla to point. This formula was refined in an attempt to eliminate liquid moisture from the monument during rebuilding by using polyester resin or PVA and sand mortar as a bedding medium, and acrylic resin mixed with stone dust as a filling and pointing medium. Once a monument has been rebuilt with a damp-proof membrane and dry materials in the core, the theory was that if it were given a coating of microcrystalline wax and Ketone 'N' (for alabaster and marble monuments), it would be completely isolated from the moisture in the building fabric and the environment. This approach was first published in 1978, and most recently in 1990.[16] What follows here is an updated approach that takes into consideration recent technological developments and changes in philosophy.

Figure 13.5 Repairs, believed to be original to the erection of the monument, to the back of the inscription panel of the Earle monument at Stragglethorpe, Lincolnshire.

INVESTIGATION AND ANALYSIS

Making an initial report to describe a monument, record its condition, look at the causes of deterioration, and make costed recommendations has, since the 1970s, been the standard first step towards an interventionist treatment. Until recently it was common practice for a conservator to quote for making a survey and report without first having seen the monument (which might be several hours drive away), or at best allowing for a ground-level inspection of the monument, a basic review of the condition of the building fabric (relative internal and external ground levels, drains and gutters, roof, and so on), perhaps with the help of a few isolated relative humidity and temperature readings, and then a few hours spent in writing the report up. In the vast majority of cases, the prognosis was the same; liquid moisture was the problem and the only realistic answer was to dismantle and rebuild along the lines of the 'dry method' outlined above. The Monuments and Furnishings Committee of the Council for the Care of Churches recognized that this approach needed refining. Since 2003, it has required a much more rigorous programme of investigation and analysis prior to making any physical intervention to a monument; permission is unlikely to be granted for work to go ahead without first submitting a report fulfilling these criteria.

It is imperative that a conservator make an initial site visit to assess what is required for a thorough survey. This can be termed a 'Phase 1 report' and should have the following aims:

- To determine what kind of access is going to be required to inspect the monument closely at all levels. A tomb chest or effigy might be inspected from ground level only, and a small wall monument set relatively near to the ground might be accessible from a stepladder, but larger or higher monuments will require a scaffold or cherry picker to allow for a full and close inspection.
- To make an initial assessment of the nature and condition of the monument.
- To arrive at a hypothesis for the cause(s) and rate(s) of any deterioration that is noted. This will require a certain amount of background information. For example, a copy of the most recent architect's quinquennial inspection report and a conversation with the architect and churchwardens will give detailed information about the condition of the fabric as a whole, and what has been done in recent years. A search for historic photographs of the monument (for example, with

the National Monuments Record) can be useful. This was the case
for the monument to Lord Campden of 1686 at Exton, Rutland, where
dated photographs of 1910–20, 1938–9, 1947, 1960, 1970 and 1992
helped map the loss of superficial marble embellishments due to
corroding iron dowels. Typically, as discussed below, liquid moisture is
the principal agent of decay – causing iron fixings to corrode and
expand, as well as causing stone decay by the action of soluble salts.
If this is the case, one needs an explanation as to how the moisture has
entered the monument, and whether the problem has now been
addressed (for example, have the rainwater goods have been overhauled,
the roof fixed, or new drains been installed?), and what the current risk
is to the monument.

- The written Phase 1 report should summarize the context and nature
  of the monument rather than describe it to the last detail, instead
  concentrating on the hypothesis for the cause(s) and rate(s) of decay.
  It should then consider how the hypothesis might be tested, and to what
  extent the time and expense of analytical work needed to do this might
  be justified. It will conclude with a detailed and costed recommendation
  for the Phase 2 report.

Two important points should be made regarding the Phase 1 report.
Firstly, it will take time and expense to prepare, particularly if a special
journey is required to visit a church some distance away (it is only
reasonable that the conservator should be paid a fair price for this
work). One of the reasons why the relatively superficial report had become
so normal until recently was that it was often seen as something the
conservator in private practice should prepare as a 'loss-leader' towards
procuring site work: it was expected to be done either for no charge or for
a fraction of the real cost. Secondly, it is often very easy to superficially
look at a monument with open joint-lines and visibly corroding iron and
jump to the conclusion that liquid moisture is the cause, and that the only
answer is to dismantle and rebuild, ensuring that the iron is replaced with
stainless steel. The reality might be that the source of high liquid moisture
levels was removed long ago, and that the iron has not corroded significantly for a century or more. This does not necessarily mean that the
monument is structurally stable, and this needs to be ascertained. However, if it is stable, then this brings into question the need to dismantle and
rebuild. Therefore, what might at first sight seem obvious can often benefit
from some further investigation prior to acting.

The Phase 2 report will involve the testing and further investigation of the hypothesis drawn up by Phase 1. Where damp is involved, this will almost certainly require a 'dispersed water survey' – that is, an appraisal of where rainwater goes in the vicinity of the building – and quite possibly, a liquid moisture survey as well. The latter can vary, from the taking of measurements of relative moisture content at measured intervals on the wall, floor and monument surface using a carbide meter, to the taking of core samples (which can be weighed, dried and re-weighed) in order to physically determine the variation of absolute moisture levels within cross-section(s) of the wall. There are advantages and disadvantages to the sampling approach. It certainly gives an accurate picture, particularly when combined with soluble salt analysis, but it is expensive (in that it is time consuming), involves the drilling of a series of holes (typically of 20 mm diameter), preferably into joint lines of the wall, and is particularly difficult in flint or cobble walls. The Phase 2 report will follow guidelines drawn up by the CCC, and will include a detailed description and condition report as well as discussion of the survey work. It may be that the hypothesis has been proved wrong, or that the testing was inconclusive, in which case other options will need to be considered. Environmental monitoring might be considered, and can be useful for determining condensation patterns, for example, but is generally less applicable than liquid moisture surveys to the issues at hand.

It is essential that as much background information as possible be obtained about the history of the monument at this stage. Is it *in situ*? This might be ascertained by looking at records held by the parish, the church's architect, the Diocese, or in the CCC's files. Antiquarian records can prove useful, and should always be consulted as part of the report writing process. Pevsner's *Buildings of England* series[17] gives an overview of antiquarian sources for the county in the introduction to the relevant volume. Some counties are better served than others: for example Leicestershire is well served by John Nichols' *The History and Antiquities of the County of Leicester* of 1811,[18] which illustrates numerous monuments. Particularly for medieval monuments, there are often more general studies, so the conservator should at least know of Gough, Stothard and Blore.[19] Also to be consulted are the *Victoria County Histories*[20] (occasionally useful) and the Royal Commission on the Historical Monuments of England (RCHME) volumes[21] (often useful), where either of these exist. Knowledge of any previous interventions gleaned by these means, and by observation of the monument itself, will help produce an informed condition assessment.

An important aspect of the Phase 2 report should be to make an assessment of the cultural 'significance' or 'value' of the monument. Its relative importance with regard to the following points should be considered:

- Is it a work of art (of local, regional, national or international importance)?
- Is it an example of a known sculptor or workshop's work?
- Who is the person (or persons) commemorated?

All of these will help make the case for grant aid and might impact upon the recommendations made.

The report will make recommendations for further work (which might simply be ongoing monitoring), and give time and cost estimates. It will also incorporate a good photographic record. The type of photographs to be used is a fairly contentious issue. Digital photographs are increasingly becoming the norm, but the National Monuments Record have recently advised that for a long-term archive their preferred form of photograph is the conventional negative. Given that these reports should be thought of as part of a long-term record, it is necessary to include both original colour photographic prints and 35 mm negatives.

THE NEED FOR STRUCTURAL INTERVENTIONS

This is probably the most fundamental question to address in determining a conservation treatment. To dismantle and rebuild any part of a monument will significantly affect its 'authenticity', particularly where background research shows that this has almost certainly never been done since the monument was first erected. Existing fixings are likely to require replacing (indeed, that may be the justification for dismantling in the first place), core material will probably not be reusable, mortar will have to be replaced, and there is, of course, a risk associated with any structural intervention. Indeed, the decision will ultimately come down to a risk and value assessment. What is the risk of not dismantling, or of only partial dismantling, and how do these balance against the gain from the intervention?

DEALING WITH DAMP

The desire to install a damp-proof membrane should rarely, if ever, be used as a justification for dismantling a monument. Furthermore, in those cases where dismantling is carried out, the argument that a monument 'is dismantled anyway, so we might as well install a damp-proof membrane' should not be entertained. At this point, the conservator should step back and look at the conclusions of the Phase 2 survey. This should have determined what levels of liquid moisture are present in the vicinity of the monument. If they are relatively low and, although ironwork may have corroded, the marble or alabaster would appear to be sound, or to have suffered only minimal amounts of decay over (say) 400 years in its present environment, then given that the ironwork is likely to be replaced with 316 grade stainless steel with a very long lifespan (far greater than any known damp-proof membrane), there seems no point in installing a damp proof membrane. The most common situation where a membrane might be appropriate is where a tomb chest sits on a floor, which, despite all efforts to improve drainage, remains unacceptably damp and the stone of the monument is deteriorating as a result. Here, there is likely to be a continuous flat surface for the membrane that is not penetrated by fixings. Wall monuments are much more problematic, since there will be numerous fixings into the wall and, almost certainly, stones corbelled into the wall; introducing a membrane in such cases could seriously affect the structural integrity of this arrangement.

The monuments at Breedon-on-the-Hill have already been noted as having had lead damp-proof membranes installed in 1974. They were reassessed in 1988 and 2000, and it was found that at least one of them was already deteriorating further as a result of liquid moisture by 1988; in 2000 it appeared that this was because the roof above was leaking. In this instance, therefore, the membrane has clearly not worked, and may even be making matters worse by allowing water to pool on top of it.[22] It is estimated that a code 4 milled-lead membrane will have a lifespan of 100 years or so. On this basis, if we were to continue to rely on membranes as an integral part of the monument conservation process, we would be creating a completely unsustainable situation for future generations.

There are often alternative (and more sustainable) approaches to dealing with relatively high liquid moisture levels. These may involve allowing for some ventilation of the core – in the case of a monument built against the internal face of an external wall, perhaps by means of an airbrick to the external wall surface, in conjunction with channels within the core and a discreetly placed vent to it within the church. Every monument presents different challenges, and there is no standard answer to this, but in four out of five cases recently examined by the author, ventilation by some means has proved to be a viable solution to the problem of damp. Each of the case studies at the end of this chapter demonstrates how this might be done.

CONSIDERATIONS IN CLEANING MONUMENTS

In the last 20 years, there has been an increasing awareness of the risks associated with the cleaning of stone buildings.[23] Parallel to this, but less widely publicized, there has been an even greater degree of caution about cleaning monumental sculpture. Any form of cleaning, even light dusting, may have risks associated when it comes to cleaning monuments – particularly where traces of polychromy survive. Against these risks, the benefits are primarily aesthetic. Neo-Classical monuments, in particular, are much easier to appreciate as the sculptor intended when 'clean' of the dust, spiders' webs and bat excreta that may accumulate over time in the average church. In addition, the conservator may have to deal with stains from condensation runs (in which case the cause of the condensation should be considered first), ingrained grease or oils from human handling, or previously applied surface treatments that may have discoloured. In the latter case, it is important to understand the nature of the surface treatment, and to ask whether or not it might have been intentionally applied at the time of the monument's erection. Background research and analysis at the survey stage can help with this.

Typical cleaning methods, their applications, and the risks posed are summarized in Table 13.1. It should be noted that the intention of cleaning is rarely, if ever, to make the monument look 'new'. A balance needs to be struck between aesthetics, the limitations of the methods available, and the risk of damage (even on a microscopic scale). It is important that this is discussed with the client from the outset, so that any unrealistic expectations are avoided.

DISMANTLING, REBUILDING AND STRUCTURAL REPAIRS

A note of caution prior to carrying out any dismantling and rebuilding has already been expressed. In many cases – particularly where severely

Table 13.1 Typical cleaning methods applied to monuments, their uses, and associated risks. The list is not exhaustive.

Method	Applications	Risks
Soft bristle brush in conjunction with a vacuum cleaner	Removing surface dust and dirt	Loss of poorly fixed polychromy and small loose fragments of stone. This can be minimized by a careful examination prior to cleaning, pre-consolidation if required, and use of a gauze over a variable power vacuum, controlling the distance of the nozzle from the surface.
De-ionized water[19] on cotton wool swabs	Removing more ingrained dirt	Dissolution of water-soluble substrate (e.g. alabaster or some polychromy); When cleaning *in situ*, might exacerbate iron corrosion.
De-ionized water poultice (acid-free paper or sepiolite)	More effective for drawing out ingrained dirt than swabs. Particularly useful for statuary marble.	Similar risks to swabbing, but more so where clay poultices (generally the most effective) are used, since residue of the clay needs to be removed using water (on swabs or with bristle brushes).
De-ionized water applied with bristle brushes and removed with tissue or cotton wool swabs.	Removing ingrained dirt. Quicker and more effective than swabbing alone.	Similar to swabbing, but more so since more water is used and the method of application is more aggressive.
Steam cleaning (typically with a Derotor cleaner), removing excess water with tissue or cotton wool swabs.	Removing ingrained dirt. More effective again than bristle brushes.	Similar to swabbing. Any method in untrained hands has a greater risk, but this one especially so, since it is easy to use it too close or for too long a dwell time, in which case micro or macroscopic damage to crystalline structure and loss of original polish is inevitable. Only to be used with great caution when less aggressive methods are inadequate.

Table 13.1   Continued.

Method	Applications	Risks
A mix of white spirit and de-ionized water with added non-ionic detergent. Applied by swab or bristle brush, as for water, ensuring that no reagent is left on the surface.	The detergent and white spirit are more effective than water at removing greasy deposits.	Leaving traces of detergent on the surface. Damage to polychromy if fugitive in white spirit or water. Damage to pitch inlay. However, can be useful on alabaster, where water on its own should not be used, particularly if used in 3:2 or 3:1 ratio of white spirit to water.
Organic solvent (typically IMS or acetone) applied by swab or brush.	Useful where water cannot be used; for removing old surface treatments; and for organic residues generally.	Risk of dissolution of polychromy. Greater health and safety risks than aqueous treatments.
Solvol paste (comprising diatomaceous earth, a methylated soap, 2–3% ammonia, and white spirit) applied by cotton wool swab or bristle brush, removing any residue with white spirit.	Can be useful where water cannot be used. Combination of reagents and mechanical action often prove effective where other methods are not. (Perhaps too) commonly used on alabaster.	Each of the components presents a different risk. The greatest issue is the mechanical nature of this method. Particularly with softer stones such as alabaster, but also with marbles, there will always be a mechanical polishing action occurring (sometimes, where a polish has been diminished, this can actually be a bonus). It can be particularly difficult to remove all residue of the diatomaceous earth from carved detail.
Linament of Soap (containing 4% camphor, 4% oleic acid, 0.7% potassium hydroxide, 1.5% rosemary oil, 63% IMS)	Can be useful where purely aqueous reagents cannot be used. Most commonly used on alabaster and on gilding.	Each of the components presents a different risk. Notable is the health and safety risk compared to aqueous reagents. Can be difficult to obtain, and relatively rarely used nowadays.

Table 13.1 Continued.

Method	Applications	Risks
Chelating agents in de-ionized water (e.g. EDTA or Tri-Ammonium Citrate)	Useful for reducing iron stains.	Risks associated with water, although only small quantities used here (typically the reagent is used at 1–5% in water in a paper poultice with a carefully controlled dwell time). The reagent will not differentiate between metal ions in the stone and those that are meant to be removed, so a degree of surface etching, albeit on a microscopic level, is inevitable.
Nd:YAG Laser	Useful where water is undesirable, particularly for removing dark deposits from light surfaces.	As the technology is developed, the reducing cost and greater ease of use (e.g. by the portability of the equipment) of this method is make it increasingly accessible. There are health and safety risks. It can be difficult to direct the laser at areas of undercut detail or where access is otherwise restricted.
Micro-airbrasive	Useful for removing surface deposits where water is undesirable and where other methods are ineffective.	Health and safety implications. Risk of mechanical damage to substrate. Difficulty in both containing spent powder and removing all residue from the monument when working on site.

corroding iron fixings are present, or a monument is structurally unstable for any other reason – a degree of dismantling and rebuilding is unavoidable. The skill required of the monument conservator is at least threefold here. Firstly, it must be judged to what extent dismantling needs to be carried out to address the problems, and how this might be done whilst causing as little disturbance as possible to the historic fabric (such as by partial dismantling or by leaving the core intact). Secondly, there is the issue of handling (what are often) very heavy, but fragile and vulnerable, elements of stone. Learning how to lever, wedge, strap, sling, pack, protect, hold and lift elements of a monument can take years of experience to do safely, since only rarely are two cases the same. Thirdly, there is the health and safety aspect. It is not always possible to simply dismantle a monument in the reverse order in which it was built, since the failure of fixings or other decay phenomena might have caused instabilities such that there is a risk of partial or complete collapse when some elements are removed. The conservator must therefore consider what might or could happen, and take measures to provide temporary support and protection as a contingency against either damage to the monument or potentially severe injury to people in the vicinity. A further risk is of either trying to lift something manually that is too awkward or heavy, and of trapping fingers when putting a heavy object down. Working on the very approximate basis that one cubic metre of stone weighs about 2 tonnes (or for those who prefer imperial, one cubic foot weighs about 130 lb, or 60 kg), it should be possible to roughly assess the weight of an element before it is handled. Structural work should never be carried out by one person working on their own – often it is desirable to have three present; the working area should be kept free of trip hazards, and there should always be a good selection of wooden runners and ethafoam pads to hand.[25]

Structural repairs typically involve pinning two or more pieces of a broken element together. Care must be taken to ensure that pieces are fixed together in the right order (so as not to 'lock' another piece out), and to align fragments together properly (a good flat bench is a necessity for flat architectural elements), especially where they might have distorted out of line. Consideration must also be given to the function of an element, and if it cannot be given sufficient structural integrity in its repair, further measures will be required – perhaps the placing of a hidden lintel, or in extreme cases the replacement of a stone. Most commonly, repairs are made using 316 grade stainless steel (either flat bars or threaded rods of various diameters), set in polyester resin or epoxy resin. Alternatives to stainless steel are Perspex (for example, close to a translucent surface) or ceramic dowels. Phosphor bronze has been used in the past, but it is not as stable in the long term as 316 grade stainless steel. One advantage of stainless steel over non-metallic materials is that it would be more easily detectable in the future, should the written record of repair work undertaken be unavailable.

Figure 13.6 Lifting a life-sized marble statue back onto the monument to Sir Richard Alibon (d.1688) and his wife in Dagenham parish church, Greater London.

Figure 13.7 Removing a huge marble obelisk from the Campden monument of 1696 (by Grinling Gibbons) at Exton, Rutland. The scaffold has been specially designed to take the weight, and original lifting holes utilized.

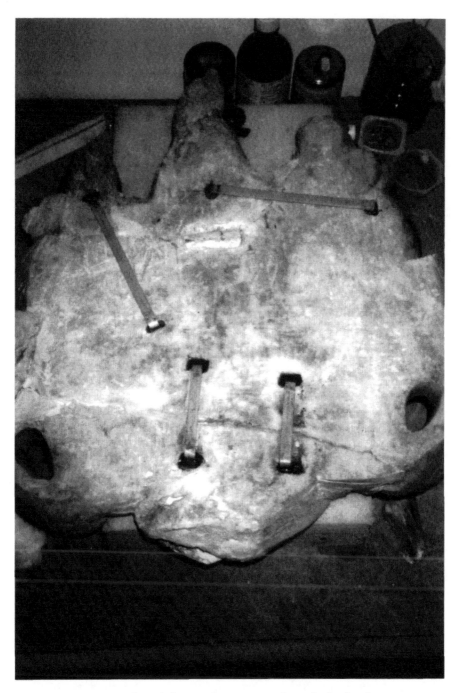

Figure 13.8   316 grade stainless steel cramps set into the back of an alabaster cartouche.

Bedding and pointing materials

Historically, either lime mortar or (almost universally from the sixteenth century onwards, except where there is an interface with the wall) plaster of Paris was used for most bedding and pointing applications to a monument. There are two schools of thought as to what should be used in conservation applications. One view is that as little water as possible should be introduced upon rebuilding or re-pointing a monument. This dictates the use of corework of dry concrete blocks, bedded in polyester resin and dry sand mortar, typically constructed over a damp-proof membrane, with polyvinyl acetate and silica sand being used to bed elements of the monument, and re-pointing being done using acrylic resin and stone dust. The other end of the spectrum is to use similar materials to those employed in the original construction – whether this be core, masonry or mortar. Contemporary thinking is steering very much towards the latter approach, although each case must be treated on its merits and the risks and benefits of the alternatives assessed.

SURFACE REPAIR AND CONSOLIDATION

To an extent, the arguments and alternatives that apply to bedding and pointing materials also apply to surface repair materials. For example, a crack or spall to a marble element could be made good with a coloured synthetic resin or with some form of plaster, either pre-coloured or painted to match the marble. Again, there are advantages and disadvantages, and each case must be taken on its merits, although the 'fashion' at the moment is more for plaster than resin fills.

Little need be said about stone consolidation here, since it is well covered in other chapters. Paraloid B72 acrylic resin has many applications to relatively dry stone, and can be particularly useful for the surface consolidation of alabaster and polishable limestones as well as for 'sugared' marble. Silicic acid esters (such as Wacker OH) have some applications (although not generally to alabaster), and acrylic emulsions and colloidal dispersions can have their uses as well. Prior to using any consolidant it is essential that trials be carried out to test its efficacy.

Applied surface coatings need consideration. Microcrystalline wax (sometimes with Ketone N) has been applied to monuments as a matter of routine as part of conservation programmes in the recent past. However, this is often unnecessary; if carried out, to be effective and to avoid the danger of cross-linking, it needs periodic removal and reapplication. In practice this is rarely considered. There is also an argument that a wax coating might actually attract dust. Therefore, it is best to start on the basis that a surface coating should not be applied, but to reconsider this if there are factors that determine that it is indeed necessary. Such factors might include: unavoidable exposure to a considerable amount of human contact or handling; unavoidable exposure to bat excreta; condensation problems; or sometimes on aesthetic grounds to re-instate the original and intended visual appearance of a (now faded) coloured marble (where the only other way of achieving the same ends would be to mechanically polish). Other issues can apply to polishable limestones such as Purbeck marble, which are covered in another chapter.

CASE STUDIES

The monument to the First Earl of Leicester at Tittleshall, Norfolk

The First Earl of Leicester, who built Holkham Hall, died in 1759 and, with his wife, is commemorated by a fine standing wall monument of various marbles by William Atkinson with two busts by Louis Francois Roubiliac, in the Chancel at St Mary's Church, Tittleshall, Norfolk. By 1997, the monument was in a perilous state of disrepair, due mainly to corroding iron fixings in the damp walls of the church. Most evident was the severe disruption and loss of veneer to the Sienna marble-clad limestone sarcophagus, but as it turned out other large sections of the monument were also extremely unstable.

Once the rainwater goods and drainage had been overhauled under the direction of the church architect, the fabric started to dry out, and attention was turned to dealing with the monument. Every possible course of action was considered, but massive disruption to the raised marble plinth, due to iron corrosion, could only be addressed by taking down all parts of the monument as described above. A carefully designed scaffold was erected by a tried and tested contractor experienced with this sort of work. It incorporated lifting beams and was built so as to take the load of several tonnes of dismantled marble that would have to remain on the scaffold. Despite every precaution being taken during dismantling, as the pediment was removed and the weight lifted from the back panel, stresses caused by heavily corroded iron bars set back into the wall caused the limestone backing to the heraldic centre section to burst apart; it collapsed

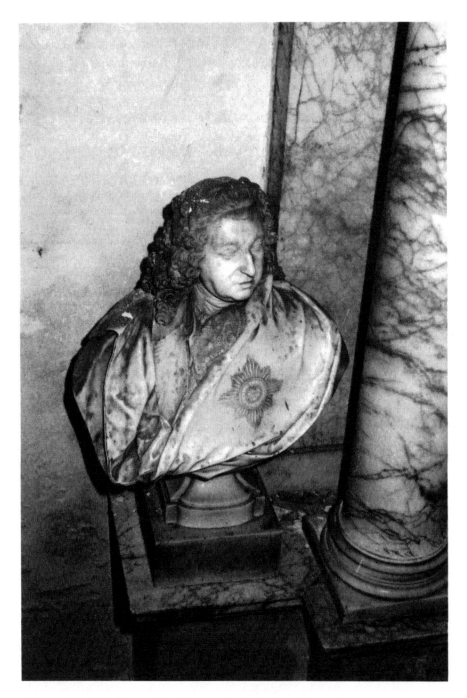

Figure 13.9   The bust of the First Earl of Leicester, by Roubiliac, on his monument at Tittleshall, Norfolk. Damage from penetrating water to the lime plaster on the adjacent wall is obvious. The level of dirt, much of it ingrained into the marble surface, is typical of that encountered on church monuments.

Figure 13.10 An arrangement used to remove large and heavy pediment stones where there is insufficient height to use a block and tackle, at Tittleshall.

Figure 13.11 The shattered heraldic panel from the First Earl of Leicester's monument.

Figure 13.12 The repaired and re-fixed heraldic panel at Tittleshall.

Figure 13.13 The external wall behind the First Earl of Leicester's monument at Tittleshall showing the airbricks inserted to allow ventilation of the core.

onto the scaffold in hundreds of pieces. Work stopped at once, and a forensic operation began. All fragments were recorded *in situ*, and then carefully lifted and laid out in order on the floor adjacent to the scaffold. The panel was in three layers: to the front was an ornately carved white statuary marble heraldic relief with painted arms (the original polychromy still largely complete and un-restored), set against a thin panel of black marble, fixed to a thick limestone backing panel. The iron fixings had been set through all three, being rebated into the back of the white marble. Fortunately, due to the careful recovery, all breaks were clean and the panel could be carefully pinned together, so that only a very careful inspection would ever reveal that it had been broken. The remainder of the monument was relatively straightforward to dismantle, although particular care had to be taken with the complex arrangement of cladding to the sarcophagus and in handling the marble busts.

Of particular interest is the approach taken to rebuilding this monument. The initial intention had been to use a damp-proof membrane, but as investigations determined that the building fabric was drying out to acceptable levels since the drainage and rainwater goods had been overhauled, and as the marble itself remained in good condition (it had primarily been the ironwork that had suffered), a method of rebuilding the monument with a ventilated core was devised in consultation with the architect. Discreet openings (covered by painted stainless steel mesh) were left to the sides of the raised plinth; air channels were built into the new core; and three air bricks set into the external wall to allow for good through ventilation. This meant that hydraulic lime mortar could be used for rebuilding the core, and any residual or excess liquid moisture in the mortar and masonry were given means of evaporating. Once clean, apart from the use of stainless steel set in epoxy resin to replace the old iron set in lead, the monument was rebuilt using methods and materials that would have been very familiar to the eighteenth-century masons.[26]

The monument to John Harpur (d.1627) and his wife at Swarkestone, Derbyshire

The Harpurs were one of the great land-owning families of Derbyshire, having their seat at Calke Abbey from the mid-seventeenth century. Sir John Harpur ran the family estate from Swarkestone for about 50 years until his death in 1627. The monument to Sir John, and his wife Isabella (Pierrepont) in the Harpur Chapel on the south side of St James' Church, Swarkestone is an alabaster tomb chest with two recumbent effigies and an

Figure 13.14 The Harpur monument at Swarkestone during dismantling, showing an exposed very heavily corroded iron fixing. This cramp had lost all structural integrity.

Figure 13.15 The Harpur monument during rebuilding, showing a new 316 grade stainless steel fixing re-using existing fixing holes, set in epoxy resin. Also note the air gap between the concrete block and hydraulic lime core and the alabaster panels.

Figure 13.16 The Harpur monument after conservation. The air gap behind is
very discreet.

inscription panel set into the wall above. The church is very close to the
river Trent, which periodically breaks its banks, allowing water to come
very close to the church. As a result of damp conditions in the church,
the iron fixings within the monument had severely corroded, leaving
it somewhat unstable and with sections of carved detail in danger of
spalling off.

Prior to any intervention being made to the monument itself the
drainage, roof and guttering were overhauled under the direction of
the church architect. A rigorous programme of research, investigation and
analysis was then undertaken under the guidance of the Council for the
Care of Churches (CCC). As well as discovering that the monument
could be attributed to a coherent group of Midlands producers, tracking
the condition of the monument through photographs dating back to the
1920s, and finding antiquarian notes which described the monument's
restoration (but crucially not dismantling and rebuilding) in the 1870s, a
comprehensive liquid moisture survey was carried out to the Chapel walls.
Considering this in conjunction with a study of surface water movement
externally, it was determined that all that could be done to provide a drier
environment had already been done, but that the walls at low level were
still too damp to allow the ironwork to remain in place. Since the background research had shown that the monument was *in situ*, the decision

to dismantle and rebuild (so as to replace the failing ironwork) was not taken lightly.

The alabaster itself had deteriorated significantly in places, and it was felt that, despite consolidation (using Paraloid B72 acrylic co-polymer), some further measure was required to protect the rebuilt monument from penetrating damp. In conjunction with the architect and the CCC, it was determined that a continuous lead damp-proof membrane between the tomb chest and the floor was appropriate. But rather than trying to place a membrane between the monument and the wall, a more satisfactory and longer-term solution was to discreetly move it approximately 40 mm away from the wall (which abutted on two sides) so as to leave an air gap for ventilation. Given that this was allowed for, the new core was built using masonry bedded in hydraulic lime mortar, and the monument itself rebuilt using a fine, feebly hydraulic lime mortar to bed and point. The inscription panel, set higher up in the wall, was left *in situ*.[27]

CONCLUSIONS: THE WAY FORWARD

The field of church monument conservation is surprisingly dynamic. By definition, such conservation work takes place in churches (although there are exceptions!), and in the majority of cases (for the Church of England), this means that any work to be carried out must go through the Faculty system, being approved by a Diocesan Advisory Committee and often referred to the CCC's Monuments and Furnishings Committee. In such cases, the work must be carried out by an approved conservator. Until very recently, this meant a contractor included on the CCC's approved list, but this has been superseded by the Conservation Register maintained by the Institute for Conservation (ICON). The Conservation Register is, in turn, closely linked to the formal accreditation of conservators, also controlled by ICON. This relatively standardized form of control should benefit the profession, and should ensure that the quality of both monument conservation work and survey and documentation continues to improve throughout the profession.

Less encouraging is the lack of opportunities for good training in monument conservation. One way forward might for firms and institutions specializing in such work to offer apprenticeships, which could be formally recognized as qualifications, and for the cost of training programmes to be taken into account where competitive tenders are sought for work.

Finally, within the UK, there is unrealized potential both in ICON and in the thriving Church Monuments Society for a greater debate on church monument conservation, and for a better record and publication of work that has been carried out. The onus for achieving this very much lies with individual monument conservators.

The author

David Carrington DPhil, ACR

David Carrington studied Archaeological Conservation at Cardiff University from 1983–86. Since then he has been involved in various aspects of building conservation, in particular sculpture and plaster. In 2000 he obtained a DPhil at the University of York in Church Monument Conservation. For the last ten years he has run a private company specializing in stone sculpture conservation.

References

1   There have been several good general studies published of the history of monuments. For example: Kemp, B., *English Church Monuments*, Batsford, London, 1980; Curl, J. S., *A Celebration of Death*, Batsford, London, 1980; and Whinney, M., *Sculpture in Britain 1530–1830*, second edition, revised by Physick, J., Penguin, London, 1988.

2   Carrington, D., *English Church Monuments to 1750: Their survival and conservation*, unpublished DPhil thesis, University of York, 2000. Volume 2 comprises a comprehensive survey of all known monuments in North Yorkshire up until 1750.

3   The best known quarries are at Totternhoe, Barrington and Burwell (no longer worked). See Ashurst J. and Dimes F. (eds.), *Conservation of Building and Decorative Stone Volume 1*, Butterworth-Heinemann, London, 1990, p. 117.

4   Much can be and has been written on alabaster monuments. The key text for medieval examples is still Gardener, A., *Alabaster Tombs of the Pre-Reformation Period in England*, Cambridge University Press, Cambridge, 1940. For the post-medieval period see in particular Bayliss, J. and Richard Parker 'The Alabasterman', *Church Monuments*, Vol. 5, 1990, pp. 39–56; and Bayliss, J., 'Richard and Gabriel Royley of Burton-on-Trent, Tombmakers', *Church Monuments*, Vol. 6, 1991, pp. 21–41. For a description of the alabaster industry see Blair, J. and Ramsay, N. (eds.), *English Medieval Industries*, Hambledon Press, London, 1991, chapter 2.

5   The mines from which it was quarried ceased to be worked in 1905. A useful history of the industry is Tomlinson, J. M., *Derbyshire Black Marble*, Peak District Mines Historical Society Ltd, Matlock, Bath, 1996.

6   To my knowledge, nothing has been published on this. It is described and a list of examples described in Carrington, D., *St. Lawrence's Church, Whitwell, Derbyshire. Report on the monument to Sir Roger Manners (d.1632)*, unpublished report, Skillington Workshop Limited, 2005.

7   The best overview of the use of Purbeck marble is Leach, R., *An Investigation into the Use of Purbeck Marble in Medieval England*, privately published by R. Leach, 1978. For a discussion of the industry see Blair and Ramsay, *op. cit.*, chapter 3.

8   The identification of marbles is a skill in itself, and beyond the present chapter. A useful reference book is Dubarry de Lassale, J., *Identifying Marble*, H. Vial, France, 2000. Although the emphasis is on both French marbles and their use in cabinet making, it is nevertheless a good guide to marbles that might be found in monuments.

9   The conservation programme is described and illustrated in an unpublished report by Harrison Hill, a copy of which is held by the Council for the Care of Churches. The monument has a complex history; it was built in its present position in 1842–3 (when the effigies were 'scraped') prior to which the effigies and tomb chest may have come from separate monuments. It is not known from what date the oak ties originate. (Kelke, W. H., 'On three sepulchral monuments at Clifton Reynes in the county of Buckingham', *Archaeological Journal*, Vol. 11, 1854, pp. 149–156; Myres, J. L., 'Materials or the history of the parish of Clifton Reynes, Bucks', *Records of Buckinghamshire* Vol. 6, 1890, pp. 386–414.)

10   The monument, upon first inspection prior to dismantling (which was necessitated by a determined attempt to lever the two busts from the monument by thieves), appeared as though it must have been previously dismantled and rebuilt, as there was no other way that the inscription panel could be accessed. However, as the monument was taken down it became quite clear that it had not been disturbed in this way since the day it was first erected. (Carrington, D., *Report on the Conservation of the Earle Monument at St. Michael's Church, Stragglethorpe, Lincolnshire*, unpublished report, Skillington Workshop Ltd, 1999.)

11   There are numerous examples of this, both documented and recorded by discreet inscriptions added to monuments. A particularly good example of the former is Richard Westmacott's (sculptor and eldest son of the better known Sir Richard) restoration of the effigies at Gonalston, Nottinghamshire (Throsby, J., *Thoroton's History of Nottinghamshire: Republished with Large additions*, second edition, G. Burbage, Nottingham, 1790).

12   Richardson published his work at Temple church and at Elford, see for example Richardson, E., *The Monumental Effigies of the Temple Church with an Account of their Restoration, in the Year 1842*, London, 1843.

13   See Jordon, W. J., 'Sir George Gilbert Scott R.A., Surveyor to Westminster Abbey 1849–1878', *Architectural History* Vol. 23, 1980, pp. 60–85.

14   Crossley, E. W., 'Alabaster tombs and effigies in the north choir aisle of Swine church', *Yorkshire Archaeological Journal*, Vol. 34, 1939, p. 329; and 'The Eighth report of the Central Council of Diocesan Advisory Committees for the Care of Churches', pp. 62–65, 1940.

15   The International Institute for Conservation of Historic and Artistic Works (IIC) was incorporated in 1950, for example.

16 Larson, J., 'The conservation of marble monuments in churches', *The Conservator*, Vol. 2, 1978, pp. 20–25; Larson, J., 'The conservation of alabaster monuments in churches', *The Conservator*, Vol. 3, 1979, pp. 28–33; Larson, J., 'The conservation of stone monuments in churches', in Ashurst J. and Dimes F. (eds.), *Conservation of Building and Decorative Stone Volume 1*, Butterworth-Heinemann, London, 1990.

17 *The Buildings of England* series, commenced by Sir Nikolaus Pevsner with the first volumes appearing in 1951, was published by Penguin but now by Yale University Press, and covers every county in England. Parallel series are covering increasing areas of Scotland, Wales and Ireland.

18 Nichols, J. *The History and Antiquities of the County of Leicester*, J Nichols & Son, London, 1811.

19 Gough, R., *Sepulchral Monuments in Great Britain*, 2 volumes, 1786–96; Stothard, C. A., *The Monumental Effigies of Great Britain*, London, 1817; Blore, E., *The Monumental Remains of Noble and Eminent Persons Comprising the Sepulchral Antiquities of Great Britain*, Harding Lepard & Co., London, 1826.

20 The *Victoria County Histories* cover various aspects of history. Unfortunately, volumes covering architectural history have relatively incomplete coverage of the country. A good example is *A History of Yorkshire, North Riding, Volume 2*, St. Catherine's Press, London, 1923.

21 There are many useful inventories published as part of the RCHME's series, particularly covering Devon, London, the Home Counties and parts of the Midlands and East Anglia. They are published by Her Majesty's Stationery Office (HMSO) and, although largely out of print, are generally not difficult to obtain.

22 See Hanna, S., *Evaluation of Conservation Work to Monuments*, Hanna Conservation, unpublished report for the Council for the Care of Churches, 1988; and Carrington, D., *An Evaluation of Conservation Work to Monuments*, Skillington Workshop Ltd, unpublished report for the Council for the Care of Churches, 2000, pp. 95–98.

23 See Webster, R. G. M. (ed.), *Stone Cleaning and the Nature, Soiling and Decay Mechanisms of Stone*, Donhead, London, 1992; and Ashurst, N., *Cleaning Historic Buildings, Volumes 1 and 2*, Donhead, London, 1994.

24 There is an argument that de-ionised water has a greater tendency to dissolve soluble substrates and dirt than water that has dissolved minerals such as tap water), and therefore is relatively aggressive as a cleaning agent. Against this must be weighed the risk of leaving traces of any dissolved minerals on or in the substrate.

25 This is not meant to be a comprehensive health and safety evaluation. Scaffolding, for example, is barely touched upon. The risks associated with structural interventions in particular really do need to be properly considered prior to carrying out the work.

26 The work was carried out on behalf of the PCC during 2003 by Skillington Workshop Limited and was generously grant-aided by the Earl of Leicester, the Heritage Lottery Fund, the CCC and the Francis Coales Charitable

Foundation. The architect was Nicholas Warns of Norwich. The scaffolding was by Merlin Services Limited of King's Lynn.

27   The work was carried out on behalf of the PCC during 2005 by Skillington Workshop Limited and was generously grant-aided by the CCC. The architect was Mark Evans of Warwick. The work carried out is fully described in Carrington, D., *A Record of Conservation Work Undertaken to the Monument to John Harpur (d.1627) and his Wife During May and June 2005*, unpublished report, Skillington Workshop Ltd, 2005.

Chapter Fourteen

Graveyard Memorials

Chris Daniels

INTRODUCTION

'God's Acre', the consecrated parcel of land that surrounds the typical English church, may often predate the building that is now its reason for existence: the early Christian preachers pragmatically sited their centres of worship on existing pagan holy places. The institution of centralized places of Christian worship spread across the land, eventually culminating in the religious building explosion of the Middle Ages. The result – a church for every 200 people, and cathedrals that could hold the entire population of the city in which they were built, the great majority surrounded by the final resting places of people loved enough by others to have had some form of memorial provided.

Our inheritance is now an estimated 20,000 churchyards in England alone, most of which contain memorial structures ranging from the simplest grave slab to great mausolea, predominantly constructed of stone. The wall enclosing each of these churchyards can often be an important structure, possibly predating the present church and perhaps incorporating a lych gate as its entrance.

From the early nineteenth century, cemeteries became increasingly common as space for burial in a churchyard ran short.

The graveyard is therefore an extremely important historical resource with regard to archaeological, material and social history.

Types of memorial

Graveyard memorials are of two basic types; monolithic pieces, such as headstones or coffin slabs, and more complicated structures, such as elaborate chest tombs, mausolea and composite headstones. Their fixings are usually iron cramps and dowels, but occasionally slate dowels were used. Chest tombs were often constructed over a vault containing the coffin. The historical development of monuments and tombs is comprehensively covered in *English Churchyard Memorials* by Frederick Burgess, and this work should be read by all those involved in this field.[1]

Materials

Most areas utilized available local materials as best they could, sometimes adapting the style of the monument to suit the stone. However, in many areas, the local stone used in building construction was not considered suitable or desirable for the construction of memorials, and stone was imported from further afield. The use of exotic, imported stones has always been an attractive proposition for those wishing to make a noticeable and significant testament to a loved one, and this often results in alien inclusions within the graveyard.

Since the advent of the global shipping trade, stones have been brought into the UK from all over the world,[2] whilst sandblasting and mechanized letter-cutting has reduced costs and the demand for hand-produced work. Interestingly this trend is being countered by a growing awareness of the possibilities of commissioning skilled artisans to produce distinctive and fitting memorials in appropriate materials, bringing liveliness and artistry back to the graveyard.

DETERIORATION OF GRAVEYARD STRUCTURES

The condition of the built structures within many graveyards is often poor, due to neglect and disrepair. Whilst monuments within a church were moved around with care and skill to make way for more important pieces or to improve the layout, those situated outside the church, once any remaining family ceased to tend the plot, were usually left to their own devices, falling prey to the ravages of nature, gravity and vandalism. It is rare for a church or burial ground to have a full complement of stones with all monuments in their original position and condition.

Stone used in graveyards may be affected by any of the usual possible causes of stone decay. However, due to the particular way that stone is used in memorials, the way the structures are constructed and the graveyard environment, there are some types of deterioration that are particularly common in graveyard memorials.

Structural deterioration

Subsidence and settlement

Settling of the ground due to the excavation and refilling of a grave may leave the soil uncompacted or unstable, resulting in subsequent subsidence or settlement of a memorial. Such movement may have been historic, occurring shortly after erection of the memorial. Often, composite memorials such as chest tombs retain their structural integrity and subside *en masse*, shortly after erection, without suffering any disruption to joints, and remain stable thereafter (once the soil has compacted).

Headstones commonly tilt out of vertical due to soil settlement. The depth and manner in which they are set in the ground are critical in determining at what point they may collapse. Monolithic headstones are usually set deeply in the soil and can lean over at an acute angle without falling over. Composite headstones, consisting of a slab set in a plinth, are usually set at a shallow depth below ground level, and can become unstable when only a few degrees out of vertical.

Figure 14.1 The level of soil around these chest tombs has risen over the years. Coupled with some subsidence it creates the impression that the tombs are sinking into the ground.

Figure 14.2   Tilting headstones.

Figure 14.3   Extreme plant growth may cause a dilemma; which is more worthy of preservation, the tree or the headstones?

The presence of trees close to structures can also undermine the ground stability through invasive root systems and drying of soil.

Structural instability

Due to the construction methods of many memorials where thin slabs and inset stones were used, there was often a reliance on iron cramps and ties to hold the pieces in place. If these are subsequently exposed to the elements due to denudation of the mortar joints, they will rust and may fail, allowing movement of the components. They may also expand, exerting enough pressure to fracture the stone.

Invasive vegetation such as ivy can disrupt structures as they grow into joints, lifting stones and moving panels.

Surface deterioration

Sulphate attack

Evidence of the pollution that attacks the stones of towns and cities can often be found on the sheltered parts of limestone monuments, for example as gypsum crusts on the underside of ledger slabs and even in the comparative shelter of incised lettering. On sandstone and granite components, dark staining can occur.

Rising damp

Most historic memorials are constructed in direct contact with the earth, and hence draw moisture up by capillary action. This can result in increased biological growth at a low level and salt crystallization damage.

Delamination

When the bed height of quarried stone was insufficient for certain applications, then stone was sometimes edge or face bedded; this is usually the case for headstones, ledger slabs and panels of tombs. Around the edges of the slab, the bedding is exposed to weathering elements, which can lead to delamination of the stone and loss of important inscriptions and carved decoration.

Figure 14.4 The ferrous cramp holding the side panels of this chest tomb has become exposed due to movement of the ledger stone. The metal has rusted away, allowing the panels to separate.

Figure 14.5 A sandstone headstone suffering extensive delamination due to soluble salts in rising groundwater in a heavily used burial ground.

Staining

Stone mats may become stained due to the rusting of iron cramps used in construction of the memorial, or due to run-off from other metal components such as metallic inscription plates or lettering.

Biodeterioration

Vegetation growth is common on graveyard memorials; flat surfaces, such as the tops of headstones and ledger slabs, and low-level stone in contact with damp earth retain moisture, encouraging growth of algae, mosses and lichens. These lower level plants are on the whole benign, but may be the precursors of higher plants by providing nutrient rich humus, or may be indicators of excessive levels of moisture within the monument material itself. A major concern regarding lower plants is their obscuring of inscriptions, and often they are 'cleaned' with liberal doses of household bleach by monument custodians or well meaning members of the parish. However, some graveyard lichens are extremely rare and should not be removed as a matter of course.

The incidence of lower plants etching stone by the creation of acids or the consumption of minerals is well documented. This may affect the legibility of inscriptions, but specialist interpretation of their effect on the stone should be sought before any remedial action is taken.

Higher forms of plants, from grasses to trees, can also inflict chemical changes by altering the pH of the mortar and stone surface, though they do most damage through their roots entering joints and cracks, with subsequent growth sometimes exerting enough internal pressure to lift and even split stones.

Human actions

The day-to-day maintenance of the graveyard and its use as a place to visit can be factors in the destruction and damage of stones and structures. Grass cutting and strimming often uses machinery that chips and abrades stones, especially those that are flush with the ground. Tidying up of small pieces of loose stone, unseated kerbs and broken pieces of slabs will make the area more presentable, but can quickly cause the loss of vital pieces. One graveyard was maintained in a tidy state by placing all loose debris and litter within the core of chest tombs. Easy access to graveyards also makes them particularly vulnerable to vandalism.

INSPECTING, REPORTING AND RECORDING

Graveyard survey

Surveys of graveyards are the first step towards appropriate care programmes, as these can highlight monuments at risk and produce a record of the overall condition of the area and its structures. These are sometimes carried out by volunteers, who should be provided with a standard recording form, which can be designed by conservators and architects to provide usable information without requiring too much technical detail. Historic Scotland has published a methodology for assessing the decay of carved stones that is suitable for use by groups or individuals undertaking graveyard surveys, and which includes recording forms.[3]

Increasingly, safety audits of graveyards are being carried out by parochial church councils (PCCs) in response to serious accidents and fatalities caused by collapse of memorials in recent years. The results of such surveys can be used as a basis for prioritizing conservation work.

Conservation report

The preliminary operation for any conservation work to graveyard structures should be detailed observation and recording of the condition of the memorial and an assessment of the causes of any deterioration. In most cases, a condition report incorporating recommendations for conservation work will be a pre-requisite to any actual work being undertaken, particularly where permission, such as faculty or listed building consent is needed, or where grant funding is sought. In such cases, the project cannot be considered finished until a full report on the complete treatment of the memorial is bound and lodged within the archives of the church authority.

There are many formats for conservation reports, but the protocol on what information is required is fairly specific with some authorities, such as the Council for the Care of Churches (CCC) publishing guidelines on what the content of a conservation report should be.[4] The report should be subdivided into the following sections:

- Description
- Condition
- Recommendations
- Specifications
- Costs and bill of quantities

Recording

As inscriptions weather and become indistinct, it may be necessary to use specialized methods to decipher the letters and text. However, the impulse to wipe the stone clean of dirt and plant life should be resisted: the dirt may be the cohesive material holding the surface of the stone together, and untended stones in graveyards are often a sanctuary for many rare lichens. It is paramount that the condition survey identifies the nature of the surface accretions, perhaps putting off the recording of underlying text until later in the project.

An effective way of disclosing text on monuments is to use raking light – a torch, shone at a low angle across the surface of the stone at dusk, can produce quite dramatic and revealing results. A refinement of this is to set up camera flashes around the stone, either at night or under a cover, and fire them with a camera set on long exposure to record the information revealed by the shadows.

Brass rubbing crayons and paper can also provide much hidden detail, as well as providing a permanent record of the surface texture, though with friable or laminating surfaces this may be damaging in unskilled hands.

Carving and decoration is often repeated on other monuments of the period or area, and it may be possible to recognize details from similar local carvings, thus allowing a fuller interpretation of any eroded work.

WORKING ON SITE

Site security and safety

One of the most important considerations for work carried out in a grave-yard is that it is a public place, usually accessible and open at all times. This can lead to potential problems of members of the public interfering with the work site, coming into contact with hazardous materials or pilfering

Figure 14.6   The site of this chest tomb under repair, photographed during a weekend, shows poor regard for safety, security and good practice. Materials are left outside, parts of the tomb are spread out on the grass and the ledger slab is balanced precariously on concrete blocks and timber. Only token attempts at security are made and the risk of theft and injury are considerable.

dismantled elements. It will be necessary to carry out risk assessments at an early stage of the project that will help to define the working area and the safety and security measures required.

If any dismantling work is carried out, there is a risk that objects may be pilfered or vandalized. A suitable form of secure fencing around the site should be erected and securely locked whilst the site is unattended. All tools and materials that remain on site overnight should be locked away; it can often be arranged with the church warden or cemetery manager that these may be stored within the church or cemetery chapel or, failing that, within the secured site compound.

Public access must be denied to the site for the duration of the project, giving particular consideration to the potential activities of children. Any hazardous materials and potentially dangerous situations must be monitored and made safe at all times. Any dismantling of memorials should be carried out in such a way as to ensure that at no time are they left in an unstable condition – reducing the risk of accident to even the most determined trespasser.

Signage to warn of prohibited areas and potential hazards must be provided by the contractor and displayed on site, along with emergency contact telephone numbers.

Site practice

Working practice must be well co-ordinated to allow maximum use of the area allocated and to minimize any disruptions to the day-to-day workings of the graveyard. Times of material deliveries or periods of loud or disruptive operations should be co-ordinated with the parish or cemetery officials to prevent any disturbances during services.

It is preferable that, when the project is completed, the graveyard environment is returned to normal as quickly as possible. Measures can be taken to reduce damage to the site. Grass abutting the monument should be lifted and cut up as turf and watered, fertilized and stacked to one side, covering it to reduce drying out. It will last about a week, and can be relaid on completion of the work.

The area that will be used to spread out the components of the monument, to stack materials and on which to carry out operations should be covered with sturdy polythene sheeting and boards to reduce churning of the ground and damage to the grass. Although the grass underneath will turn yellow, it will survive for two to three weeks, and if watered and fertilized prior to covering it will recover within a week. If possible, uncover

Figure 14.7   At this site turf is stacked haphazardly and stones are left unprotected on the grass, both of which may cause irreversible damage to the grass.

the grass during weekends to extend its life. Routes for the transportation of materials and regular foot traffic should be similarly protected.

REMEDIAL WORK

Introduction

When considering conservation work to graveyard memorials, there are various special considerations that need to be taken into account. There are the requirements of health and safety legislation, as the project, once finished, is an artefact that is readily accessible to the public with little or no supervision. This might necessitate more extensive work being carried out than might be the case for a structure on private land. A graveyard monument will, unless it is of some significance, almost certainly lapse into a state of neglect once the work has been finished; the conception may be that the monument, once repaired, does not need further attention, and attention will move on to more deserving monuments in the graveyard. It may therefore be prudent to intervene to a greater extent in order to

Figure 14.8 This headstone has been repaired using iron cramps which are now rusting and risk damaging the headstone. However, they form part of the history of the monument and careful thought should be given to whether or how they should be replaced.

safeguard the artefact better in the future. There are also the needs of relatives and friends of the deceased to ensure that the memorial's effects (inscription, stature and presence) are all maintained to the fullest.

Any intervention should be preceded by documentary research to establish the repair history of the memorial. Often, it is the case that an apparently crumbling or precarious structure has had changes implemented in the past, and all that is practically necessary is surface treatment to the accessible elements, thus reducing the need to dismantle and rebuild.

Some parishes run 'Living Churchyard' projects concentrating on the biodiversity of the churchyard, and the PCC should be consulted about the impact any work will have on the environment and ecology of the area.

Dismantling

Monuments should be inspected carefully, and a judgement made on the necessity of dismantling. Many tombs and headstones can tilt as complete units, and may well be structurally sound in such positions. Monitoring of

Figure 14.9   Subsidence of poorly founded monuments does not necessarily mean that they must be rebuilt. Comparison of past and current photographs will help to establish whether the memorial is still moving.

monuments at regular intervals may help to determine whether any movement is ongoing. It is also imperative to check whether there is an underground vault beneath a monument, as this may collapse, causing subsidence. If vaults are discovered, they should be inspected as soon as possible, and any remedial work to them undertaken before the tomb is reassembled. Work such as this can often require the services of a structural engineer to determine loads and material performance. During the process of dismantling or removing parts of a monument, it may reach a point of instability that can be dangerous to the conservator, where it might damage other parts of the structure or allow other parts to collapse; it is important to set out a method statement and risk assessment in this regard before work starts.

Temporary protection

If the stone is undergoing decay, has a delicate surface, or there is a chance that damage will occur to inscriptions, 'facing up' (reinforcing the surface using layers of acid free tissue paper and a water-soluble acrylic dispersion) may allow the piece to be safely moved. If a very delicate panel is to be moved, it may be necessary to provide extra support by applying a reinforced plaster layer over the facing up tissue.

For safe transport of delicate dismantled items, it may be necessary to construct a wooden box around the item and to provide cushioning and support using foam rubber or expanding foam adhesive (isolated from the stone surface using plastic film). If the surfaces of the stone are sound, it may be safe to simply lay the slabs onto foam as the monument is dismantled. When slabs or elements are fractured or prone to breaking, then they can be temporarily strengthened using wooden splints strapped securely in place, taking care to protect arrises.

Lifting ledger slabs

Lifting of ledger slabs can allow their side panels to fall out or in once the restraint has been removed; a cushioned strap around the panels before lifting should be provided, with judicious soft-wood wedging to prevent the panels toppling inwards.

Ledger slabs, being both of considerable weight and size, and yet carved with delicate mouldings, are very awkward to manoeuvre. They should always be lifted using the correct equipment, such as an A-frame gantry with block and pulley, and should be placed on to a solid support built

Figure 14.10 Demonstration of vacuum lifting equipment. This might be suitable for lifting and replacing ledger slabs provided the surface of the slab is sound and is not deeply contoured.

from blocks and planks, and never laid directly on the ground. There are also other methods, such as vacuum lifting or inserting inflatable raising bags underneath to raise the slab.

Digging out headstones

The stones should be checked to ensure they are strong enough to remove. If pieces are loose, or in danger of breaking, then suitable precautions should be taken, such as temporary pinning, strapping or dismantling piecemeal. Headstones should be shored up prior to digging out any supporting material from the base. As material is excavated, it should be stored in a manner that allows sensible re-use; soil and infill material can

Figure 14.11   A headstone being lifted using a hoist and gantry. The strops must be strong enough to lift the estimated weight of the stone and used correctly to minimize damage to the stone. (Richard Mortimer)

be placed in buckets or on a tarpaulin; footing material such as bricks should be stacked in reverse order for re-use.

Repairs

Repointing

Open joints should be re-pointed with lime-based mortar. Care must be taken that any water used for damping the stone to take the mortar, does not affect any ferrous cramps.

Repairing fractures

Fractures in sound stone can be repaired by pinning, using threaded stainless steel rod set in resin. The main criteria for rejoining slabs is that they are aligned properly and that the repair diverts any forces that may cause it to hinge on the break into the main body of the stone. Headstones may be repaired *in situ*, provided the stone is soundly set in the ground and that none of the repair techniques used will cause it to become unstable. Do not use percussive drills on monument slabs when drilling dowel holes. In the case of panels that will only be visible from one side (such as the side panel of a chest tomb) it may be possible to provide an external support of stainless steel mesh or glass reinforced plastic (GRP), attaching it to the back of the panel to hold disparate pieces in position.

Strengthening vaults

Where a vault beneath a chest tomb is starting to collapse, it may be possible to insert reinforced concrete lintels to reduce the pressure on the masonry or spread the loading. Empty vaults may be filled with clean stone, with a reinforced concrete raft cast on top to form a foundation for a chest tomb. Any remedial work of strengthening or adding elements should be carried out by skilled operatives, according to the recommendations of a structural engineer.

Rebuilding chest tombs

In order to prevent future subsidence of a chest tomb, it is advisable to provide a new concrete footing. A damp proof membrane is an option that should be considered if the monument has been affected by rising moisture; it should be installed in such a way as to allow moisture to drain to the outside of the tomb. A suitable material is lead sheeting, as this will take up irregularities whilst allowing simple channels to be formed. If the original core was poorly constructed or is missing, then a new core can be built from modern concrete blocks and lime mortars to prevent future misinterpretation of the structure. The side panels should be tied together or to the central core, using non-ferrous cramps recessed into the stones and fixed in resin or calcium caseinate cement. Fine joints can be buttered with pure lime putty as construction proceeds, but wider joints should be pointed with lime mortar, which can be colour matched to the stone if required. If the side panels are weak, the core should be built fractionally higher than the side panels to take the weight of the ledger slab. Pads of lead or an injected resin can be applied to the top of the panels to prevent rocking without overloading. If the stone is to be supported by the panels, then a cushion material should be used to prevent pressure points on the edges of the panels. Mortar is the most effective material if there is sufficient width on the upper edge of the panel to support it; otherwise a

Figure 14.12   Sympathetic repair using a stainless steel support to strengthen the structure without replacing any of the broken side panels.

compressible flexible gasket material can be used (a maintenance note should be made regarding the projected lifespan of this material).

Re-setting headstones

Headstones should be re-fixed on a new footing. A Code of Practice has been drawn up by the National Association of Memorial Masons (NAMM), which suggests several different methods and provides specifications.[5]

If a stone is of historic or architectural significance and it is undergoing irreversible decay in its original position that threatens its significance, there may be a case for re-siting in a sheltered environment such as a porch or within a cemetery chapel or the church. It should be securely fixed, and not just propped against the wall. An explanatory notice should be placed nearby to aid in future interpretation and enjoyment of the graveyard.

Drainage

Drainage, and the removal of unwanted water around memorials, is very important. The most obvious method of controlling the movement and amount of water coming into contact with a structure is to ensure that there is adequate drainage to the surrounding ground. It is pertinent to know the character of the soil, its moisture retentiveness, and drainage levels. Around the base of monuments, the simplest method of providing relief from standing and moving water is to construct a French or land drain. Archaeological advice may be needed prior to excavation for a drain.

Surface repair

Delicate and hollow areas of stone may require facing up, whilst some form of consolidant or adhesive can be injected into voids behind any flaking stone. The material used for grouting voids or for consolidating delaminating stones will depend on the mineralogy of the stone and the size of the void. Hydraulic lime is suitable for lime and calcareous sandstones. Epoxy resins can be used for hard, impervious stones such as blue Lias or granite. Acrylic resin in various viscosities, and silane-based consolidants can be used for micro-fissures. Depending on the size of the void, a filler may be added to the grout, such as fumed silica, glass micro beads or silica sand. Alternatively, the filler can be fed into the void dry, and a binding solution, such as Paraloid B72, poured in afterwards.

Vacuum impregnation can be of use here: a simple Melinex (polyester film) shroud and nozzles placed to feed the consolidant into the areas most in need would probably suffice, and possibly be reusable for other panels.

Cleaning

The cleaning of churchyard memorials raises slightly different questions than the cleaning of buildings. It may be argued that the purpose of a memorial is commemorative, and as such legibility of the inscription is of paramount importance. Removal of soiling that is neither disfiguring nor harmful is therefore sometimes undertaken for such aesthetic reasons. However, the removal of dirt and staining on memorials should be based upon the same premises as those for buildings – always carry out trials to ascertain the most appropriate method to use. Almost without exception, chemical cleaning should not be used on monuments to remove pollution and general staining.

Metals used in construction can cause brown or green staining to the surface of the stone; this can be reduced and sometimes removed by the use of chemical poulticing, once the type of stone and staining is identified and the appropriate trials carried out.

Brushing to remove loose soiling is once again only to be undertaken after expert consideration of all the factors involved, such as condition of the stone and nature of the soiling. It is tempting for volunteers to attempt to clean up memorials, but this should only be allowed following expert consideration of all the factors contributing to soiling, and then only after trials have been carried out by a conservator. Some lichens growing on graveyard memorials are extremely rare and further advice should be sought before their removal.

Inscriptions

When a carved inscription on a stone begins to deteriorate, it is through the loss of stone as the surface erodes away. It is tempting to commission the recutting of the letters deeper into the stone. But this practice should be avoided, as it is detrimental to the integrity of the monument, results in a false impression of the stone's history, and will always be aesthetically incorrect. Letter-cutting is a skill that must follow the correct process to produce a good letter, and cannot be carried out on eroding stone with any hope of success; it is also against conservation ethics to re-enhance work in such a way that the original material is lost. It is possible to

Figures 14.13 This church uses Bath stone for the dressings and it
was assumed that this churchyard cross was also Bath stone.
Fortunately the stone was eventually correctly identified as sandstone.
A suitable cleaning method was used rather than the air abrasive
system which was originally proposed and which could have resulted
in over-cleaning and loss of detail. These pictures show the carvings at
the base of the cross before (above) and after (below) cleaning using
water and bristle brushes.

highlight letters using paint applied by a skilled hand to form painted edges on the stone, thereby approximating their original form without damaging the stone. Acrylic paint is recommended, as it can easily be removed in the future. Significant inscriptions should be recorded fully for archival purposes, and if there is a need for the inscription to be read then

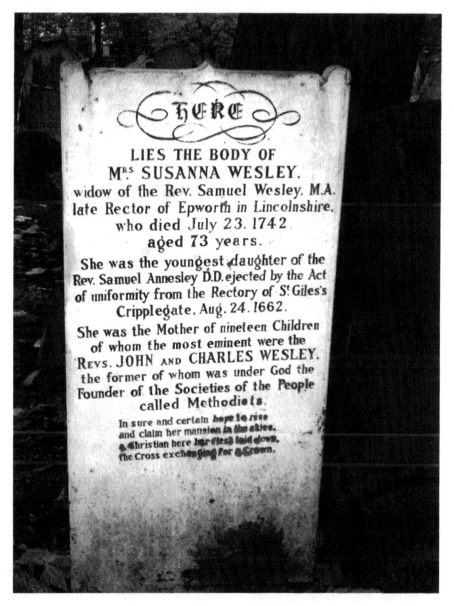

Figure 14.14   A painted headstone in an urban environment. This has probably be repainted because of the association of the deceased with a famous person.

a new stone or plaque, with the inscription freshly cut, can be sited close to the original stone, perhaps on the reverse.

Raised lead letters are often lost through the effects of time or picking fingers, but they can be replaced successfully by monumental masons or letter-cutters versed in this traditional craft.

Painted stones should never be touched up without a thorough investigation into why the paint is deteriorating, what the original paint is, and how it was applied. It is also necessary to obtain a licence from English Heritage if traditional lead-based paint is to be used on a Grade I or Grade II* listed monument.

EMERGENCY WORKS TO GRAVEYARD STRUCTURES

In the light of recent serious accidents caused by collapsing graveyard memorials, many local authorities and PCCs are understandably concerned about safety in the graveyard. It is advisable to inspect all memorials, even comparatively recently erected ones, for stability. Testing for stability should comprise a visual inspection, including taking photographs, gentle hand pressure, and testing using a 'Topple Tester' applying a force of 35 kg. Some monumental masons and gravediggers have undergone the training provided by the NAMM in the testing of headstones using a 'Topple Tester'. The force applied is intended to be similar to that applied by a man leaning on the stone. For chest tombs, a visual examination will determine if there is any mortar missing, or if there are any hair-line fractures that may indicate expanding metals or stress loading within the structure.

Memorials that are found to be unstable should be cordoned off immediately, and warning signs erected. Unstable headstones and chest tombs can be shored up as a temporary measure, using timber frames with cushioning to isolate the stone from the timber (which might otherwise stain the stone), and to prevent damage to the stone surface. The shoring must be competently constructed for it to be effective. Once made safe in this way, attempts can be made to trace the owner of the memorial.

It is often tempting for a PCC to lay unstable monuments flat on the ground. However, consideration should be given to longer-term repair. Laying a stone flat replaces a falling hazard with a tripping hazard, and will also require cordoning off and warning signs. Laying a stone down will almost certainly lead to more rapid decay, as water will be retained for longer on a flat surface. Also, simply dismantling and laying stones flat will incur costs, and consideration should be given to putting this expense towards the cost of safe re-fixing instead.

If the decision is taken to dismantle a memorial, it should always be isolated from the ground. When stones are placed into a different

Figure 14.15   An 'L' or box section external support reduces the risk of a headstone hinging around the break after dowelling. Cushioning in the form of polytetrafluorethylene (PTFE) can be placed between the support and the stone.

Figure 14.16   Restoration of damaged stone using a replacement piece cast from a clay maquette, modelled *in situ*. The lines of the break are followed exactly so that no stone had to be removed from the memorial. The repair is reversible.

environment, such as in contact with the ground along their length, then changes will occur, such as increased damp penetration or mobilization of soluble salts, which will invariably introduce new factors of decay. Historic Scotland has published a useful document suggesting alternative methods for making memorials safe, such as laying on clean sand and timber runners, which will help to reduce the risk of further deterioration.[6] It is important to consider that any emergency work to monuments will cost money, and it may be more economical to engage a conservation contractor to carry out these safety and emergency tasks, as they can undertaken the work with the future repair and reinstatement as a prime consideration.

MAINTENANCE

The simplest method of looking after a monument is to remove any vegetation that may be causing damage through disruption by invasive root systems. Woody growth and extensive roots should never be pulled or levered out of joints; always treat with a biocide prior to commencing work, and carefully cut back when dead with sharp bladed implements. Chainsaws and brushcutters used to remove heavy woody growth can damage the face of the stone as well as causing vibratory damage. Ideally, woody growth should be cut back by hand.

Graveyard maintenance is often a neglected area, but drawing up a maintenance plan can help focus on particular problems and in prioritizing work. The maintenance plan should take into account the resources and funds available to carry them out. A cost effective approach is to draft plans that can be followed by volunteer members of the community without the need for specialists. This will involve training and education as to the best methods for controlling vegetation without resorting to biocides, how to record changes in the condition of the memorial, and what to do if pieces become detached.

Quinquennial inspections by the church architect should include the churchyard monuments, noting the condition of the memorials and any significant changes since the last inspection.

Each graveyard will have its own requirements as to how they present the whole area and what is important to the community, and tending and cleaning instructions should take this into account. Creation of a wildlife area within a graveyard should never be used as an excuse for not maintaining memorials.

CONCLUSION

Graveyard memorials are set in an unusual and difficult context from the point of view of stone conservation. Memorials that were erected as private acts of remembrance are often perceived now as public property. Twenty-four hour unsupervised access renders them susceptible to unwitting damage by visitors and children and, at worst, to wilful vandalism. Many graveyards provide habitats for rare flora and fauna, and maintaining a well-tended memorial with a legible inscription is often at odds with conservation of the picturesque wildlife sanctuaries that many graveyards have become.

Care of individual memorials competes for scarce resources with other aspects of graveyard maintenance, such as grass cutting and upkeep of paths.

Grants for conservation of graveyard memorials are rare, and much of this work is done by volunteers, whose efforts must be supported with appropriate training. In some graveyards, experienced conservators have trained volunteers in tasks such as crack filling and re-pointing, enabling much preventative conservation to be undertaken at reasonable cost.[7] Preparation of a graveyard conservation plan, in which the significance of individual memorials and of the graveyard as a whole is considered, will help to identify threats to that significance and provide a framework for developing an integrated approach to graveyard management, and a cost effective programme of expenditure. This type of work should only be undertaken or supervized by suitable accredited and experienced professionals.

The author

Chris Daniels PGdip Arch Cons, Europe Diploma Conservation Architectural Heritage, C&G Advanced Stone Masonry, PACR

Chris Daniels has worked on historic buildings for over 20 years since training as a City & Guilds Advanced Stonemason. After working for St Blaise in Dorset he moved to Italy to study conservation at the Centro di Artigni, Venice. He then became Senior Conservator at Rattee & Kett followed by Senior Conservator with Herbert Read Ltd. A Professionally Accredited Conservator with the Institute of Conervation (ICON), he is currently Programme Leader of the Applied Architectural Stonework and Conservation Foundation Science Degree at Weymouth College, visiting lecturer at Plymouth School of Architecture and Consultant for Architectural Conservation.

References

1   Burgess, F., *English Churchyard Memorials,* Lutterworth Press, Cambridge, 2004.
2   A Welsh letter-cutter recently bemoaned to the author the fact that it was cheaper to buy a cut and polished piece of Granite imported from South Africa, than to purchase an unworked slate slab from his local quarry.
3   Maxwell, I., Nanda, R. and Urquhart D., *Conservation of Historic Graveyards,* Historic Scotland, Edinburgh, 2001.
4   www.churchcare.co.uk (accessed 21 June 2006); www.conservationregister. com/guidancereports.asp?id=3 (accessed 21 June 2006).
5   Memorial Specifications Guide is published by the National Association of Memorial Masons (NAMM) and can be downloaded from www.namm. org.uk.
6   Historic Scotland, *Emergency Measures for Historic Memorials: A Short Guide for Cemetery Managers,* Historic Scotland, Edinburgh, 2003.
7   Historic Scotland, *Conference Proceedings: Conservation of Historic Graveyards 2001,* Historic Scotland, Edinburgh, 2002.

Appendix

Practical Application Procedures for Putty Lime Mortar Repairs and Sheltercoat

TYPICAL PROCEDURE FOR APPLYING PUTTY LIME
MORTAR REPAIRS

- Prepare a sound, well keyed surface ready to receive the repair,
- Flush loose dust from surface and wet stone several times with limewater,
- Remix matured repair mortar to plastic state, and add 5–10% pozzolanic additive if required.
- Prepare slurry of diluted mortar,
- Paint slurry onto area to be repaired; when it starts to turn matt (as water is absorbed into the stone) it is ready for mortar application.
- Apply mortar by hand (wearing rubber gloves), or by wooden or metal spatula to a maximum thickness of 12–15 mm. For deep cavities, broken pieces of pre-wetted stone can be pressed into the mortar, or a coarser aggregate used.
- Compress mortar after it has stiffened slightly – typically 5 to 15 minutes after application.
- A second coat can be applied when the first is leather hard – typically 12 to 24 hours after the first application. The surface of the first coat should be keyed before a second coat is applied. Build up and compress further layers as required, using mortar slurry between each coat.
- The mortar surface can be textured when leather hard by scraping back or compressing with a bristle brush. An open granular texture can be

obtained by pressing coarse limestone aggregate into the soft mortar surface, with a damp brush or shaped piece of stone. A smooth surface can be obtained by using appropriately sized and shaped wooden floats.

- Protect mortar repair after initial compression using damp cotton wool, hessian or cloth. Ensure mortar remains damp for at least 3–4 days. Periodic rewetting of mortar during first few weeks after application is thought to aid carbonation.

TYPICAL PROCEDURE FOR APPLYING SHELTERCOAT

- Ensure stone surfaces are clean,
- Wet stone several times with limewater,
- Remix matured sheltercoat putty to a plastic state,
- Add 5% by volume of lactic acid casein powder, and mix well into the sheltercoat mixture until it the calcium caseinate reaction occurs and the mixture becomes liquid.
- Add water to thin the liquid to a thin cream consistency,
- Apply with a soft, short haired bristle brush to damp (not wet) stone surface, working the sheltercoat well into the surface (especially pits and hairline cracks).
- As the sheltercoat application starts to turn matt (as water is absorbed into the stone), work in the sheltercoat a second time with a dry bristle brush. Timing is imperative – if the sheltercoat is too wet it is just moved around the surface, if it is too dry it gets brushed off. When done well, the brushstrokes should be barely visible.
- When the surface has completely dried, a small brush can be used to remove any excess that may have built up in undercut areas and areas of fine detail.
- Protect sheltercoat immediately after initial application with damp hessian/cloth and polythene. Ensure sheltercoat remains damp for at least 2 days. Periodic rewetting of sheltercoat during first few weeks after application is thought to aid carbonation.

Index

Page numbers include text and figures, except those in *italics* which contain only figures.